Edward Ball is Lecturer in
Old Testament and Hebrew,
University of Nottingham, UK.

Ronald E. Clements was
formerly Samuel Davidson
Professor of Old Testament
Studies at King's College,
University of London.

JOURNAL FOR THE STUDY OF THE OLD TESTAMENT
SUPPLEMENT SERIES
300

Sheffield Academic Press

In Search of True Wisdom

Essays in Old Testament Interpretation in Honour of Ronald E. Clements

edited by
Edward Ball

Journal for the Study of the Old Testament
Supplement Series 300

Copyright © 1999 Sheffield Academic Press

Published by
Sheffield Academic Press Ltd
Mansion House
19 Kingfield Road
Sheffield S11 9AS
England

Typeset by Sheffield Academic Press
and
Printed on acid-free paper in Great Britain
by Bookcraft Ltd
Midsomer Norton, Bath

British Library Cataloguing in Publication Data

A catalogue record for this book is available
from the British Library

ISBN 1-84127-071-7

CONTENTS

6   *In Search of True Wisdom*

PREFACE

The essays in this volume are presented with respect, admiration and affection to Ronald Clements on the occasion of his seventieth birthday. The contributors are drawn principally from the universities with which he has himself chiefly been associated, and from his own former pupils; but there is representation, too, from the wider world of British and international Old Testament scholarship to which Ronald has contributed so liberally and inspiringly.

For he has been known for over 30 years as a prolific and creative scholar and teacher, who has also been generous in his encouragement and support of younger scholars, and always ready to share the fruits of his own latest research. A person of wide sympathies, he has followed no party line, established no school, and has encouraged his pupils as they have gone their own ways. It is, even so, a tribute both to the fertile stimulus of his work and to his kindness and friendship, that so many have found their own study richly influenced by his. A pointer to a new approach or conclusion has often been indicated by his unassuming question, 'Don't you think that...?' More often than not, this is indicative of a fresh direction in Ronald's own work: he has never been afraid to move beyond previously accepted positions (I think, for instance, of his recent questioning of traditional critical forms of the 'Deutero-Isaiah' hypothesis); and he has shown himself able to make use, both critical and creative, of what he has presciently seen as positions likely to establish themselves firmly (such as the proposal of a 'Josianic redaction' in the preceding chapters of Isaiah). In several areas he has been something of a trail-blazer: think, say, of the wide impact of his work on the redactional patterning of the Old Testament prophetic books.

A (select) bibliography of Ronald's published writings appeared in his 1996 collection of essays, *Old Testament Prophecy: From Oracles to Canon*, pages 265-70, and he has continued to add to it. There are, for example, (yet) more essays on the later chapters of Isaiah, and his substantial commentary on Deuteronomy in the *New Interpreter's Bible* (1998). The merest glance at the bibliography will show how focused his concerns have always been in the broad, central heartlands of Old Testament literature and theology; one will search in vain for published notes on isolated textual or philological issues.

If the present collection is entitled *In Search of True Wisdom*, that is intended to create a number of resonances. In recent years, Ronald has himself devoted considerable attention to what is usually (but perhaps not altogether happily or helpfully) referred to as the 'wisdom litera-ture' of the Old Testament. But a good deal of contemporary research has suggested how 'wisdom' has been deployed as a kind of interpreta-tive framework for understanding the nature of the Old Testament as a whole, at least in the later stages of its canonical formation—and Ronald has commented on that in his essays in the *Festschriften* for the late Barnabas Lindars and for Professor John Emerton. In that sense, to study the Old Testament is to be in search of that wisdom which it seems to present itself as expressing—like the personified figure of wis-dom herself, a reality of both heaven and earth, transcendent gift and matter for human quest. More generally, it is the common conviction of the contributors to this volume that the Old Testament has its con-tinuing part to play, not only in shaping the ongoing human quest for meaning and truth, but also in mediating in rich and luminous, if not necessarily simple, ways something of the reality that is sought. In other words, it may yet bring us to Jacob's ladder, to the significance of which Ronald called out attention in his London inaugural lecture in 1984.

The central concerns of the present volume, then, are with Old Tes-tament theology and hermeneutics, and this quite deliberately in so far as it reflects the wider but far from peripheral aspects of Ronald's own work. A first group of essays focuses chiefly on approaches and methods in constructive theological interpretation; later ones consider specific books through the lens of such interpretative interests.

It is a matter of particular sadness that Professor Norman Whybray did not live to see the appearance of his contribution. As his opening comments indicate, he was delighted to participate in this tribute.

I would like to express my thanks to all the contributors, and espe-cially to Eryl Davies and Bill Bellinger for their assistance in the early stages of planning for this book. My gratitude goes also to those at the

Press who have with care and efficiency overseen the book's production, especially Rebecca Cullen.

It remains only to express again our deep regard for Ron, with the hope that he (and maybe a few others) will find these essays of interest. We pray for him, and for Valerie, God's continued blessing in the years ahead.

Edward Ball
Department of Theology
University of Nottingham

ABBREVIATIONS

ABD	David Noel Freedman (ed.), *The Anchor Bible Dictionary* (New York: Doubleday, 1992)
AnBib	Analecta Biblica
ATD	Das Alte Testament Deutsch
AV	Authorized Version
BDB	Francis Brown, S.R. Driver and Charles A. Briggs, *A Hebrew and English Lexicon of the Old Testament* (Oxford: Clarendon Press, 1907)
BETL	Bibliotheca ephemeridum theologicarum lovaniensium
BHS	*Biblia hebraica stuttgartensia*
Bib	*Biblica*
BibInt	*Biblical Interpretation: A Journal of Contemporary Approaches*
BJRL	*Bulletin of the John Rylands University Library of Manchester*
BKAT	Biblischer Kommentar: Altes Testament
BWANT	Beiträge zur Wissenschaft von Alten und Neuen Testament
BZAW	Beihefte zur *ZAW*
CBQ	*Catholic Biblical Quarterly*
ConBOT	Coniectanea biblica, Old Testament Series
CTA	A. Herdner (ed.), *Corpus des tablettes en cunéiformes alphabétiques découvertes à Ras Shamra–Ugarit de 1929 à 1939* (Paris: Imprimerie nationale Geuthner, 1963)
DTC	*Dictionnaire de théologie catholique*
EvT	*Evangelische Theologie*
ExpTim	*Expository Times*
FRLANT	Forschungen zur Religion und Literatur des Alten und Neuen Testaments
HTR	*Harvard Theological Review*
HUCA	*Hebrew Union College Annual*
Int	Interpretation
JBL	*Journal of Biblical Literature*
JJS	*Journal of Jewish Studies*
JSOT	*Journal for the Study of the Old Testament*
JSOTSup	*Journal for the Study of the Old Testament*, Supplement Series
JTS	*Journal of Theological Studies*
KAT	Kommentar zum Alten Testament

NCB	New Century Bible
NIV	New International Version
NJB	New Jerusalem Bible
NRSV	New Revised Standard Version
OBT	Overtures to Biblical Theology
OTG	Old Testament Guides
OTL	Old Testament Library
PG	J.-P. Migne (ed.), *Patrologia cursus completa...* *Series graeca* (166 vols.; Paris: Petit-Montrouge, 1857–83)
PL	J.-P. Migne (ed.), *Patrologia cursus completus...* *Series prima [latina]* (221 vols.; Paris: J.-P. Migne, 1844–65)
RB	*Revue Biblique*
REB	Revised English Bible
RSV	Revised Standard Version
RV	Revised Version
SBLDS	SBL Dissertation Series
SBLSP	SBL Seminar Papers
SBT	Studies in Biblical Theology
SJOT	*Scandinavian Journal of the Old Testament*
SJT	*Scottish Journal of Theology*
ST	*Studia theologica*
ThWAT	G.J. Botterweck and H. Ringgren (eds.), *Theologisches Wörterbuch zum Alten Testament* (Stuttgart: W. Kohlhammer, 1970–)
TTod	*Theology Today*
TynBul	*Tyndale Bulletin*
TRE	*Theologische Realenzyklopädie*
VF	*Verkündigung und Forschung*
VT	*Vetus Testamentum*
VTSup	*Vetus Testamentum* Supplements
WBC	Word Biblical Commentary
WMANT	Wissenschaftliche Monographien zum Alten und Neuen Testament
ZAW	*Zeitschrift für die alttestamentliche Wissenschaft*
ZDPV	*Zeitschrift des deutschen Palästina-Vereins*

LIST OF CONTRIBUTORS

Graeme Auld (New College, University of Edinburgh)

Edward Ball (University of Nottingham)

John Barton (Oriel College, University of Oxford)

W.H. Bellinger, Jr (Baylor University, Waco, Texas)

Walter Brueggemann (Columbia Theological Seminary, Decatur, GA)

Brevard S. Childs (Yale University)

R.J. Coggins (formerly King's College, University of London)

Eryl W. Davies (University of Wales, Bangor)

Graham Davies (Fitzwilliam College, University of Cambridge)

Knud Jeppesen (University of Århus/The Ecumenical Institute, Tantur)

Paul M. Joyce (St Peter's College, University of Oxford)

Rex Mason (formerly Regent's Park College, University of Oxford)

Iain W. Provan (Regent College, Vancouver)

Rolf Rendtorff (Emeritus, University of Heidelberg)

J.W. Rogerson (Emeritus, University of Sheffield)

the late R.N. Whybray (Emeritus, University of Hull)

H.G.M. Williamson (Christ Church, University of Oxford)

RONALD ERNEST CLEMENTS: AN APPRECIATION

Rex Mason

Ronald Clements was born on 27 May 1929 and grew up in that not unpleasant part of 'Outer London in Essex' flanked by Epping Forest. He was educated at Buckhurst Hill County High School, where he was recognized as one of their most outstanding pupils. However, he did not continue into the Sixth Form and so aim for a direct route to university but went instead into banking. In that postwar period National Service was still obligatory and his time of service in Barclays Bank was interrupted as he served in the RAF from 1947–49, an experience he greatly enjoyed and which left him an enthusiast for travel of almost every kind, with a great love of aeroplanes and flying. This was a taste he could indulge later in Cambridge, surrounded as it was, especially in earlier years, by so many aerodromes and flying fields. He was a keen glider and still loves to fly in light aircraft. Once, after addressing a conference in South Africa, he stayed on for a week in order to travel its remaining steam train network. When the Society of Biblical Literature met in New Orleans, two of the great attractions for him were the paddle steamers on the Mississippi and the Charles Avenue streetcar.

However, this is to anticipate, for the road leading from a bank desk to participation in international conferences of biblical scholars might not seem a direct or easy one. That it was taken is the result of another major influence in his life in addition to Buckhurst Hill County High School, and that was the Baptist church in South Woodford. The Minister during Ron's formative years was the Revd Herbert Hunter, a delightful and enthusiastic Northern Ireland Protestant whose devotion to evangelical doctrines was matched only by the strength of his suspicion of deeply-laid papal plots! He was a deeply caring and sensitive pastor, however, who saw the great potential in this young church member and who encouraged in him a sense of call to the Baptist Ministry. No one will understand Ron Clements's later work as a scholar who does not see in it a marriage of great erudition and love of scholarship with a concern for sharing with others his own love of the Bible and the faith it nourished in him. Coming from the tradition he did it was natural that this candidate for ministerial training should apply to Spurgeon's College, the Baptist theological college in London founded by the great nineteenth-century Baptist preacher Charles Haddon Spurgeon, an institution which has always embraced a deep commitment to scholarship with the evangelical emphasis imprinted on it by its founder. It is the college which, among others, has also produced Arnold Anderson for Old Testament, and George Beasley-Murray for New Testament scholarship.

Lack of formal sixth-form education does not seem to have hindered Ron in any noticeable way, for his own industry and intellectual ability led him to prepare for entry to theological college with a thoroughness that few others could have matched. He attended extra-mural studies in French, Greek and Hebrew, and before his entry into college he was able to inform the college Principal, Dr F. Cawley, that he had completed his Greek grammar book and was working through Davidson's Hebrew Grammar. This latter, in particular, was no light enterprise, for it is a book which poses formidable barriers even for undergraduates, many of whom today have turned gratefully to more user-friendly substitutes or successors.

Ron entered Spurgeon's College in 1951 and in 1954 gained the London BD. In those days it was the custom for Baptist ministerial candidates with obvious academic abilities to go on from their first college to Regent's Park College in Oxford, since it was (very sensibly) seen that, with its attachment to the Theological Faculty in Oxford, it could provide scope for them in a way others then could not. Towards the end of his time at Spurgeon's, therefore, Ron applied to Regent's. At this point, however, a complication arose. He had by this time met his wife-to-be, Valerie Suffield, and after the protracted period of National Service and three years at Spurgeon's they naturally wished to get married without further delay. Regent's, however, had at that time a strict rule that ordinands were not to marry until the end of their college course. Pleas for the rules to be waived in this particular case were met with flinty hearts, not least that of the then Principal, Robert Child, who, a bachelor himself, perhaps had little sympathy with such a headlong dash for the altar. How good it is to report that Ron and Valerie put love before rules and regulations and, with a commendable show of that independence which has also often characterized his later work, Ron applied instead to Cambridge. Oxford's loss was Cambridge's gain, for thus began an association with Cambridge which has been broken only relatively briefly ever since. And, it is well worth recording, so also began a marriage which has been a long and happy one, a firm and secure base for all Ron's multifarious activities. It has produced two gifted daughters, Gillian and Marion, both of whom achieved success in their respective careers and who have in their turn presented Ron and Valerie with grandchildren who are a source of great delight to them.

In 1954 Ron went, then, to Christ's College, Cambridge. Among his teachers were J.N. Schofield, who was soon setting him two pages of Hebrew a day, and D. Winton Thomas, who taught him Hebrew prose composition. In such surroundings and inspired by such tutelage no wonder he was later writing to say how much he was 'enjoying the riches that Cambridge offers'. In 1956 he gained a first-class degree, and then proceeded to a pastorate in Southey Green Baptist Church, Sheffield, a church situated on a new housing estate. During this time his academic work forged ahead at a quite stupendous rate for one who was settling into a new ministry. He continued preparation for the Cambridge University Hebrew Prize which entailed mastering Aramaic for the Targums, but which he won the following year. At the same time he began work on a PhD at Sheffield under the supervision of F.F. Bruce. This he gained as early as 1961 upon the submission of a thesis entitled 'The Divine Dwelling Place in the Old Testament', a work subsequently published in 1965 as *God and Temple: The Idea of the Divine Presence in Ancient Israel*, and which has always been highly regarded and has exercised considerable influence.

It was inevitable that such industry and such ability would come to be more widely recognized, and so it was that in 1960 he was appointed as Assistant Lecturer in Old Testament Language, Literature and Theology at the University of Edinburgh, a post which became permanent in 1964. It was a significant move in which Ron may be said to have found his true 'ministry'. He had found the three years' work in the Sheffield church in some ways frustrating, and although he had received another invitation to a congregation in Stratford-upon-Avon and had just started his ministry there, he had little hesitation in moving to Edinburgh. With hindsight we can see how right this decision was, although at the time it ruffled a few official feathers in the high eyries of the Baptist Union! It was greatly to the credit of the then General Secretary of the Union, Ernest Payne, that he defended Ron's choice and insisted on keeping him as an accredited Baptist Minister, a choice which has greatly enriched Baptist circles in this country and throughout the world since.

At Edinburgh he worked with Professor Norman Porteous, a happy conjunction, since the interests of both were very much in the *theological* issues raised by study of the Old Testament. This was an interest well reflected in Ron's next book, *Prophecy and Covenant*, which also appeared in 1965. This, perhaps unsurprisingly in a young scholar at an early stage of his career, reflected very much the 'Covenant Theology' prevalent at the time, which saw the prophets as exponents of early covenant ideas rather than as innovators who helped to blaze the trail for such concepts. The appearance later of another book, *Prophecy and Tradition* (1975), in which some of these earlier opinions were revised in the light of later scholarship, showed, however, that his was by no means a closed mind but one always open to new exploration and to fresh insights.

In 1967 his growing reputation was recognized by the University of Cambridge which appointed him as Lecturer; and thus began, not only his long association with that university, which later was to confer upon him the degree of Doctor of Divinity, but also his association with Fitzwilliam College, one which he has always enjoyed greatly. The college gave him a base from which to influence generations of students, not only by his teaching and scholarship, but also by his pastoral care of them as individuals. These individual students have included by no means only those reading Theology, or ordinands. The circle has been diverse enough to include an England cricketer, Phil Edmonds, and another who was appointed a Master of Foxhounds immediately upon completing his Theology course! Cambridge was also the setting for the publication of a formidable array of books, articles and contributions to works of composite authorship, a scholarly output which has firmly established Ron's international reputation. Here one may record particularly his study *Abraham and David: Genesis 15 and its Meaning for Israelite Tradition* (1967) and his contributions to the study of Deuteronomy (e.g. *God's Chosen People* [1968] and *Deuteronomy* [1989]) and Isaiah (both *Isaiah and the Deliverance of Jerusalem* and *Isaiah 1–39*, his contribution to the New Century Bible series of commentaries, were published in 1980). All these works and many others have fully demonstrated both his love of the biblical texts and his interest in the theological issues they raise. This concern for theology was certainly evident in *Old Testament Theology: A Fresh Approach* (1978). Ron is one of very few British Old Testament scholars to have attempted such a work in recent years, and if there was criticism that the book somewhat neglected the Wisdom literature of the Old Testament this 'neglect' was more than amply compensated for in *Wisdom for a Changing World: Wisdom in Old Testament Theology* (1990) and *Wisdom in Theology* (1992).

It was fitting that such a scholar should come to occupy a professorial chair, and this duly occurred with his appointment in 1984 as Samuel Davidson Professor of Old Testament Studies at King's College, University of London. The appointment coincided with a period of ill-health for his wife, Valerie, and this was doubtless one of the reasons why he continued to reside in Cambridge. Happily, Valerie's health recovered and since Ron's slightly early retirement from London, they have both continued to live near Cambridge and in close touch with the university where he has been so happy for so many years. And there, fortunately for us all, his literary output seems to continue unabated.

He served as Foreign Secretary of the Society for Old Testament Study from 1973 to 1983. It was indeed fortunate for the Society to be served by him in this way for so long, since his overseas connections are so extensive and his own international reputation so strong. His knowledge of academic literary output in a formidable variety of languages is encyclopaedic, and his reputation is perhaps even more firmly established abroad than it is in Britain. Shortly after he retired from that post the Society elected him as its President for 1985.

His is a quiet personality, although friends very quickly find him to be a man of great warmth and humanity. There can be no doubt that Ron is an outstanding scholar whose work has made an invaluable contribution to many facets of Old Testament study. In this respect he stands worthily in that remarkable long line of outstanding Baptist Old Testament scholars which has included T.H. Robinson, H. Wheeler Robinson, H.H. Rowley and A.R. Johnson. But it is his human personality which has also contributed to the effectiveness and influence of his scholarly work. There is, first, the close relation he has established with generations of students, relationships which have included personal friendship and a real pastoral care to which many of them testify. Every one of them mattered to him and they were made to feel they were valued for what they were and for their own insights. One has also only to reflect on those of his past students who currently occupy significant posts in Old Testament studies to realize how wide has been the range of his influence as teacher. And when one further reflects on how diverse they are and how varied their approaches to their work, one sees here the mark of a truly great teacher who does not merely seek to reproduce clones of himself but encourages individuals to be themselves and helps to release their own individual powers and insights. And such a relationship has been effected, not merely because of his own meticulous and well-informed scholarship, but by his 'fullness' as a human being. For example, in addition to his interests in flying and all forms of travel he is also an enthusiastic photographer and takes a keen interest in the cinema. One distinguished Old Testament teacher who was taught by him put it exactly this way: '...he has always seemed the most down-to-earth and generally approachable of my eminent teachers and colleagues'. Nor is it only the intellectual élite of Edinburgh and Cambridge whom he has helped. He never considered himself too great to help as tutor, for example, in such lay educational schemes as those organized by the Baptist Union. A Cambridge minister told me of one young man in his church, who had received little formal education, to whom Ron gave great time and attention. The boy was so enthused by his teaching that he went on to tackle and pass the A-Levels needed to apply to university to read Theology.

Nor is it only students who have benefited from his erudition and his personal readiness to give time and encouragement to others. One of our most outstanding Old Testament scholars who was formerly a Cambridge colleague made the interesting remark to me, 'If you want to assess the value of Ron's contribution to scholarship look not only at his own books, but at the number of times he is mentioned in the prefaces of the books of other scholars'. That is because fellow scholars are always glad to be able to talk over their own work with Ron, partly because of his immense knowledge of current scholarly trends (perfectly illustrated in his *A Century of Old Testament Study* [1976, rev. edn, 1983]) but also because of his interest and concern and ability to provide new shafts of insight into a wide variety of issues.

In 1971 Ron was asked by his old college, Spurgeon's, to contribute a short article about himself as part of a series on illustrious former students in the college magazine, *The Record*. With characteristic self-effacement he wrote, not about himself, but about his work. He began,

'The lecture halls of a historic university may sound like a very sheltered place in which to exercise a Christian ministry...' However, he continues, '...teaching the Old Testament to men [this *was* 1971!] who have committed themselves to read a course of Theology has its spiritual excitement and interest... The Bible can only seriously continue to hold the affections and faith of men, so long as it also holds their intellectual convictions. A scholarly and critical investigation therefore is always a searching out of faith'. That is a remarkably succinct statement of how Ron has always seen his 'ministry', of holding faith and scholarship together, each employed in the service of the other, a process illustrated in all his work and particularly in such a book as *The Prayers of the Bible* (1986).

The present book is an expression of indebtedness by many who have gained immeasurably from this 'ministry' in many different ways. And those who write here are but representatives of many others who are grateful for this rare combination of scholar, man of faith and man of humanity.

HISTORY–INTERPRETATION–THEOLOGY: ISSUES IN BIBLICAL RELIGION*

Graeme Auld

1. A whole set of recently controversial issues clusters round the topics of history and meaning in the Bible.

How 'do-able' is ancient Israelite history? How serviceable are the biblical materials as historical sources? Can we at least write—or attempt to write—a history of the biblical material? Must we so attempt, because that is simply our principal way of organizing our thinking in the modern world?

Are we dependent for 'history properly so called' on written documentation? Is study of the past by means of other sources 'pre-history', or simply non-history?

Are biblical history and ancient Israelite history interchangeable terms? Should they be? If a choice must be made, does 'ancient Israel' refer first and foremost to the people about whom the Bible speaks, or to the people who produced the Bible? And what about biblical theology? Is that something done in the Bible, or to or with the Bible?

How historical—how history-focused—is biblical faith or religion? Is a strong positive answer demanded by the oft-repeated biblical injunction to remember or memorialize the past? And how otherwise may we understand the concern with their own time and their own world that seems prominent among the biblical prophets?

What does 'biblical religion' mean? Should answers be sought first from the Psalms, where overt interest in history is less (and the memory

---

*   It is a pleasure to offer these remarks to one of my teachers, half his lifetime ago, whose influential monographs on *Abraham and David*, *God's Chosen People*, and *Prophecy and Covenant*, were all prepared in his Edinburgh period. A first version of this paper was presented as the 1998 Ethel M. Wood Lecture at the University of London, where Ronald Clements completed his career as Samuel Davidson Professor.

most mentioned is God's), rather than from Torah and Prophets?

Recent controversy on the aims and the possibility and the means and the ethics of writing histories of ancient Israel is well documented, and need only be selectively mentioned here.[1] Some of the discourse is very bitter. Raw nerve ends of individuals or of corporate bodies are clearly being exposed. Important values are held to be—or feared to be—at stake. For at least some of the participants, it is 'us' and 'ours' that are being slightingly discussed; and careless talk matters.

Elements of the conversation I want to grapple with include:

The compelling review (by Barstad) of historical methodologies, although I remain less persuaded than he that Solomon was an historical figure.[2]

The biblical narrative as propaganda rather than history (Carroll).[3] I take it he means propaganda in the older ecclesiastical sense of 'congregatio de propaganda fide' (a 'congregation for the "advancing" of faith'). However, I grant it that the politics in question is adversarial, rather than consensual.

If we say (with Philip Davies[4]) that there is no neutral history, do we thereby shorten our distance from the Bible? If we agree with him that we should not trust anyone who claims to offer a neutral history (and is his analogy for neutrality Switzerland or No-Man's-Land?), that does not preclude an attempt at greater inclusiveness, at an account of the past that could be more widely shared.

Just as the history of Palestine (its past and our discourse about its past) must be given back to all of its inhabitants (Lemche,[5] reviewing Whitelam[6]), so too, one hopes, the (history of the) Bible must be made

1.   It is conveniently attested and explored in L.L. Grabbe (ed.), *Can a 'History of Israel' be Written?* (JSOTSup, 245; European Seminar in Historical Methodology, 1; Sheffield: Sheffield Academic Press, 1997).

2.   H.M. Barstad, 'History and the Hebrew Bible', in Grabbe (ed.), *Can a 'History of Israel'*, pp. 37-64 (on Solomon see p. 60).

3.   R.P. Carroll, 'Madonna of Silences: Clio and the Bible', in Grabbe (ed.), *Can a 'History of Israel'*, pp. 84-103 (on propaganda see pp. 101-102).

4.   P.R. Davies, 'Whose History? Whose Israel? Whose Bible? Biblical Histories, Ancient and Modern', in Grabbe (ed.), *Can a 'History of Israel'*, pp. 104-22.

5.   N.P. Lemche, 'Clio is also among the Muses! Keith W. Whitelam and the History of Palestine: A Review and a Commentary', in Grabbe (ed.), *Can a 'History of Israel'*, pp. 123-55.

6.   K.W. Whitelam, *The Invention of Ancient Israel: The Silencing of Palestinian History* (London: Routledge, 1996).

available to all of its readers. And, throughout, there is the nagging question of involvement and detachment: whether the historian can be the physician or only the pathologist of memory. Yerushalmi relates the flowering of contemporary Jewish historiography to the widespread loss of memory and faith.[7] An important related question is whether the sort of truth-telling envisaged (at least) in (the setting up of) the South African Truth and Reconciliation Commission can lead to a future—and a history—with which people in a radically divided society can more readily live.

After such a scatter of questions, are we reaching a place, finally, at which discussion of the relatedness of historical criticism and biblical theology can begin? There is so much variety, so much ambiguity, there are so many contrary strands, in the Hebrew Bible that biblical interpretation or biblical theology, however defined, must be given wide scope.

A first biblical illustration of several of the issues at stake, and one with continuing resonance, is provided at the end of Exodus 17. 'Then Yahweh said to Moses, "Write this as a memorandum in a book and recite it in the hearing of Joshua: Nothing less than "blot out" from under heaven is what I will do to the memory/ial of Amalek." And Moses...said, "...Yahweh will have war with Amalek from generation to generation".' The words of Moses ('from generation to generation') appear to be in tension with those of his God ('I will utterly blot out the memory'). Yet they also offer a consistent reading of Yahweh's own words, which appear to subvert each other: put on record—and recite the record—that I will erase the record. At the very minimum the whole passage represents a confidence—or a deeply-held longing—that Amalek, a contemporary cipher in Israel for the Palestinians or at least the PLO, will never win; that it does not belong alongside Israel. Put more mythologically: Israel's divine champion is committed to denying Amalek a place in heaven's book. The memory, the memorial, the record is of a future pledge. As such, it is rather like Isaiah's Maher-shalal-hash-baz, attested by reliable witnesses (8.1-4), or his document inscribed 'for a later day, as a witness for ever' (30.8). When we recognize that our historiography is for the present and the future, we stand in continuity with biblical memory. 'It is I AM/I SHALL BE who has sent me to you' (Exod. 3.14).

7.   Y.H. Yerushalmi, *ZAKHOR: Jewish History and Jewish Memory* (Seattle: University of Washington Press, 1982).

2. The stories of Joseph in Egypt model for us two different sorts of interpreter: the sort Joseph himself was, and the sort he did not need. Joseph was able, by virtue of divine gift, to explain the significance of their dreams to his family, his fellow prisoners and Pharaoh himself (Gen. 37; 40-41). On the other hand, he needed no translation facilities to understand what his brothers were saying among themselves in his presence—they themselves were unaware of this because their communication with the Egyptian vizier was through an interpreter (Gen. 42.23).

A story set early in Genesis sees God punish overweening human ambition by turning linguistic intercourse into a confusing babble (Gen. 11.1-9). Yet interpretation as translation is seldom an explicit issue within the pages of the Hebrew Bible. With half an eye already open to our topic, we might offer different explanations. The tales of any country seldom delay to tell us how their characters communicate, even where one of them is a traveller from a distant land: they simply speak to each other. Wherever we find such material in the Bible, we should not expect evidence of communication difficulties. Alternatively, in the ancient Levant as in the same area today, 'real' people may have been more competently multi-lingual than most native English-speakers would suppose possible.

We might conveniently continue our approach towards issues of history and biblical interpretation via two narratives from the books of Luke and Acts in the New Testament. These tales are apparently related, and are certainly cautionary. Two puzzled followers of Jesus, walking homewards away from Jerusalem, are trying to make sense not only of his death, despite their hopes for him, but also of reports that he is alive. Someone they meet chides them for their slowness to 'believe all the prophets have declared', interprets for them all the Scriptures, breaks and blesses bread for them, and vanishes as they recognize him as the risen Jesus (Lk. 24.13-32). The eunuch in charge of an African queen's treasury is also on a road down from Jerusalem after worship at the temple. He is reading Isaiah. His interlocutor asks him if he is understanding what he is reading. 'How can I, unless someone guides me?' Philip starts from the passage of Isaiah the eunuch is reading, and proclaims the good news about Jesus. Seeing water, the eunuch asks for baptism; after administering that, Philip is snatched away by the Spirit of the Lord (Acts 8.26-40).

In both cases, Scripture is interpreted, or a reader is led to understand

Scripture, as being about Jesus. The one tale moves from Jesus to
Scripture and the other from Scripture to Jesus: the starting point matters less than the relatedness. And each story ends with what has
become one of the sacraments of Christianity, and the immediate disappearance of the interpreter. Was no further interpretation required, once
the code was broken? Or was further interpretation now the business of
the (Christian) community?

The eunuch in the story knew he needed a guide to help him read
Isaiah no less than Pharaoh's cup-bearer and chief baker needed an
interpreter for the dreams that worried them. And history is important in
pesher or *pitron*. Yet the history that is vital in such interpretation is the
contemporary history that is illumined by the divinely-provided dream
or text. The history or the reality that is important to each of the New
Testament tales is in part the good news about Jesus—but also in part
how that good news bears on those who come to know it. However, in
order for the interpretation to 'work', the (books of) 'Moses and the
prophets' which are 'interpreted' need be no more historical in part or
whole than the dreams and visions which required interpretation by
Joseph and Daniel in the first book of Moses and the last book of the
prophets.

Yet to say that the biblical means of illumination may be no more
real than a dream or a vision or a story is to give a misleadingly negative impression. For the means of 'real' illumination will be dream-like
or story-like. Plain speaking about God is no more possible in most of
the Hebrew Bible than straightforward looking at God. I am suggesting
that these two New Testament stories, by featuring an interpreter or a
guide at work on the Bible, should actually permit a latter-day Theophilus to remove the historicity of Moses and the prophets of the Hebrew Scriptures from the agenda of Christian theology.[8] The implication
of such an attitude to biblical history is more fashionable in some
contemporary quarters than others—and is quite a recent fashion. For
many, the historicity of Old Testament materials is much more important theologically than I have suggested.

3. It may readily be conceded that New Testament interpretation of
Scripture is largely a matter of contemporizing exposition. But much
contemporary biblical interpretation is closer to translation: the kind of

8. Theophilus in P. Carey, *Oscar and Lucinda* (London: Faber and Faber,
1988) would not readily have been so encouraged. For the Lucan Theophilus, see
section 3 below.

interpretation Joseph did not require. It is more concerned with better understanding of documents from a strange culture in unfamiliar language: with developing competence in reading. A whole clutch of books from the current decade have addressed the issue. I draw attention first to three of these: two by Christian academics of different persuasions and one by a Jewish scholar.

Bartlett's 'critical enquiry into the nature of biblical history'[9] reports on and discusses what was widely taught in the 1980s, as indeed still in the 1990s, about the production and development of much of the Bible: how greater awareness of the history of the text should induce greater sensitivity to such history as is reported in the text. I suspect he is perceived by conservative readers as too ready to argue that much of the biblical text is other than history pure and simple. Many will be impatient over his agreement with Oscar Wilde that history is 'rarely pure and never simple'. And I wonder at his optimism that dating individual books is 'for the most part...not particularly difficult'.[10] Yet he is enthusiastic himself to talk up the importance of substantial historicity for the believer, even if not for belief itself:

> While it is true that what matters for faith and theology is Israel's perception of what happened, her understanding of her history, it is also true that what matters for our peace of mind is that Israel's perception of her history was not too far removed from what actually happened.[11]

Yet that depends on which part of the history is under review: the peace of mind of many readers (for example Calvin on Joshua[12]) would have been eased had what happened been more remote from the perception.

Long has contributed a confessedly conservative evangelical but also very irenic discussion of *The Art of Biblical History*.[13] He writes well, though in very general terms, about the need to develop 'ancient literary competence'—only on his last page does he mention ancient Near Eastern and Hellenistic literature—; and about the ambiguity of history no

---

9. J.R. Bartlett, *The Bible: Faith and Evidence. A Critical Enquiry into the Nature of Biblical History* (London: British Museum Publications, 1990).

10. Bartlett, *The Bible*, p. 17.

11. Bartlett, *The Bible*, p. 5.

12. See D.F. Wright, 'Accomodation and Barbarity in John Calvin's Old Testament Commentaries', in A.G. Auld (ed.), *Understanding Poets and Prophets* (JSOTSup, 152; Sheffield: Sheffield Academic Press, 1993), pp. 413-27.

13. V.P. Long, *The Art of Biblical History* (Foundations of Contemporary Interpretation, 5; Leicester: Apollos, 1994).

less than of fiction.[14] Yet there is a good deal of 'persuasive definition' in his argument. Remarkably few biblical authors claimed divine inspiration for their writing, despite the impression he gives; and Luke's preface (1.1-4), one of the few explicit statements of intent in all of the Bible, does not so much make a truth claim as assert that the author has taken care and been orderly.[15]

Brettler's *The Creation of History in Ancient Israel*[16] is in many respects not dissimilar in aim to Bartlett's critical enquiry. He endeavours to 'show what various biblical authors were 'trying to do' when they wrote works which we typically categorize as historical'. Yet he is more radical than Bartlett: he continues-

> The approach I suggest questions the traditional assumption that ancient Israelite and early Jewish religions were fundamentally historical religions in the sense of being primarily concerned with, and based on, actual events in history. A strong impetus for my dissenting perspective comes from a study by Moshe David Herr, 'The Conception of History among the Sages'. He points to an idiom in rabbinic literature: 'what was, was', which shows the rabbis' complete disregard for actual events of the past. Based on the use of that idiom and other rabbinic evidence, he notes, 'there was no question more meaningless or boring [to the rabbis] than the purpose and usefulness of an exact description of what actually transpired.'[17]

Although their religion is important to each of them, these three scholars are addressing a wider readership. Each is facing the less partisan, more disinterested questions of the public: not (just) what is the Bible for (us) believers, but what is the Bible in itself? The studies by Bartlett, Long and Brettler all use the books of Samuel and Chronicles as worked examples.

Bartlett aptly sketches the difficulties in assessing the contents of 1 and 2 Samuel as historical. His remarks are typical of a historian assessing the quality of evidence. Few of the materials could possibly be archival. The source-material available to the author exhibited more of the character of popular story-telling. As to the character of the final writing: 'who but a novelist could recount the many private conversa-

14. Long, *The Art of Biblical History*, pp. 33, 226, 58-63.

15. Long, *The Art of Biblical History*, pp. 75, 92.

16. M.Z. Brettler, *The Creation of History in Ancient Israel* (London: Routledge, 1995).

17. Brettler, *The Creation*, p. 2.

tions given in these chapters?'. His account of the Chronicler's work, which he states to be 'clearly based on the earlier books of Samuel and Kings', pinpoints its leading ideas and notes indicators, such as coinage, that it dates from the fifth or even fourth century BCE.[18]

Long's interests seem more those of the expositor than the historian. He directs our attention first to a synoptic view of Samuel and Chronicles, with Nathan's oracle to David as his main example.[19] Alternative accounts are less historical problem, and more historian's opportunity. The Chronicler offers not so much a repainting (on the same canvas) as a second painting of the subject matter of Samuel–Kings. This new version explains and updates the earlier work for a later age, but with no intention to replace it. What it does allow us is a richer appreciation of the shared subject matter.

Long's final main chapter reviews 'the rise of Saul' as an extended example of the argument of his book. He is concerned to rebut the widely-held conclusion that the events by which Saul came to the throne 'are and will remain a mystery'.[20] He recognizes that the issue is not so much the paucity of relevant archaeological evidence, or the lack in the ancient Near East in the tenth century BCE of suitable historiographic parallels. 'By far the most frequently cited reason for the historical agnosticism regarding Saul's kingship is the belief that the biblical narratives recounting Saul's rise simply do not make sense as a story'.[21] This issue he faces with some success; and he concludes that, since the books of Samuel as a whole have a historiographical character, the narrative of Saul's rise (when correctly read as a coherent account) does make truth claims.

Bartlett begins with Samuel, Long with Samuel and Chronicles together, but Brettler very deliberately with the Chronicler. Since we have his main source (Samuel–Kings), we can learn most clearly from the Chronicler how a biblical historian worked. He commends Cogan's view that the Chronicler should be assessed not only as a theologian, 'but also as an example of historiographic writing which mirrors the canons of ancient Near Eastern literature'. And after a very useful review of the Chronicler and recent study of him, he concludes:

18. Bartlett, *The Bible*, pp. 69, 150-53.
19. Long, *The Art of Biblical History*, pp. 76-87.
20. *The Art of Biblical History*, pp. 201-23, 202.
21. Long, *The Art of Biblical History*, p. 204.

> The Chronicler in many ways was like the official newspapers that are
> published by some non-democratic regimes—the people writing them
> are often so convinced of a particular doctrine that dissenting sources
> have little impact on their reporting... It is only because we no longer
> subscribe to the Chronicler's ideologies that we so clearly perceive the
> Chronicler's bias, and suspect that his history diverges significantly from
> the actual past.[22]

Brettler's main point should elicit considerable sympathy, though I
am far from persuaded that ideological bias in the press is a failing particular to 'non-democratic' regimes. He returns to a similar analogy in a
later chapter where he starts his discussion of ideology in the books of
Samuel with reference to *The King David Report* by Stefan Heym of
the (then) German Democratic Republic.[23] His reading of Samuel is
both careful and suggestive. But it should, I think, be brought closer to
his analysis of the Chronicler.

4. The long-standing consensus, reproduced again by each of Bartlett,
Long and Brettler, is that the Chronicler's source history was the books
of Samuel and Kings. I see my own historical-critical studies of recent
years on Samuel–Kings and Chronicles as contributing also to a fresh
theological appropriation of these materials. I have been arguing that
Samuel–Kings and Chronicles are something like two originally-identi-
cal cuttings from the same plant: cultivated in different soils and in different climates, trained differently, and grown to twice their original
size—and very different now in aspect. That organic analogy covers
some of the divergence; but it needs to be corrected by another. Two
drawers of paper files in different departments of a single organization
each began half full, and with identical sections and contents. But, as
the departments went about their separate work, their files accumulated
quite differently. Sometimes only a single sheet was added to a folder;
sometimes much more; and sometimes whole new folders had to be
added to one or other drawer to cope with entirely fresh business.

If my part-organic, part-archival analogy offers a more appropriate
model of the relationship between Samuel–Kings and Chronicles, the
original from which each has developed to double the size was made up
of two very different halves. The second was often little more than an
annotated list of the kings that followed Solomon in Jerusalem over
some 350 years. Here and there it could extend to chapter-length detail.

22. Brettler, *The Creation*, pp. 20, 23, 47.
23. *The Creation*, pp. 91-111.

Such material would have had some relationship to the official royal records of Jerusalem. But, after the collapse of the city, it could readily have been reconstructed from the memory of one of the royal scribes: the basic genealogical information supplemented by a sentence here and a story there, as recollection enabled or importance required. The first half was extended narrative, devoted to an account of David and Solomon: David, the founder of the dynasty; and Solomon, the great builder of Jerusalem. This had been much more largely legendary. Such a judgment can readily be heard as pejorative. But it is precisely in these more extended narratives, I want to argue, that key issues and attitudes are sketched which are vital for the interpretation of divine house and royal house in Jerusalem that follows.

My earlier studies concentrated on two aspects of the evidence: the portraits of Solomon, and the development of religious polemic.[24] A more recent article has looked at the role prophets and seers play in the source common to Samuel–Kings and Chronicles.[25] I have found that tracking the few prophets in what I am calling the Book of Two Houses leads very close to the heart of that fundamental work. When working on a short commentary on the books of Samuel,[26] I have found many more pieces of a complicated jigsaw slotting into place.

Two of the shared stories involving seers and prophets may serve as helpful examples. One is from the founding days: the report of David's census; the other is one of the longer narratives that slow down the summary treatment of Jerusalem's kings, and stars critical Micaiah ben Imlah ranged against four hundred more compliant or supportive prophets. For most scholars, these very different stories share the same problem: they do not fit where they are—they are erratic boulders in otherwise straightforward landscapes. David's census is widely seen as one of several appendices to the books of Samuel that wrench apart from each other the troubles in David's family (2 Sam. 13–20) and their proper conclusion in the machinations that ensure the succession of Solomon (1 Kgs 1–2). As for Micaiah (1 Kgs 22), his vision of the heavenly court, so like Isaiah's, and the presence in the story of a king of Judah alongside Ahab of Israel, mark this story off from the long

24. A.G. Auld, *Kings without Privilege* (Edinburgh: T. & T. Clark, 1994).

25. 'Prophets Shared—and Recycled', in T. Römer (ed.), *The Future of the 'Deuteronomistic History'* (BETL [forthcoming]).

26. For J.D.G. Dunn and J.W. Rogerson (eds.), *Commentary 2000* (Grand Rapids: Eerdmans [forthcoming]).

Elijah/Elisha cycle at the heart of the two books of Kings (1 Kgs 17–2 Kgs 10).

Yet I also want to argue that these two stories are among those more extended narratives in the Book of Two Houses which bear the main weight of religious explanation in that book. Am I describing something like the famous ambiguous drawings? You can see it as a duck or as a rabbit; you can see it as opposing faces in profile or as a classical urn—but not both at the same time. If you concentrate on one way of looking, you stop seeing the other. Two characteristics tip the balance and settle the argument to my satisfaction: the inter-connectedness of the 'erratic boulders', and their classic status. I suspect that they are not so much rooted in the tradition, as part of the root-system of that tradition.

For many scholars, the central section of the books of Kings dominated by Elijah and Elisha had been drawn from prophetic rather than royal sources. That had been true of the story of Micaiah as well, though it had derived from a different prophetic source. It is widely held that Ahab was not the original anti-hero involved: how could Ahab have had recourse to four hundred prophets of the Lord (1 Kgs 22 // 2 Chron. 18) when Elijah already knew that only he was left in that role (1 Kgs 19.10, 14)? But look away from Jezebel's husband and a cast of many prophets, and concentrate on Jehoshaphat king of Judah, and the story fits well the whole record of David's line. From its anchorage there it has had wide influence. Micaiah, one against four hundred, is Elijah's role-model rather than a problem for his story. When Zedekiah, spokesman for the four hundred, slaps Micaiah's face and asks him, 'Which way did the spirit of the Lord pass from me to speak to you?', he supplies the (later) author of 1 Samuel with the language that explains Saul's loss of divine support in favour of David (1 Sam. 16.14).

David is divinely incited to count his people (2 Sam. 24 // 1 Chron. 21). Joab suggests it is wrong, but is overruled and must himself organize the count. Only when the tally is complete is David's heart 'stricken'. He has sinned; he asks for his guilt to be removed; he has been very foolish. Yet, when Gad, his seer, comes to him in the morning, he asks only which of three divine punishments David will choose. The question how, or whether, whichever punishment chosen will relate to the removal of his guilt is left unaddressed. David chooses, but hopes for divine mercy. When the deity sees the destroying angel about to strike Jerusalem, he has him stay his hand. When David sees the destruction of his people, he protests that only he has sinned—only he and his household should suffer: not 'these sheep'. (Micaiah in his vision sees 'all Israel scattered like sheep without a shepherd' [1 Kgs 22.17]—one of the many internal connections between the prophetic stories in the Book of Two Houses.) Gad comes again, and instructs the building of an altar: when sacrifice is offered, the plague is averted.

Many of the questions that it poses, great story that this is, it also leaves unanswered. As the Book of Two Houses was being expansively rewritten to become Samuel and Kings, later additions to the royal story anticipated some of these issues and suggested resolution. When Nathan condemns David's adultery, David also confesses he has sinned. Nathan does respond directly to the confession: the Lord has removed his sin—he will not die, but a member of his household will (2 Sam. 12.13-14). The earlier census story has raised the big issues; the later story, though we come to it sooner in the book, addresses some of them in expected ways. Still earlier in the books of Samuel, some of the distinctive language and issues relating to David's census are tellingly recombined in stories about Saul.

The second time fugitive David has Saul in his power, Saul says to him: 'I have sinned... I have been foolish and very mistaken'. David responds, even if rather bleakly: 'The Lord rewards everyone for his righteousness and faithfulness' (1 Sam. 26.21, 23). But it is the story of Saul's very first campaign as king (1 Sam. 13) which gives the strongest hint that we should read Samuel from back to front. Saul at Gilgal offers the same sacrifices as conclude the census story, without waiting as he had been told to for Samuel to come (13.9, 10). Samuel tells him he has been 'foolish' (part of David's admission) and warns him that his kingdom will not survive (13.13, 14). And Saul then counts the people who were with him (13.15b)! When you already know the census story, you do not need Samuel to tell you that Saul is done for before he is properly begun. But, when you know the census story, you also hear in the report of Saul at Gilgal a new threat against the house of David: one that is not explicitly voiced when he counts the people—it is the hold of his house over the very kingship that is at stake.

Each variation on the theme of David's confession in the census-story, each narrative commentary on that text, supplies what is found lacking in the text itself: an explicit acknowledgment by Gad or by any-body that David has confessed—and comprehensively so. Response is lacking in the theme; and that lack in the theme is pointed up by being supplied in each of the variations. But the very beginning of 1 Samuel does suggest an explanation for that lack. It reports as follows on old Eli rebuking his no-use priestly sons at Shiloh: 'If one person sins against another, God will mediate for the sinner; but if someone sins against the Lord, who can make intercession?' The author adds, 'they would not listen to the voice of their father; for it was the will of the Lord to kill them' (2.25). In the variations on the confession theme from the census, Saul sinned or behaved foolishly against Samuel and David, and David against Bathsheba and Uriah—all of them, person to human person. But in the theme itself, David did not listen to Joab's warning and sinned against the Lord.

Exodus offers a remedy (30.12-13). Its prescription is appropriate to a scattered community no longer resident near the temple:

> When you take a census of the Israelites to register them, at registration all of them shall give a ransom for their lives to the Lord, so that no plague may come upon them for being registered...half a shekel according to the shekel of the sanctuary.

A tax to finance the appropriate *lustratio* or *tebetu*. And Deuteronomy may hint at a reason:

> Take care that you do not forget the Lord your God... When you have eaten your fill and have built fine houses and live in them, and when your herds and flocks have multiplied, and all that you have is multiplied, then do not exalt yourself... Do not say to yourself, 'My power and the might of my own arm have gained me this wealth' (8.11-17).

Yet Deuteronomy actually talks about the multiplication of everything they possess, and not their own numbers.

The authors of Deuteronomy and of Exodus both knew what David had done, and what the consequences had been. The census story itself ends: 'David...offered burnt offerings and offerings of well-being. So the Lord answered...' (2 Sam. 24.25 // 1 Chron. 21.26). So far so good—but how far does this conclusion engage with David's own request that he and his house bear the iniquity? The story of Eli may be relevant again. The Lord's first message to Samuel had included this statement: 'The iniquity of Eli's house shall not be expiated by sacrifice or offering for ever' (1 Sam. 3.14). Did the averting of the plague from Israel, did David's successful supplication for the land, include a solution to his own problem? Neither does the old Book of Two Houses say, although it underscores the question by accusing of sin only David and the wicked Manasseh (2 Kgs 21.16 // 2 Chron. 33.19) out of all the kings who ruled in Jerusalem—David is in bad company in the source. Nor do the new books of Samuel say. But they do help us ask the question whether David's house was already doomed like Eli's. Excellent commentary: commentary that does not get in the way of the text!

5. Solomon and Manasseh, religious polemic, the role of prophecy—the hypothetical Book of Two Houses, though largely mechanically reconstructed from its two expanded successors, comes through each test of its coherence and artistry. Most of the discussion in my earlier studies was based on Kings and Chronicles. I have included the foregoing discussion here, in part at least, as a down-payment on the demonstration that the Book of Two Houses was also the seedbed from which our books of Samuel grew; the theme on which they played variations; the classic text on which they and other biblical books so brilliantly mused.

Robert Carroll's powerful and touching tribute to Ronald Clements's predecessor in the Samuel Davidson chair in King's College notes that there is no biblical story.[27] We are told in the Bible (in the main example Carroll uses) that the temple vessels from Jerusalem were destroyed—and also that they were available to be restored. Faced with such discrepancy, we readers have to make our own biblical story. I want first to support his argument by adding the case of Saul at the opposite end of our 400-year story of the houses of David and Yahweh in Jerusalem. The Book of Two Houses reports simply that Saul and his sons perished on Mt Gilboa and that Israel made David their king in Hebron. The Chronicler, following his source in that book, reports of Saul that he with his three sons and all his house died together on the northern mountain—as complete an end as the destruction of the temple vessels. However, another author spins in 1 Samuel, as a foil to his new introduction to David, a brilliant and tragic life for the Saul whom his source simply let die. Not content with that, he contrives in 2 Samuel another son and a son's son and further descendants: Saul's family, rescued like Sherlock Holmes by the narrator from a fatal fall, returns to continue testing David.

Yet, exactly as we note the greater freedom to retell, at the beginning

27. R.P. Carroll, 'Razed Temple and Shattered Vessels: Continuities and Discontinuities in the Discourse of Exile in the Hebrew Bible', *JSOT* 75 (1997), pp. 93-106.

and after the end of our story, we must also note that in this Book of
Two Houses there did exist a biblical story of the kings of Jerusalem. It
did not inhibit elaboration; but it gave structure to further development.
Some of its powerful and integral chapters, like David's census,
resonate with other classics like the divine testing of Abraham and of
Job—and may have influenced them.

6. The example I have followed through the books of Samuel also
provides a basis for discussion with a point important to Philips Long—
a discussion essentially independent of the history I am advocating of
the development of the material. He cites Vos at length[28] on the indis-
pensability of history for valid Christian faith that takes sin seriously. I
am not concerned here to dispute that main point. But I do doubt
whether one should extrapolate backwards from it, and insist on the
importance of the maximal historicity of the books of Samuel for valid
Christian faith. Sin, identification and confession of sin, and removal of
sin are very important topics in the books of Samuel, as in the Book of
Two Houses before them. But the treatment of these leaves us not with
eternal credal verities related to the happened-ness of certain events, but
rather with big questions: Did sacrifice by God's chosen David on the
site of his chosen altar in Jerusalem achieve for David's house the expi-
ation denied to the house of Eli? Or, despite the promise to him, was
David's house doomed before ever the first of his descendants succeeded him?

The issues had been of great moment, political and religious and
theological, for a community wondering whether and how its present
and future well-being were bound up with the remnants of the house of
David or with sacrifice on an altar in front of the house of Yahweh. And
what it means to be tested by God, and whether there is a sin more terrible than those we practise on each other, are issues that did not die
with the passing of that community—and may address readers who are
neither Jewish nor Christian. But the writing which explores these
questions is no more—and also no less—historical than a Dostoevsky
novel.

---

28. *The Art of Biblical History*, pp. 94-95.

CANON AND OLD TESTAMENT INTERPRETATION

John Barton

When the history of twentieth-century biblical interpretation comes to be written, will the various movements known as 'canonical criticism' or 'the canonical approach' be assessed as major or minor events in biblical studies in the last two decades of the century? At one level they can hardly be said to have started 'schools': the number of biblical scholars who are card-carrying members of the canonical criticism union is really quite small. On the other hand, to change the metaphor, they have succeeded in moving the goalposts. This is especially true, I think, of Brevard Childs's canonical method,[1] which because it is superficially rather like some literary movements in biblical criticism, particularly in its concern with the 'final form' of the biblical text, is very much in tune with the spirit of biblical study in our day. While few scholars declare themselves canonical critics, many feel the force of Childs's argument that we should be much more interested than biblical criticism has traditionally been in the text as it lies before us, and want to ask about the relationship between different books within the canon of Scripture rather than acting as though the canon were essentially an irrelevance. We find scholars asking about the overall structure and theology of the Pentateuch,[2] the shaping of the book of the Twelve,[3] the

1. For Childs's approach see B.S. Childs, *Introduction to the Old Testament as Scripture* (Philadelphia: Fortress Press; London: SCM Press, 1979); *Old Testament Theology in a Canonical Context* (London: SCM Press, 1985); and *Biblical Theology of the Old and New Testaments* (London: SCM Press, 1992).

2. Cf. D.J.A. Clines, *The Theme of the Pentateuch* (JSOTSup, 10; Sheffield: JSOT Press, 1978).

3. Cf. J. Nogalski, *Redactional Processes in the Book of the Twelve* (BZAW, 218; Berlin: W. de Gruyter, 1993). See also my discussion in J. Barton, 'The Canonical Meaning of the Book of the Twelve', in J. Barton and D.J. Reimer (eds.), *After the Exile: Essays in Honour of Rex Mason* (Macon, GA: Mercer University Press, 1996), pp. 59-73.

meaning of the book of Isaiah in its complete form.[4] Such interests, though they do not necessarily amount to the canonical approach as Childs himself understands it, do owe a lot to his influence in changing the questions it is thought sensible to ask about the Old Testament.[5]We should not measure Childs's importance simply in terms of adding up his disciples, who are admittedly few, but should credit to him at least part of the great sea-change which has come over Old Testament study in our day, as a result of which the exegesis of whole books and even of the Old Testament as a whole is now on the agenda in a way unthinkable in, say, the 1950s or 1960s.

Obviously, then, the canonical approach is a new approach to the Old Testament: indeed, it defines itself by contrast with the historical-critical movement which was dominant before its arrival on the scene. Yet there is a certain ambivalence in Childs's own assessment of his approach. At the same time as he emphasizes its novelty by contrast with historical criticism, he also wishes to assert its substantial continuity with what are usually called 'pre-critical' approaches to the biblical text. Childs is not saying that we should begin to look at the finished form of the canonical text, but rather that we should *get back* to looking at this form. Historical criticism, on his view, has been one long bad dream, separating two periods of a real waking attention to the text, the first represented by the classic Christian commentators of the past—the Fathers, the Reformers—and the second by his own programme of canonical reading. Thus the canonical method, though in one sense new by comparison with historical criticism, is in another sense much older. It

---

4.   See E.W. Conrad, *Reading Isaiah* (OBT; Minneapolis: Fortress Press, 1991) and other works cited in J. Barton, *Isaiah 1–39* (OTG; Sheffield: Sheffield Academic Press, 1995), pp. 121-22.

5.   Childs's concerns were anticipated in a highly creative article by Ronald E. Clements, 'Patterns in the Prophetic Canon', in G.W. Coats and B.O. Long (eds.), *Canon and Authority: Essays in Old Testament Religion and Theology* (Philadelphia: Fortress Press, 1977), pp. 42-55. This article was a contribution to the historical development of the canon of the prophets, and is not an exercise in the 'canonical approach' in the sense discussed in the present article. It is a great pleasure to dedicate this article to Ronald Clements, who has done so much for biblical scholarship, and who greatly encouraged me when I was beginning my academic career and has been unfailingly kind and gracious ever since.

is an attempt to recapture, in a postcritical world, the genuine theological engagement with the Bible that characterized what we dismissively call the pre-critical era.

In this essay I want to examine this dual claim to be both new and old. My argument will take the form of trying to show that, though both sides of the claim have some validity, the canonical approach as a form of biblical interpretation is neither so new nor so old as it appears. I shall then go on, however, to suggest that this rather negative conclusion points not in the direction of suggesting that the canonical approach is therefore rather unimportant, but on the contrary that it is too important to be understood purely within a biblical studies context. The canonical method is a method within systematic theology, and it is as such that it should be evaluated.

The Alleged Novelty of the Canonical Approach

So long as we stay within the world of Old Testament study, it is not hard to show that Childs's approach is in fact less novel than he himself claims. It is indeed a sharp departure from the normal approach of historical criticism. But it is a mistake to think that historical criticism has been so enormously dominant in twentieth-century interpretation as Childs suggests. Part of the rhetoric of all the newer methods—canonical criticism, the newer literary approaches, poststructuralist and postmodernist movements of all sorts—is that historical criticism has had an unchallenged dominance in our field since the late nineteenth century or perhaps for even longer, and that it is only in the 1980s and 1990s that anyone has begun to see through it. This, however, is a distortion of the history of twentieth-century biblical interpretation. It rests on a memory (but in many cases, I think, a false memory) of being told by a lecturer or professor that now one was at university one was to ask only historical questions of the Old Testament: that in his class no theological interpretation of the Old Testament was allowed. I can think of teachers of Old Testament of whom this was probably true, but I greatly doubt whether they were ever in the majority. Most Old Testament teachers in the twentieth century have been religious believers (it is only in the last couple of decades that this has ceased to be true, if indeed it has even now), and they have seldom been uninterested in the possible religious meaning of the texts they have studied. Jewish critics of Christian biblical interpretation argue, indeed, that the historical-critical approach itself was mostly a cover for Christian theological pre-conceptions, and though I believe this in general false, I think its plausibility seriously undermines the claim that historical critics operated without theological interests.

This has two aspects. On the one hand, most historical critics probably thought their historical conclusions were in themselves of religious importance. Since the God Christians believed in was continuous with the God worshipped as Yahweh in Old Testament times, what was then believed about him, as it could be reconstructed through historical criticism, could not be a matter of indifference to the modern believer. Paradoxically, the suggestion that the Christian God is not continuous with Yahweh, who is simply an ancient Near Eastern god of a fairly standard type, has come to be made only in the same period that has witnessed the rise of such movements as canonical criticism. It would not have occurred to most of the scholars who taught me that one should use a small 'g' in referring to this god, since he was, after all, ultimately the same as the God and Father of our Lord Jesus Christ. And many scholars quite untouched by postcritical movements continue happily in this tradition. Whether or not it is ultimately compatible with a historical-critical approach, it was certainly perceived as being so. The idea that historical criticism emptied out the enduring religious value of the Old Testament text is now common, but it was generally not a conscious part of the self-understanding of actual historical critics. It would be easier to construct a case against them as having been too pious, than to show them up as radically untheological and irreligious. Historical-critical questions were being asked of texts which were *taken for granted* as sacred texts: most historical critics were far from seeing themselves as iconoclasts.

But, on the other hand, the desire to move beyond historical criticism to a more systematically theological interpretation of the Old Testament has also been a recurring theme in Old Testament studies. For most of this century this has not been linked to a rejection of historical criticism, but more to a feeling that historical criticism gets us only so far along the road to a theological appreciation of the text's meaning, and that something more is needed. One sees this very clearly in a scholar such as Gerhard von Rad. Von Rad was fully committed to critical scholarship, and himself contributed substantially to critical analysis of the Pentateuch. But he was also convinced that critical investigation, especially of an analytical kind, was not enough. Beyond analysis there must be synthesis; beyond the critical investigation of how texts came to be, there must be an exploration of their finished form and the theology which that form expresses. Hence his commentary on Genesis,[6] which clearly distinguished J from P and yet was interested in the work of the redactor who made J and P into the text of Genesis we have inherited, the redactor (R) whom following Franz Rosenzweig he calls Rabbenu, 'our Master'. Hence also his work on the narrative art of the Succession Narrative and the Joseph Story, and his concern for the overall message of the book of Deuteronomy. Childs's canonical approach has many anticipations in von Rad, whom it is far from adequate to call simply a 'critical' scholar.

We can see the drive to synthesize and theologize even more clearly than in the case of von Rad if we consider the work of the 'Biblical Theology Movement'. It was the demise of this movement that provided the first impulse for Childs's own work, as set out in his book *Biblical Theology in Crisis*.[7] Biblical Theology, in this technical sense, was a primarily North American phenomenon, and to a much greater extent than the work of von Rad, which is similar in some ways, it reflected a disillusionment with critical scholarship. The Biblical Theologians were not concerned simply to move on beyond the historical-critical method while fully accepting its findings. Rather, they tended to argue that historical criticism was in any case a defective approach to the study of the Old Testament: that, after a century or more of the method, it had got us nowhere, or at least nowhere worth getting. What was needed, they said, was to turn away from minute analysis of the biblical text and instead synthesize, putting back together the pieces that had been taken apart. Then the Bible would once again be able to communicate a properly theological message applicable to our own day. We would, to use Krister Stendahl's terms, be able to move from what the Bible *meant* to what it *means*.[8]

Childs's recipe for what should replace historical criticism is different from that of the Biblical Theologians in many respects, and to that extent his programme is undoubtedly new. But the underlying theory

6.   G. von Rad, *Das erste Buch Mose, Genesis* (ATD; Göttingen: Vandenhoeck & Ruprecht, 1956) (ET *Genesis* [OTL; London: SCM Press, 1961, rev. edn 1963]).

7.   B.S. Childs, *Biblical Theology in Crisis* (Philadelphia: Westminster Press, 1970).

8.   K. Stendahl, 'Biblical Theology, Contemporary', *The Interpreter's Dictionary of the Bible*, I (ed. G.A. Buttrick; Nashville: Abingdon Press, 1962), pp. 418-32.

about how the Bible ought to be treated by the biblical scholar is much the same as theirs. Respect for the whole should replace concern for the parts; theology should replace history; a religious frame of reference should take the place of the essentially secular norms of historical criticism. The Bible ought once again to become the Church's book, to which we go for inspiration and revelation, and should cease to be seen as the proper province of rationalist critics. All this the canonical approach shares with the Biblical Theology Movement.

Thus it is fair to say that, already in the generation before Childs, many biblical scholars perceived historical criticism much more negatively than people nowadays seem often to think. It is not that there was a time before Childs when everyone regarded the historical-critical method as the Holy Grail. On the contrary, at least as early as the late 1940s doubts were being expressed about its dominance, and proposals were being made for outflanking or superannuating it, in the interests of a mode of biblical study more congenial to the kind of theological use to which the Church wanted to put the Bible. A sentiment that could be roughly formulated as 'The historical-critical method is all very well *but...*' can thus be found long before Childs. Moreover—and I shall return to this—polemic against what Robert Alter calls the 'excavative' character of historical criticism[9] can also be found before the Second World War, especially in the work of Karl Barth and biblical scholars who agreed with him, such as W. Vischer. I doubt in fact whether historical criticism ever enjoyed the undisputed hegemony against which people nowadays protest, and suspect that phrases such as 'the assured results of historical criticism' were always easier to find in the work of opponents of such criticism, where they were used sarcastically, than in the historical critics themselves. Most historical critics themselves worked in an avowedly religious environment, and had a generally reverent attitude towards the biblical text: how often does one read a classic of biblical criticism in which a given Old Testament book is debunked or even mildly criticized, or in which a critical analysis is presented as detracting from its religious value? Wellhausen, certainly, was notoriously disrespectful towards some books and strata, as in his robust demolition of the ideas in P. But how many scholars ever followed Wellhausen in this freedom towards the text? The history of scholarship since his day is largely a history of increasing respect for

9.	See R. Alter, *The Art of Biblical Narrative* (London: George Allen & Unwin, 1981).

the Old Testament, not of ever sharper criticism of it, if criticism is taken to imply hostility. The modern notion that biblical scholars spent their time emptying the Old Testament of religious value until people like Childs came along to give it back its rightful place is, I believe, a straw man, a useful foil with which to demonstrate the importance of canonical criticism, final-form exegesis, and other recent trends. And it is an unnecessary straw man, for these modern trends, whether one likes them are not, are of undoubted intellectual seriousness, well worth taking seriously and evaluating carefully. They do not need to rest on the foundation provided by a tendentious and unfair reading of all that went before.

The Alleged Antiquity of the Canonical Approach

But a canonical approach does not only claim novelty; it also, paradoxically, claims antiquity. It says that there were no 'canonical' readings during the 'historical-critical' period which, as we have seen, is at best partially true. But it maintains that there were such readings in pre-critical times. The programme of the canonical approach as argued for by Childs is to reclaim the biblical hermeneutic of the era before historical criticism—in effect, before the Enlightenment. When in his great Exodus commentary Childs surveys the interpretations of the Fathers and the Reformers, he is not practising mere reception history, out of a historical interest in what people in the past made of the Bible. He is setting out an agenda for the modern interpreter, in the belief that commentators nowadays ought to be sensitive to the interpretations of their 'pre-critical' predecessors, who may not have possessed as much historical knowledge about the Bible as we do, but who had a far clearer sense of the text as Holy Scripture and felt impelled to interpret it as such.

This respect for interpreters of the past may be seen in modern Old Testament study even where there is no explicit commitment to canonical criticism. One sees it clearly in much literary interpretation, where rabbinic and patristic exegesis is enjoying a renewed respect—in Robert Alter[10] and Gabriel Josipovici,[11] in Frank Kermode[12] and Jack Miles.[13]

10. Alter, *Art of Biblical Narrative*.
11. See G. Josipovici, *The Book of God: A Response to the Bible* (New Haven: Yale University Press, 1988).
12. See F. Kermode, *The Genesis of Secrecy: On the Interpretation of Narrative*

There the reason is perhaps a sense that these interpreters read the biblical books as 'texts' in the pregnant sense that term has in modern literary criticism, or even as *works*, an equally important term. Jack Miles, for example, tries to see how the Hebrew Bible would look if one interpreted it as a single work with a unified plot and consistent characterization: hence his title *God: A Biography*. Both here and in more theological canonical criticism one finds a drive towards holistic reading, resisting the historical-critical tendency to divide texts up into sources and interpret them piecemeal, and concentrating instead on the text in its present form.

Now it is in their holism, it seems to me, that theological and literary interpretation in our day fail to make good their claim to be recovering the scriptural vision of the Fathers, the rabbis or the Reformers. It is true that pre-critical interpretation regarded books of the Bible as a unity, in the sense that they did not think they were composed from pre-existing fragments or even longer source-documents: Isaiah was by Isaiah, not by First, Second and Third Isaiah together with a whole heap of other contributors. But it is not true that they therefore interpreted the biblical texts holistically, as having a beginning, a middle, and an end, a plot, a shape, a *Gestalt*. Rabbinic exegesis, for example, often sees no divisions in the text where critical commentators find dislocation—they do not find any disjunction between Isaiah 39 and 40. But at the same time they do find it possible to break the text down into verses and half-verses and to comment on each as if it were a text in its own right. The Midrashim are apparently serial comments on biblical books, proceeding verse by verse. But any reader of these texts knows that it is folly to try to find any progression of thought within a midrash, still less any progression which is an attempt to mirror the 'ductus' of the book being commented on. The principle that 'there is no before and after in the Torah' justifies any amount of jumping from text to text, in a way that negates any idea of plot, the development of arguments, or narrative shape. It is rather as though every biblical book were like Proverbs, and like the sentence literature of Proverbs 10–29 at that: isolated atoms of communication, each to be interpreted in its own right. Where rabbinic exegesis *is* holistic is in its interpretative framework, which is provided by the whole tissue of rabbinic assumptions about theology and ethics.

(Cambridge, MA: Harvard University Press, 1979); cf. R. Alter and F. Kermode (eds.), *The Literary Guide to the Bible* (London: Collins, 1987).

13. See J. Miles, *God: A Biography* (London: Simon and Schuster, 1995).

The framework, not the scriptural text, is the unified whole to which the rabbis pay attention. Similar things could be said of patristic and Reformation exegesis; for the former it is the rule of faith which provides a unifying scheme, into which any and every text can be fitted: the internal organization of the individual books is of far less interest than their concord with Christian doctrine. And for the Reformers, who evince more concern with biblical books in their own right, it is still an external theological scheme—albeit claimed as deriving from Scripture itself—that controls the interpretation of individual books. Holistic reading in the modern sense is very hard to detect.

I think myself that the claim to be recovering pre-critical attitudes to the Old Testament is concerned more with reverence and respect for the text than with particular ways of reading it, whether holistic or (as I believe is more commonly the case in pre-critical exegesis) atomistic. The sense one gets from Childs is not so much that he is reading the Old Testament in the way pre-critical interpreters read it, as that he is reading it with the same attitude. The details of the interpretative method are really neither here nor there—this is one reason why Childs (rightly) dislikes it when his approach is described as canonical 'criticism', suggesting a method parallel or alternative to form criticism or redaction criticism. What matters is the state of mind with which the text is approached. Historical criticism approaches texts with suspicion, with an interest in historical reconstruction, with a reductionist view of them as merely human products; whereas the canonical reader is seeking to read the text as the Church's Holy Scriptures, and therefore as speaking truly of God. It is in this, rather than in any preference for holistic interpretation, that the similarity to pre-critical approaches lies. If this is true, then we ought probably to distinguish more sharply than is currently normal between canonical and holistic readings, since, though they can of course be combined, either can exist in the absence of the other. A desire to read the Old Testament as Scripture need not predispose one to prefer holistic readings, for it certainly did not so predispose the rabbis. And on the other hand holistic reading can easily belong to some other, quite non-theological, programme—hence its prevalence in practitioners of the newer literary approaches who could not care less about the Bible's theological claims. Even to read the Old Testament in its final form, as Childs insists we should do, is not necessarily to read it holistically: St Paul certainly took the Old Testament to be God's revelation exactly as it stood, but there is precious little evidence of holism in his reading of it—rather a digging out of proof-texts in a manner deeply unwelcome to practitioners of holistic interpretation.

One can understand, from this perspective, why Childs is annoyed to find his canonical approach equated with a modern literary style of scriptural reading, and even when critics who do not make the equation nevertheless point to the resemblances (as I myself have done). The similarity between canonical 'final form' exegesis and literary 'holistic' exegesis is essentially accidental, the chance confluence of two very different attitudes to the Bible. But if this is true, then it is in its theological commitment rather than in the details of its method that the canonical approach resembles pre-critical exegesis. I shall return to this point later, since it seems to me extremely important.

The point can also be made that the canonical approach is by no means simply a return to the kind of biblical interpretation current before the rise of historical criticism, but depends on the critical method as a foil for its own proposals. This is something James Barr has stressed: Childs's interpretation of Isaiah, for example, depends on our knowing that Isaiah 40–55 is later than 1–39, in order then to be able to see how the 'canonical shaping' of the book has decontextualized it.[14] No-one who simply believed unreflectively that all of Isaiah was from the pen of the eighth-century prophet would be able to appreciate this point. It is a mystery concealed from generations of Fathers and rabbis, and revealed only in these last days to those who have first sat at the feet of the historical critics.

This point may, however, conveniently lead into the more positive things I should now like to say about the canonical approach. For, we may reason, it is a fairly obvious point: it is hardly likely that Childs himself does not realize how often his 'canonical' readings rest on critical positions, and indeed he is perfectly willing to concede it, and not only to concede it but to state openly that he regards the historical-critical method as important and by no means simply evacuated of significance by the canonical approach. It might be that in this he is simply being inconsistent. But before attributing inconsistency to a scholar of his intellectual stature, perhaps we should do well to pause, and ask whether we may have been evaluating the canonical approach from the wrong angle, or through the wrong focus. How is it possible for Childs to maintain that the historical-critical method remains both valid and

14. See J. Barr, 'Childs' Introduction to the Old Testament as Scripture', *JSOT* 16 (1980), pp. 12-23.

important, when he is all the time trying to show how desirable it would be to get back into a state of mind for which it had not yet been discovered? I believe that it is by probing this puzzle that we may come to a more useful assessment of what canonical criticism is really about, and thus to a juster evaluation of it.

The Canonical Approach and Theology

The truth about the canonical approach is, I think, that it is a proposal about how theologians should use the Bible, rather than about how biblical critics should study it. The difference may seem unimportant, and of course the same person may be both a biblical critic and a theologian—many people, myself included, believe that this is desirable. Nevertheless there is a conceptual distinction to be drawn between what the critic does when studying the Bible, and what the theologian does when drawing on biblical materials in the process of producing systematic theology, preaching or apologetic; and it seems to me that it is the latter which Childs is really concerned with.

The canonical approach does not begin with the biblical text, asking, What can we say about this text if we apply a critical intelligence to it? The canonical approach begins with the need to formulate theological truth, and it asks how the Bible can be used in that context. The canonical theologian is one who, coming from a broadly Reformed background, takes the Bible very seriously indeed as the source of theological truth, but has at the same time a confessional framework within which the Bible's teaching is to be received. The question for such a person is how the Bible can actually be fruitful, but also how we can do it justice: how we can ensure that we hear its whole witness to Christian truth, not just the parts we choose for ourselves, and how we can ensure that we are not diverted by apparent (or even real) discrepancies within the text from assimilating it as a coherent whole.

It is, broadly speaking, fair to say that this amounts to a return to a 'pre-critical' reading of the Bible, in that interpreters during the patristic or Reformation periods shared the concern to assimilate the Bible as a whole, and to show that all of it was fruitful for Christian faith. It is equally true to say that it is not far from the concerns of many in the Biblical Theology Movement to seek out 'the biblical doctrine' of this or that theological theme and to present it as an integrated whole. Above all, I think, it would be true to say that the hand of Karl Barth may be seen very strongly at work in a canonical approach to the text, something that I imagine Childs would not wish to deny. Barth lay behind much of von Rad's concern to move beyond source analysis to an appreciation of biblical books as a whole, and he is also at work in the background of canonical criticism. For a 'canonical reading' of the Bible one need look no further than many of Barth's excurses on biblical passages, where the reading of the Bible is carried out within a clear doctrinal framework and where it is taken as a given that the Bible will speak with a consistent voice on any given subject.

It might, indeed, be argued that canonical reading is what not only theologians but ordinary Christian believers instinctively engage in whenever they open a Bible. They assume that what they will get from any given portion of Scripture is religious truth; and since there cannot be mutually inconsistent versions of such truth, they assume that any other passage will help to elucidate the same message. This is not to be confused with a fundamentalistic insistence that there cannot be the slightest inconsistencies in the Bible: ordinary Bible readers, like canonical critics, have enough breadth of mind to realize that the biblical books were written at different times and have different concerns. But they assume, in approaching Scripture, that it will be reasonably consistent and coherent, and also that the message it conveys will be important and serious, not inconsequential or trivial. On matters that deeply concern us, we expect the Bible to have things to say that are worth hearing, and we also expect that it will speak, to a great extent, with a single voice. These assumptions are probably given in the very term 'Scripture': they are assumptions made in many religions that have sacred books, not just in Judaism and Christianity. The canonical approach is essentially an attempt to formulate carefully and programmatically the attitude towards the biblical text that most believers share.

This partially explains what sometimes seems the rather ambivalent attitude of canonical critics towards historical criticism. On the one hand, they are clear that we must move beyond it; on the other, that it has a legitimate place. The mystery is solved when we see that the agenda of the canonical approach is essentially how to read Scripture in a way that is religiously edifying and helpful. Sometimes historical criticism can be useful in this, as for example in showing us that the book of Isaiah comes from a diversity of periods and therefore in its finished form is not to be located in any of them, but has a certain 'timeless' quality. This could not be known so long as people thought it was all the work of the eighth-century prophet whose name it bears. It is precisely the historical-critical insight into the book's provenance that shows us how the tradition has freed it for applicability in ever new situations. On the other hand, when historical criticism seeks to insist that passages are to be read against the background of their times, and hence as having a narrower applicability or truth than the Christian believer would like to see in them, it is to be regarded as having exceeded its brief and led us astray. There is no inconsistency here, once we grant that the canonical approach is concerned with what is profitable for the Christian reader, *ergiebig* in the useful German shorthand expression.

As observed above, it is probably not the case that a canonical approach necessarily leads to a final-form reading of any given text. The association is close, in most people's minds, and Childs himself often speaks of the need to respect the final form. But that means, on the whole, the text as it is presented to us, not necessarily the text understood as an aesthetic or theological whole. I do not think that a canonical reading of Proverbs, for example, is committed to finding order and sequence in the sentence literature of chs. 10–29; what it is committed to is making sense of the book we now have, rather than of putative earlier collections that may lie beneath it. And 'making sense' means making religious sense, treating the text 'as Scripture', not just as an ancient document, and hence asking questions about its intertextual relations with other books in the canon and its theological relations to Christian doctrine.

On this understanding the canonical approach is really rather simpler than it is sometimes thought to be—and none the worse for that. Its agenda is to show the Bible's relevance and significance for religious readers by an appropriate style of interpretation. Is that not what all students of the Bible are really concerned with anyway?

It is tempting to answer 'yes' to this, and indeed it may almost seem so obvious as hardly to need stating. But biblical criticism, as traditionally conceived, is not really directed to that aim, as Childs, I believe, sees only too clearly. What drives 'historical criticism' so called is not theology, but a concern to let the text speak for itself. Religious believers who engage in biblical criticism hope that what they discover through their critical studies will support rather than undermine their faith; and since until recently virtually all biblical critics were religious believers, we may assume that they generally found it did, unless they were dishonest. But biblical criticism dies at birth if it is told to find in the text only what will support the critic's faith. In that sense its role is genuinely critical: to establish what is the case, prescinding for the time being from the question of whether this is religiously edifying or not. And, unfortunately for the canonical approach, there comes a point where biblical critics cannot rest content with inhabiting the restricted world of biblical studies, but have necessarily to interfere in the activities of doctrinal and systematic theologians. This they have to do when such theologians make a use of biblical materials which the biblical critics believe the text cannot sustain. When they do this, it is not enough to reply that the theologian is making a constructive and edifying use of the Bible and therefore is not subject to the verdict of mere biblical critics: for the use cannot really be as edifying as it looks if it rests upon falsehood in exegesis. Error is never truly 'helpful': any scholar who believes that it is has given up his or her claim to be called a scholar.

This is to put the matter in a very sharp and polemical way, and for the most part, of course, the difference between critical and canonical readings will be slight, if they even exist at all: but I believe it is important to see what is at stake. The canonical approach ultimately tells the student of the Bible what to think the text says on doctrinal grounds, rather than on the basis of the philological and textual criteria which historical criticism has developed. It says, for example, that since the overall drift of the Bible is in the direction of monotheism and the framework within which we are meant to read it is that of Judaeo-Christian monotheism, any given text in Scripture should be interpreted as a witness to such monotheism, for by definition any non-monotheistic interpretation can only be of a level of the text which is sub- or not-yet-canonical and therefore is ruled out by the canonical approach. Hence when Ps. 97.7 says that 'all gods bow down to' Yahweh, this must 'canonically' be read as a metaphorical way of saying that Yahweh is the only God (or, better, that there is only one God), since in a canonical perspective the assertion that there are other gods who bow to Yahweh cannot be tolerated. The traditional biblical critic, on the other hand, will at least ask whether the verse is not meant literally, and whether it does not imply the existence of many gods, of whom Yahweh is the chief. There may be good critical grounds for preferring the monotheistic reading, but they will not owe anything to the fact that the interpreter who is deciding between the two readings is himself or herself a monotheist. Only think how we should react if a modern 'pagan' insisted that the polytheistic interpretation must be preferred because, as we all know, there are in fact many gods and the Bible can be trusted to get this right! The essence of biblical criticism is that the Bible is not 'owned' by anyone, not even by orthodox Christians, but should be interpreted according to publicly available criteria of the meanings of words and sentences. It will not do to say that this is true when it is being read 'critically', but that different standards of evidence apply when it is being read 'canonically'.

The Task of Biblical Criticism

What then is the place of 'canon' in biblical interpretation? At one level, there is none. Biblical criticism has always been, and rightly so, of its essence anti-canonical in the sense that it refuses to allow for the framework within which the Church has placed the Bible when asking about the Bible's meaning. In practice very few biblical critics have actually spoken against or criticized the existence of the Bible as canonical Scripture, since most biblical critics until our own day have been Christian believers, and they have not seen their work as tending to undermine the canon at all. But their work has always contained the possibility of finding things in canonical Scripture which are incompatible with this or that theme in Christian theology, and when this has been the case they have been willing to say so. Where they have tried to be 'helpful' to religion, it has often been by attempting to synthesize what is in the Bible into an 'Old/New Testament Theology'; but the results have seldom proved able to feed systematic theology very successfully, except perhaps when they have themselves been conceived on a model drawn from systematic theology in the first place (compare Eichrodt's very 'Reformed' Theology of the Old Testament).[15]

To retain its cutting edge, biblical criticism needs to remain on the alert for any sign that it is being dragooned into the role of edifying helper to doctrinal theology; and when a systematic theologian is also a biblical critic—as in a sense is true of Childs—then the critical side of the personality needs to be, precisely, critical of the other, not subordinate to it. Once we suspect that the systematic tail is wagging the critical dog, our confidence in the whole system is undermined. It is this

15. W. Eichrodt, *Theologie des Alten Testaments* (vols. I–III; Leipzig: Hinrichs, 1933–39) (ET *Theology of the Old Testament* [vols. I (from sixth German edn) and II (from fifth German edn); London: SCM Press, 1961–67]).

that lies behind the widespread neglect among students of the Bible of
so much in Karl Barth's immensely detailed and careful exegesis of the
Bible: the suspicion that, however deeply he delves into the text and
however much he knows about it, we already know what he will find
there, because it is dictated by his prior theological convictions.

In short, Christian theologians do have an obligation to take account
of the Bible, because it is an acknowledged source of authority within
Christianity. That does not mean, however, that everyone who studies
the Bible has an obligation to help them by providing readings easily
assimilated into a systematic theology. Biblical critics' obligations are
to the text, not to the Church or to theology, and they have the duty of
reporting what the text says, not what the theologian wants to hear. The
idea that there is a special 'canonical' level of meaning above the natural sense of the text has been widespread in Christian history and has, of
course, an extremely distinguished pedigree; but it is not compatible
with biblical criticism as this has developed since the Reformation, and
nothing is gained by pretending that it can be made compatible. The
best service biblical critics can render to religious believers (among
whom they are often numbered themselves) is to tell the truth about
what the text seems to them to mean, not to be talked into believing that
it means something more helpful, more edifying or more theologically
correct than it does.

ENABLING SILENT LIPS TO SPEAK: LITERARY CRITICISM
IN THE SERVICE OF OLD TESTAMENT INTERPRETATION*

W.H. Bellinger, Jr

Introduction

The hermeneutical debate in contemporary biblical scholarship shows
no signs of resolution. One noticeable division is among those who
continue to insist on the centrality of historical-critical and reconstruc-
tive work and those who announce the demise of the historical method.
Those who would press beyond the historical-critical approach that carries the Enlightenment stamp often work under the rubric of 'literary
criticism,' but contemporary 'literary criticism' includes a bewildering
diversity of methods.[1] It is thus difficult to construct a comprehensive
view of either component in the title of this paper—literary criticism or
Old Testament interpretation. The title does, nonetheless, suggest a
relationship between the two. The first task, then, is to shape working
definitions of the two and seek to gain some perspective on how scholars have construed this relationship. It will then be important to tie the
conversation to a variety of biblical texts before distilling concluding
reflections.

The term 'literary criticism' is familiar in biblical studies. It has often
been associated with the work of source criticism, especially in the

* With gratitude and pleasure I contribute to this volume celebrating the work
of my mentor and friend Ronald E. Clements. I learned much of form-critical matters as well as issues relating to biblical theology while studying with Professor
Clements in Cambridge. But even more, I learned of decisions biblical interpreters
make in the course of their work. Professor Clements's thoughtful reflection, teaching, and scholarship continue to influence my work.
  1.   It may even be outdated to describe 'literary criticism' as a discrete
approach. The methods are ever changing.

Pentateuch.[2] We will need to attend to historical-critical methods, for many of them are literary in the sense that they deal with Old Testament texts, which are literature in the most obvious sense.[3] The term in more recent times, however, has referred to approaches that take many of their clues from the broader field of literary criticism as often practised in university departments of English and literature. A distinction between source criticism and more recent attempts at literary approaches to the Bible is useful. James Barr makes the distinction well:

> In general literary study we mean by literary criticism a study of the structure and the imagery of works, their modes, symbols and myths, their poetic, dramatic and aesthetic effect; but in technical biblical scholarship the same term means the separating out of historically different layers in composite works, the history of the tradition during the period of its development in written form, as distinct from its development in a spoken form before it was written down.[4]

My use of the term approximates Barr's first approach, from the broader field of literary criticism. By literary criticism I mean the serious, critical analysis of literary dimensions of biblical texts.[5] This essay will pursue various dimensions of this simple working definition.

We also need to articulate a basic working definition of Old Testament interpretation. The title of this essay uses a phrase from Leo Perdue's *The Collapse of History* as a way to envision the task of interpretation.[6] Interpreters articulate important information about the text.

---

2.   N.C. Habel, *Literary Criticism of the Old Testament* (Guides to Biblical Scholarship; Philadelphia: Fortress Press, 1971) assumes that literary criticism is equivalent to source analysis.

3.   See M.A. Powell (compiler), *The Bible and Modern Literary Criticism: A Critical Assessment and Annotated Bibliography* (with the assistance of C.G. Gray and M.C. Curtis; Bibliographies and Indexes in Religious Studies, 22; New York: Greenwood, 1992), p. 3.

4.   J. Barr, 'Reading the Bible as Literature', *BJRL* 56 (1973), pp. 10-33 (20-21).

5.   M. Minor, *Literary-Critical Approaches to the Bible: An Annotated Bibliography* (West Cornwall: Locust Hill, 1992) includes a helpful introduction (pp. xiii-xxv) which suggests elements of a literary approach. It treats the final form of the text, not so much as a window to a world behind the text as part of a world the text creates and invites readers to enter. See also M. Minor, *Literary-Critical Approaches to the Bible: A Bibliographical Supplement* (West Cornwall: Locust Hill, 1996).

6.   L.G. Perdue, *The Collapse of History: Reconstructing Old Testament Theology* (OBT; Minneapolis: Fortress Press, 1994), p. 10.

Perhaps a good description of the task is to make explicit what is implicit in the text.[7] Interpreters make explicit what is implicit in texts so that readers may at some level encounter a 'world' the text creates.[8] It stands to reason that the interpreter's view of the text will then determine how interpretation proceeds.

A Question of Perspective

The question of how to proceed while interpreting a biblical text is, of course, not new. A brief rehearsal of the movements of the history of interpretation can provide us with some perspective and tie interpretation to hermeneutical issues.[9] In the era before the Enlightenment,[10] biblical interpretation was done in the context of the church and sought some higher spiritual reality in the text. The locus of meaning was in the church's concerns. Language and history were studied to find spiritual meaning.[11] The Reformation brought something of a break in

---

7. R.A. Culpepper, 'Commentary on Biblical Narratives: Changing Paradigms', *Forum* 5 (1989), p. 89.

8. The language comes from Paul Ricoeur, *Interpretation Theory: Discourse and the Surplus of Meaning* (Fort Worth: Texas Christian University Press, 1976); *idem, The Rule of Metaphor: Multi-disciplinary Studies of the Creation of Meaning in Language* (ET; London: Routledge and Kegan Paul, 1978); *idem, Essays on Biblical Interpretation* (Introduction and ed. L.S. Mudge; London: SPCK, 1981); *idem, The Conflict of Interpretations: Essays in Hermeneutics* (ed. D. Ihde; Evanston: Northwestern University Press, 1974); J.D. Crossan (ed.), *Paul Ricoeur and Biblical Hermeneutics* (Semeia, 4; Missoula: Scholars Press, 1975).

9. See W.H. Bellinger, Jr, *A Hermeneutic of Curiosity and Readings of Psalm 61* (Studies in Old Testament Interpretation, 1; Macon, GA: Mercer University Press, 1995), pp. 1-23. Powell, *The Bible and Modern Literary Criticism*, pp. 4-16, provides a helpful discussion of the basis and theory of literary-critical approaches to the Bible. Also helpful is his taxonomy of the various methodologies included.

10. These centuries are often labeled 'pre-critical', but the term 'pre-Enlightenment' is more appropriate.

11. See E.V. McKnight, *Postmodern Use of the Bible: The Emergence of Reader-Oriented Criticism* (Nashville: Abingdon Press, 1988), pp. 29-44; R.M. Grant with D. Tracy, *A Short History of the Interpretation of the Bible* (Philadelphia: Fortress Press, 2nd edn, 1984); Culpepper, 'Commentary', pp. 90-91. For a different perspective, see D.C. Steinmetz, 'The Superiority of Pre-Critical Exegesis', *TTod* 37 (1980), pp. 27-38. Minor, *Literary-Critical Approaches*, pp. xiv-xix, is quite right to note literary study of Scripture prior to the Enlightenment. The

this approach. The work of Luther and others after him brought attention to additional human and literary dimensions in the text. Attention had begun to shift toward what the texts were about rather than what the church was about.

With the rise of the Enlightenment, further change came into view. Focus shifted from concerns of church and Spirit to concerns of reason, science and history.[12] Scholars began to discover artifacts and literature from ancient cultures and see the differences in historical eras. Historical contexts became central in biblical studies as the Enlightenment project inspired confidence in the human ability to discover the historical contexts from which texts arose. Empirical observation was the hallmark of the Enlightenment; external historical background came to dominate biblical studies, and the historical-critical approach was born.[13] Source criticism became the dominant tool of historical critics in the search for the historical processes that gave rise to biblical texts. This search especially dominated the study of the Pentateuch with the documentary hypothesis.[14] The task of interpretation was cast in terms of the historical processes from which texts originated. Form criticism originated by Gunkel sought to go further behind the texts to a setting from which oral traditions arose to contribute finally to documents that made up the Pentateuch. Form critics also sought to discover an original *Sitz im Leben* for poetic texts. Events and settings that gave rise to texts dominated the concerns of scholars. Redaction critics began to reverse the historical movement to ask how these texts were then edited together. The approach of tradition history sought to trace the process by which these texts were gathered. Still the focus was on what was behind the texts, often the purpose or intent of the writer or redactor. With historical-critical studies using source criticism, form criticism, redaction criticism and tradition history, the hermeneutical key for the interpreter

work of Bishop Robert Lowth is especially noteworthy; see Bellinger, *Hermeneutic*, pp. 9-10.

12. See McKnight, *Postmodern Use*, pp. 44-53.

13. Various works chronicle the rise of historical-critical studies: see, e.g., Grant with Tracy, *A Short History*; R.E. Clements, *A Century of Old Testament Study* (Guildford: Lutterworth Press, rev. edn, 1983); R. Davidson and A.R.C. Leaney, *Biblical Criticism* (The Pelican Guide to Modern Theology, 3; Harmondsworth: Penguin Books, 1970).

14. See Clements, *A Century*, Chapter 2.

is found in the origin of the text.[15] When one finds the original context, one has the key to meaning.[16]

In recent years the hegemony of the historical-critical approach has begun to fade. This development has come from several directions, including the influence of the Anglo-American literary-critical movement called the New Criticism.[17] Its advocates reacted against biographical or historical criticism, arguing that elements internal to the text itself should be the interpretive keys rather than influences external to the text. New Critics argued that interpreters cannot really divine the intention of an author and can seldom be confident about the circumstances of the origin of a text. Rather, it is the shape of the text itself that is at issue. The search is for strategies the text uses to communicate: plot, tone, paradox, irony, humor, other literary devices. A text coheres as a system of values, as an autonomous whole. Such a text-immanent approach raises questions about the historical-critical approach.

Not unrelated to this development is the canonical approach pioneered by Brevard Childs. His canonical analyses move beyond questions of origin to questions of canon and the texts as we have them in the canonical context.[18] Muilenburg's rhetorical criticism has a similar influence in moving beyond questions of origin to questions of the shape of the text itself.[19] The work of formalists would also fit in this

---

15. Textual criticism is also, in a sense, a historical-critical endeavour, but it was also practised prior to the Enlightenment.

16. See Culpepper, 'Commentary', pp. 92-93. D.J.A. Clines, *The Theme of the Pentateuch* (JSOTSup, 10; Sheffield: Sheffield Academic Press, 2nd edn, 1997), pp. 9-13, has labeled the approach 'geneticism'. A classic statement of the historical-critical approach is K. Stendahl, 'Biblical Theology, Contemporary', *The Interpreter's Dictionary of the Bible* (4 vols.; ed. G.A. Buttrick; Nashville: Abingdon Press, 1962), I, pp. 418-32.

17. See R. Wellek and R. Warren, *Theory of Literature* (Harmondsworth: Penguin Books, 3rd edn, 1963); W.K. Wimsatt, Jr, *The Verbal Icon: Studies in the Meaning of Poetry* (London: Methuen, 1970); D. Newton-de Molina (ed.), *On Literary Intention* (Edinburgh: Edinburgh University Press, 1976).

18. See B.S. Childs, *Introduction to the Old Testament as Scripture* (Philadelphia: Fortress Press, 1979), especially p. 74; J. Barton, *Reading the Old Testament: Method in Biblical Study* (Louisville: Westminster/John Knox Press, 2nd edn, 1996), pp. 153-54, though Barton fully admits that Childs distances himself from the New Criticism. Barton's description and critique of the New Criticism is on pp. 140-79.

19. J. Muilenburg, 'Form Criticism and Beyond', *JBL* 88 (1969), pp. 1-18.

category, especially the work of Robert Alter.[20]

A similar move away from the historical-critical is found in structuralism. Structuralists are concerned with the structures or system of human communication reflected in texts.[21] In each of these approaches the basis for interpretation has shifted from origin to text.

Recent hermeneutical developments have witnessed a further shift in poststructuralist interpretations of various kinds to an emphasis on the reader.[22] Reader-response criticism, whether of the phenomenological stripe or the ideological stripe, fits here.[23] So the hermeneutical movement since the Enlightenment has been from an emphasis on origin to text to reader.

I have elsewhere argued for a hermeneutic of curiosity in which interpreters attend to all three of these dimensions: origin, text and reader.[24] Certainly a text originated from some setting with an author or authors, and the text is somehow related to that origin. The text has a shape of its own and its meaning is only completed in the act of reading.[25] All three aspects are inherent in the task of interpretation, and each aspect subsumes various methodologies. One of the hallmarks of the contemporary, postmodern context of interpretation is methodological pluralism.[26] No single aspect can provide *the* interpretation of a text.

20. R. Alter, *The Art of Biblical Narrative* (New York: Basic Books, 1981), and *The Art of Biblical Poetry* (New York: Basic Books, 1985); R. Alter and F. Kermode (eds.), *The Literary Guide to the Bible* (Cambridge, MA: Harvard University Press, 1987).

21. See F. de Saussure, *Course in General Linguistics* (ET; New York: Philosophical Library, 1959); R. Detweiler, *Story, Sign, and Self: Phenomenology and Structuralism as Literary-Critical Methods* (Missoula: Scholars Press, 1978); J. Culler, *Structuralist Poetics: Structuralism, Linguistics and the Study of Literature* (London: Routledge and Kegan Paul, 1975).

22. See Culpepper, 'Commentary', p. 94. I agree with Barton, *Reading*, pp. 104-39, that structuralism is properly a theory about reading texts. It provides transition to other methods such as deconstruction.

23. See Bellinger, *Hermeneutic*, pp. 89-107.

24. Bellinger, *Hermeneutic*, pp. 3-7.

25. W.R. Tate, *Biblical Interpretation: An Integrated Approch* (Peabody, MA: Hendrickson, 2nd edn, 1997) speaks of the world behind the text, the world within the text, and the world in front of the text.

26. The term 'postmodern' can be confusing. 'Post-Enlightenment' or 'poststructuralist' might be helpful alternatives. By the term I do not imply a splintering of biblical interpreters into isolated camps with no dialogue between them. I refer rather to our context in which a plurality of methods and interpretations is the order

Instead, the text invites the hermeneut to investigate its various aspects.[27] It is, of course, impossible for a single interpreter to converse with all the approaches, but it is possible to approach the task with an awareness that no single approach will answer all the questions and with an awareness of the contributions various approaches can make.[28]

My task here is to reflect on the place of literary criticism in the interpretive task. I have defined 'literary criticism' as serious, critical analyses of literary dimensions of texts. There are many ways to approach these literary dimensions, and a startling diversity of methods operates in contemporary biblical studies under the rubric of 'literary criticism'. I may be accused of limiting the term,[29] but I propose in this essay to concentrate on formal literary features in biblical texts, in the tradition of Alter.[30] Such features can guide readers. So an important dimension of the task of an interpreter is to help readers see the clues in the text. Meaning is then produced in an interaction between text and reader with responses, insights and emotions. Diversity in interpretations reflects the diversity of contemporary interpretive communities. Historical and cultural codes reflected in the text will call for explanation

of the day. See The Bible and Culture Collective, *The Postmodern Bible* (New Haven: Yale University Press, 1995), pp. 1-19. Perdue, *Collapse*, chronicles the move from modern to postmodern in Old Testament theology, and W. Brueggemann's *Theology of the Old Testament* (Minneapolis: Fortress Press, 1997) operates in that context.

27.　I agree with J. Barton, 'Classifying Biblical Criticism', *JSOT* 29 (1984), pp. 19-35, that we are in a time in which hermeneuticians produce 'readings' of texts.

28.　The multiplication of approaches in recent decades is dizzying. Good introductions are provided by Tate, *Biblical Interpretation*, and Barton, *Reading*. See also The Bible and Culture Collective, *Postmodern Bible* and J.C. Exum and D.J.A. Clines (eds.), *The New Literary Criticism and the Hebrew Bible* (JSOTSup, 143; Sheffield: Sheffield Academic Press, 1993).

29.　The Bible and Culture Collective, *Postmodern Bible*, pp. 110-11, has fairly accused Alter of methodological escapism and M. Sternberg of a kind of biblicism. Contemporary literary criticism includes a wealth of diverse methods, and I believe the tent of biblical interpretation includes places for these approaches. In this essay, I have made a more practical decision to concentrate on one aspect of biblical interpretation—as necessary for the discussion to proceed in a meaningful way.

30.　See n. 20 above. M. Sternberg, *The Poetics of Biblical Narrative: Ideological Literature and the Drama of Reading* (Bloomington: Indiana University Press, 1985), also attends to such features. Note the description of Alter and Sternberg as practical literary critics in Barton, *Reading*, pp. 205-12.

as will literary devices of language use, narration, plot or sequence, and characterization. Attention to such clues can enable readers to enter the symbolic world produced in interaction with the text. It is a world associated with the origin of the text and now in conversation with readers and their worlds. Readers can envision that world by following the direction of the text and relating to its characters and responding to its images. Interpreters help readers see those textual clues. Readers are then to make decisions about texts, and those texts can influence their lives.[31] The task of interpretation is to help readers identify with the literary world of a text. Historical issues may well be part of the task but interpreters cannot equate historical investigation with interpretation. Rather, interpretation's primary focus is the movement of the text that can elicit responses from readers. Biblical narratives purport to commend a world pervaded by faith and so speak to readers of faith.

I have spoken of interpretation in terms of making explicit what is implicit in texts so as to help readers envision the full import of texts. Readers expect much from commentators, an interesting reading that articulates the movements, patterns, characters and features of texts so readers can entertain a world in conversation with their worlds. That is a significant task. It is now important to relate this theoretical discussion to some biblical texts.

A Question of Praxis

While the interpretation of the Old Testament appears in a variety of forms, one of the standards is still the commentary. To illustrate the place of literary criticism, I will consider three commentaries' treatments of texts in Numbers. The first is the Word Biblical Commentary by Philip J. Budd.[32] The second is the New Century Bible Commentary by Eryl Davies[33] and the third is by Dennis Olson in the Interpretation series.[34] The treatments of the spy narrative in Numbers 13–14 provide good samples of interpretation. Budd's interpretation is best cast as a history of traditions.[35] There is evidence of both Yahwistic and Priestly material. After a lengthy discussion, Budd suggests that the tradition in

31. See Culpepper, 'Commentary', pp. 95-100.
32. P.J. Budd, *Numbers* (WBC, 5; Waco: Word Books, 1984).
33. E.W. Davies, *Numbers* (NCB; Grand Rapids: Eerdmans, 1995).
34. D.T. Olson, *Numbers* (Int; Louisville: John Knox Press, 1996).
35. Budd, *Numbers*, pp. 140-64.

Numbers 13–14 has a long and complicated history in which the Yah-wist has adapted earlier Calebite settlement traditions and a tradition of a reconnaissance and successful invasion from the south, in order to cast the story as one of disobedience. A further exilic expansion empha-sizes Moses' intercession. The final expansion of the story is a Priestly one extending the reconnaissance and emphasizing Joshua's faithful-ness in contrast to the people's murmuring.[36] The literary-critical tools Budd uses are tied to a history of traditions or redactional approach. He suggests a literary pattern in the stories of disaffection in Numbers, but even that is in a hypothetical construction of an earlier Yahwistic source.[37]

Davies's treatment of Numbers 13–14 begins with an outline of the basic plot of the narrative.[38] Then he says, 'This brief outline of the content of chs. 13f. must not be allowed to disguise the fact that the narrative, in its present form, is by no means unified, for it is replete with inconsistencies, redundancies and duplications'.[39] Davies concludes that the narrative is a composite of J and P. He then treats the composition of the two narratives, J and P, and the content of each, as well as other questions of tradition history, supporting Martin Noth's perspective. Literary criticism is again source criticism.[40]

Olson's treatment of Numbers 13–14 is rather different.[41] He sees the spy narrative as decisive for the book and as an elaborate narrative that is carefully constructed. He outlines the movement of the narrative as a whole, suggesting several scenes, confrontations and movements.[42] Olson is aware of the source-critical and tradition-historical problems associated with the text and alludes to them,[43] but his treatment is of the canonical text as a whole, a reading that concentrates on the suspense, irony and dramatic dialogue in the narrative. Olson understands the spy story to be central in the structure of Numbers; the narrative seals the fate of the old, wilderness generation. He argues that the main theme of the book is the death of the old, rebellious generation and the birth of a

36. Budd, *Numbers*, p. 155.
37. Budd, *Numbers*, p. 162.
38. Davies, *Numbers*, pp. 126-49.
39. Davies, *Numbers*, p. 127
40. Compare the quotation from Barr, n. 4 above.
41. Olson, *Numbers*, pp. 75-90.
42. Olson, *Numbers*, pp. 75-76.
43. Olson, *Numbers*, pp. 76-77.

new generation of hope. Olson's treatment of Numbers 13–14 is strikingly different from those of Budd and Davies. The three commentators are reading the same text but moving in different directions and drawing different conclusions. Olson often finds narrative flow and movement where Budd and Davies find different sources.

The difference in approach is perhaps even more striking in Olson's comment early in his treatment of Numbers 7–8:

> Most scholars see this section in Numbers 7–10 as a late editorial addition of a miscellaneous collection of material. But the narrative effect of this flashback is to rehearse the careful preparations that all the tribes of Israel have obediently made in regard to the tabernacle, its personnel, and other cultic matters. The flashback forces the reader to slow down, to wade through the repetitive lists of tribes and their offerings, to sit through the consecration of the Levites, to take time to celebrate the second Passover, and to prepare the lampstand and silver trumpets. We may want to get on with the journey to the promised land. But this attention to matters of the sanctuary, priests, Levites, and the worship life of the people reminds the reader that Israel's hope and trust is properly centered on God's presence in their midst.[44]

Davies notes the problem: 'the date presupposed here is a month earlier than that mentioned in 1.1. Yet, curiously, the following verses presuppose that the events of chs. 1-4 had already taken place…the most probable explanation is that the present chapter is the work of a later editor who had simply failed to notice the inconsistency'.[45] Budd agrees that the text is a late one, though he does suggest that the repetition in these first chapters of Numbers has the literary effect of emphasis on the massive proportions of things.[46]

The commentaries by Budd and Davies are of the historical-critical stripe; they hardly seem aware of the movement to a newer kind of literary analysis or to postmodern perspectives. Both offer much insight in the verse-by-verse analysis. They work toward our task of interpretation—making what is implicit in the text explicit—in the treatment of terms in the text but not in the overall point of view. One comes out with a history of traditions that *might* have formed the book of Numbers, not with a commentary on the narrative which Numbers now is.[47]

---

44. Olson, *Numbers*, p. 44.
45. Davies, *Numbers*, pp. 71-72.
46. Budd, *Numbers*, pp. 81-82.
47. For a similar evaluation of a commentary on the New Testament side, see

The commentaries tend to equate interpretation with historical investigation.[48] The comparison with the volume by Olson confirms the earlier description of a newer literary approach. The interpretation treats the text as it now stands and understands the language to create a world with which readers can interact. Handling the inner workings of the text helps readers encounter the specifics of the text. The task is not primarily the attempt to reconstruct some world behind the text.

I am not suggesting that we abandon historical investigation. Budd published a commentary on Leviticus in 1996, a commentary that also takes a historical approach;[49] but this commentary has a much greater emphasis on cultural codes that might help readers envision the world of Leviticus. The Leviticus commentary early on raises issues of holiness and sacrifice and theology,[50] issues that help readers grasp the Priestly world commended in the book. In his treatment of the Manual of Sacrifice (Lev. 1–7), Budd certainly attends to issues of the historical development of the various offerings, but he also addresses the structure and significance of each offering in a section concluding the treatment of the relevant chapter in Leviticus.[51] The commentary is still a historical enterprise, but it is not focused solely on historical-critical issues that are unresolvable and which offer little help for understanding the text of Leviticus. The commentary rather concentrates on cultural codes that can help readers glimpse how ancient auditors could have heard or read this text and which can help contemporary readers comprehend the unfamiliar world this Priestly text is commending. The work also has a holistic perspective emphasizing the ambiguity present in Leviticus.[52] The commentary is quite helpful to readers of the biblical text. It comments on the text of Leviticus rather than some hypothetically constructed text and it deals with cultural codes embedded in the book. The method borrows from cultural anthropology as much as liter-

C.H. Talbert's review of F. Bovon's *L'évangile selon saint Luc 9.51–14.35*, in *Bib* 78 (1997), pp. 425-28.

48. Budd does give some attention to the final form of the book.
49. P.J. Budd, *Leviticus* (NCB; Grand Rapids: Eerdmans, 1996).
50. Budd, *Leviticus*, pp. 24-39.
51. Budd, *Leviticus*, pp. 53-54, 64-65, 75-76, 97-98.
52. See Budd, *Leviticus*, pp. vii-viii. Budd articulates his goals in the preface. See also W.H. Bellinger, Jr, 'Leviticus and Ambiguity', *Perspectives in Religious Studies* 25 (1998), pp. 217-25.

ary criticism, but that decision flows from the nature of the material.[53] The book's focus on sacrifice, holiness, purity and atonement chart unfamiliar ground for contemporary readers, and attention to those issues helps readers interact with the world Leviticus is structuring. Attention to those issues helps make explicit what is implicit in the text.[54]

Commentaries often say little about their purposes but presumably they all seek to present information that will in some way help readers understand the biblical text. Olson's commentary is a different kind of commentary from those in the Word and New Century series. The Interpretation commentary series is explicitly designed to facilitate preaching and teaching, and Olson's commentary is much shorter than the other two. The goal of interpretation clearly has an impact on approach. Interpretations for the sake of a community of faith will likely emphasize a different set of directions than will interpretations in the context of (say) the Society of Biblical Literature. The usefulness of an interpretation for its audience is an important hermeneutical component.[55]

A Question of Meaning

Another component in the interpretive task is genre. Many newer literary studies have emphasized narrative texts in the Hebrew Bible, as has this essay. Much of the Hebrew Bible, however, is in poetry. How might one proceed with a literary approach in such texts?

In *How Does a Poem Mean?* John Ciardi and Millar Williams have strongly argued that *what* a poem means is the wrong question.[56] The language of classification so often leads to a search for a paraphrasable message in a poem and leads readers away from experiencing the poetry. A more exciting and productive journey is to try to experience *how* a poem means. Form criticism is one of the central methods bibli-

---

53. Interdisciplinary approaches are characteristic of the postmodern.

54. This essay barely hints at the place of history in interpretation, a particularly complex problem.

55. See D.J.A. Clines, 'A World Established on Water (Psalm 24): Reader-Response, Deconstruction and Bespoke Interpretation', in Exum and Clines (eds.), *The New Literary Criticism*, pp. 79-90.

56. J. Ciardi and M. Williams, *How Does a Poem Mean?* (Boston: Houghton Mifflin, 2nd edn, 1975).

cal scholars have used in analysing poetry. Form criticism trades on classification. A more contemporary literary analysis gives focus to how a poem means and thus enables readers more fully to encounter the poem and the world it achieves. Poems bring to expression powerful parts of life and often do so playfully but with profound impact:

> For the poem is not a statement but a performance of forces, not an essay on life but a reenactment, and just as [people] must search their lives over and over again for the meaning of their deepest experiences, so the performance of a true poem is endless in being not a meaning but an act of existence.[57]

A poem is an event that calls upon readers to enter the fray and live in the event by living with the use of language: repetition, images, use of words, rhythms and symbols.[58] I illustrate with two texts.

Most historical-critical readings of Psalm 61 concentrate on the cultic setting from which the text arose.[59] I have treated this text elsewhere and there expended energy on constructing a setting from which the psalm might have originated in ancient Israel.[60] The newer version of literary criticism gives attention to matters of poetic sequence for the reader.[61] Poetic structures, repetition, imagery, sequence and characterization provide helpful anchors for the reader to make sense of the poetic composition.

Psalm 61 echoes other lament psalms by speaking a plea from the edge of the world. The speaker is in pain but looks forward. The text moves to God's past protection and calls for renewed protection in Yahweh's house. The emphasis shifts to hope in v. 6 and the latter part of the text gives a hopeful context for the prayer. The text closes looking forward to the future fulfilling of vows to God. The speaker has called God to task for not delivering and the speaker's call has been heard. God has acted to move the speaker from the margin to the tent or shelter, to the community of order and renewal. The poetic form of

57. Ciardi and Williams, *How Does a Poem Mean?*, p. 10.
58. Note the assertion of Ciardi and Williams, *How Does a Poem Mean?*, p. 105: 'With a few exceptions every word traced back far enough is either a metaphor or an onomatopoeia'.
59. See, e.g., H.-J. Kraus, *Psalms 60–150: A Commentary* (ET; Minneapolis: Augsburg/Fortress Press, 1989), pp. 7-10; A. Weiser, *The Psalms: A Commentary* (ET; OTL; Philadelphia: Westminster Press, 1959), pp. 442-45.
60. Bellinger, *Hermeneutic*, pp. 39-55.
61. Bellinger, *Hermeneutic*, pp. 71-107.

Psalm 61 with its parallelism and intensifying structure makes possible a dynamic unfolding of a pilgrimage from crisis to hope, and it does so with only 16 lines of poetry. The poetic imagery is also striking. It moves from the image of fainting, wax melting, to the cry to God, to the contrasting pole of the rock in v. 3. God is now refuge and strength. The shelter of God's wings has moved the poet to the protection of home. The text moves from fainting to sheltering protection to praise in the context of community, from Sheol to sanctuary to thanksgiving, from lament to divine response to human response. The immediate purpose of the prayer is to persuade God to protect the worshiper in this crisis, but the rhetoric flows in another direction—to persuade the hearing/reading community, both ancient and modern, to join with the speaker in addressing God in times of trouble and in claiming the declaration that God hears and responds. The psalm thus nurtures faith. So the poetry has two purposes. It affirms God's response and awaits the community's.

Another good example is Amos 1–2. Most of the work done on this text consists of form-critical or redaction-critical studies. The attempt is to find the editorial setting, often somehow tied to the book's editorial introduction, or to describe the form of these foreign-nation oracles and explore their *Sitz im Leben*.[62] The specific references in these oracles certainly invite historical investigation, but literary analysis also has much to contribute. What is the relationship between the divine roaring in Amos 1.2 and the oracles that follow? What is the impact of repetition and variation in the poem?[63] What is the import of the nature of the sins catalogued here as crimes against humanity, war crimes? The cumulative effect of trying to get inside the poetry and see its rhythms, use of language and images leads to the portrait of the coming divine warrior who will bring fitting punishment for the crimes catalogued. Theophany will bring a measure of justice. When interpreters work with the literary dimensions of such poetry, they make explicit what is

---

62. See J.L. Mays, *Amos: A Commentary* (OTL; Philadelphia: Westminster Press, 1969); H.W. Wolff, *Joel and Amos* (ET; Hermeneia; Philadelphia: Fortress Press, 1977).

63. See Sternberg's helpful treatment of repetition, *Poetics*, pp. 365-440. R.C. Tannehill, 'The Composition of Acts 3-5: Narrative Development and the Echo Effect' (SBLSP, 23; Atlanta: Scholars Press, 1984), pp. 238-40, describes various functions of repetition.

implicit in the text by inviting readers to enter the poetry with them and play with the poetry—and thus encounter a horrible world of pain and oppression and the dreaded coming of a divine warrior to exact justice. Historical investigation can inform interpretation but it tends to be about the poem rather than serving to invite readers into the poem to encounter the world the text creates.

It is difficult to make universal statements about poetry because each poem is a world of its own. The literary dimensions of each poetic text create a unique composition.[64] Attention to those specific dimensions— how the poem means—enables readers to enter the poem and its world and encounter it. The task of interpretation is to help readers make that move. An interpreter makes explicit what is implicit in the poem by working with and articulating the specifics of the poetic composition.

Conclusions

I have suggested that the interpretation of biblical texts attends to the three dimensions of a text: origin, text and reader. Each text derives from a setting and comes from an author or authors. The text itself has a shape and dimensions of its own. The reading of the text is completed with the reader and the process of reading. The first conclusion of this essay is that biblical interpreters today need to examine their efforts and determine on which of these dimensions their interpretations turn. We live in a postmodern era of methodological pluralism, and so it is incumbent upon us as interpreters to be aware and explicit about our hermeneutical assumptions. This essay has maintained that the task of interpretation is to make explicit what is implicit in the text. It only stands to reason, then, that the interpreter's perspective on the location of the text's meaning will have a significant impact on interpretation. If meaning comes from the original setting or the author, then interpretation will in the main take a historical turn. If meaning is in the text itself, interpretation will focus on the shape of the autonomous whole that is the text. If the locus of meaning is the reader, interpretation will attend to the reading process and context of readers. The locus of meaning might be in a combination of these. Interpreters today cannot

---

64. See Ciardi and Williams, *How Does a Poem Mean?*, p. 305.

simply proceed without indicating their hermeneutical assumptions.[65] We must state our purpose.[66]

A second conclusion is that the dominance of the historical-critical approach is at an end. One cannot presume the equation of historical investigation and interpretation. Such a modern perspective does not take into account the postmodern moves in hermeneutics and literary criticism.[67] Many today would suggest that meaning is produced somehow in an encounter between reader and text. Arcane historical treatises contribute little to interpretation. Awareness of this new context is essential in the interpretive task.

A third conclusion has to do with the purposes of interpretation. If the task of interpretation is to make explicit what is implicit in a text, that interpretation is carried out in light of the purposes at hand. If the purposes relate to some community of faith, the interpreter will need to emphasize certain dimensions and move in certain directions. If the purposes are tied to literary or archaeological contexts, the interpreter will follow a different path. The path of interpretation is tied to the purposes of interpretation.

Many biblical scholars have resisted the turn to our postmodern context because they hold to the myth of objectivity for historical investigation.[68] The fear is that subjectivity will somehow corrupt the interpretation, but there is no such thing as disinterested interpretation. Our own location and view of the nature of the text affect our interpretation. Some subjectivity is inevitable. Our interpretive context determines the shape of that subjectivity, and location in an interpretive community provides some check on our idiosyncrasies. While interpretation is of necessity subjective, it is also placed in a community for evaluation and conversation.[69] Such interpretation has wider impact and effect.[70]

65. Stating one's hermeneutical assumptions provides a starting point for considering the ethics of interpretation.

66. B.W. Anderson, 'The Problem and Promise of Commentary', *Interpretation* 36 (1982), pp. 341-55, provides a helpful treatment of the history of commentary-writing and an evaluation of the commentary genre. He supports the view that commentators need to state their hermeneutical perspectives and purposes for writing. He also suggests that interpretation is a communal task.

67. In this essay, I have tied historical-critical interpretation to modernism and literary criticism to postmodernism. A literary critic could, of course, exhibit a modernist approach by rejecting the notion of a plurality of meanings.

68. See Powell, *The Bible and Modern Literary Criticism*, pp. 16-17.

69. See S. Fish, *Is There A Text in This Class? The Authority of Interpretive*

Some of these interpretive communities will be confessional communities; the postmodern context makes a place for them.[71] And so the interpretive task may attend to confessional concerns. The biblical text has through its history been tied to a community of faith, as have biblical interpreters. If the task of interpretation makes it possible for readers to encounter a world the text creates, then members of communities that affirm the efficacy of Scripture would want to encounter that world. That kind of encounter with the text is precisely what informs and nurtures faith.

Finally, this essay suggests that literary analysis has a particular contribution to make in Old Testament interpretation. Attention to literary dimensions of narratives and poems is especially helpful in making explicit what is implicit in texts. This articulation of the point shows that the question of genre is also relevant. Interpretation of narrative and poetry will be distinct. Still, analysis centering on literary characteristics will provide essential material for interpreters.

Literary criticism serves Old Testament interpretation well. It makes fresh readings of texts possible.[72] Certainly, one of the responsibilities incumbent upon an interpreter is to craft an interesting interpretation. Otherwise, readers of interpretations will not likely encounter the world of the text. Literary analysis provides a means for further adventures with texts.[73]

Communities (Cambridge, MA: Harvard University Press, 1982).

70. See Steinmetz, 'Superiority', p. 38. His stunning conclusion aptly describes a significant part of the context of contemporary biblical scholarship.

71. See Powell, *The Bible and Modern Literary Criticism*, pp. 18-19.

72. I am aware that this essay has hardly touched on ideological readings. Such approaches also lend themselves to creative interpretations.

73. An earlier version of this paper was presented to the Southwest Regional Biblical Studies Seminar in Fort Worth in February 1998.

THE ROLE OF OLD TESTAMENT THEOLOGY IN OLD TESTAMENT INTERPRETATION*

Walter Brueggemann

I

In a summary way, it is possible to distinguish in scholarship four rather distinctive phases of critical study, each of which hosted theological interpretation in a way peculiar to its horizon:

1. *The Reformation Period*

It was in the Reformation that 'biblical theology' became a distinct enterprise, as theological interpretation was undertaken apart from the sacramental system of the church, and to some extent outside the conventional categories of the dogmatic tradition.[1] In that context, 'biblical theology' had as its role the attempt to voice the fresh, free, live word of gospel, completely uncontained and unfettered by any hegemonic categories of established church tradition. Different traditions in the Reformation, of course, gave different accents to this newly 'evangelical' interpretation, best known in Lutheran *grace* and Calvinistic *sovereignty*. In all these cases, however, the effort was made to deal directly with 'the things of God' in the text, without mediating forms and structures that worked toward domestication and containment. Thus 'biblical theology' had a distinctly 'evangelical' impetus.

---

*   I am pleased to join in a salute to Professor Clements, from whom I have learned much and whose hospitality I have greatly appreciated.

1.   It was Luther's intention to interpret the Bible and its Gospel apart from the interpretive controls of the church. Thus 'biblical theology' became an enterprise distinct from church theology. It is instructive that H.-J. Kraus, *Geschichte der historisch-kritischen Erforschung des Alten Testaments* (Neukirchen–Vluyn: Neukirchener Verlag, 3rd edn, 1982), pp. 6-24, begins his study of *biblical criticism* with the rubric '*sola scriptura*'.

2. *Enlightenment Historicism*

While the forms and cadences of Reformation 'biblical theology' persisted into the seventeenth century, the notion of unfettered witness to the things of God was exceedingly difficult to maintain. In both Lutheran and Calvinist circles (not to speak at all of Trent), the great claims of unfettered gospel were eventually reduced to new scholastic formulation, surely as domesticated as the scholastic formulations against which the primal Reformers had worked.[2]

In that context, the move from *dogmatic* to *historical* questions was an attempt to emancipate biblical interpretation from the deep domestication of Scripture. It is exceedingly important to recall that the emergence and appropriation of 'the historical' was an effort to maintain the free availability of scriptural claims against the new theological scholasticism. It is common to cite the lecture of Johann Philip Gabler in 1787 as the decisive articulation of this new approach, whereby Gabler insisted that Old Testament study was primally an historical and not dogmatic enterprise.[3] As Ben Ollenburger has shown, however, Gabler's intention is more subtle than the simple categories of dogmatic-historical may indicate.[4]

Focus upon 'the historical' brought with it the subsequently developed notion of 'God acts in history'. But the primary energy released by this new category was devoted to historical *criticism* and the effort to situate every text according to its date and recoverable context. This movement culminated in Wellhausen's great synthesis that is aptly entitled *Prolegomena to the History of Israel*.[5] That is, the documentary

---

2. See H. Graf Reventlow, *The Authority of the Bible and the Rise of the Modern World* (ET; Philadelphia: Fortress Press, 1985).

3. Gabler's decisive lecture is available in its pertinent parts in English by J.E. Sandys-Wunsch and L. Eldredge, 'J.P. Gabler and the Distinction between Biblical and Dogmatic Theology: Translation, Commentary and Discussion of his Originality', *SJT* 33 (1980), pp. 133-58.

4. B.C. Ollenburger, 'Biblical Theology: Situating the Discipline', in J.T. Butler, E.W. Conrad and B.C. Ollenburger (eds.), *Understanding the Word: Essays in Honor of Bernhard W. Anderson* (JSOTSup, 37; Sheffield: JSOT Press, 1985), pp. 37-62. See also R.P. Knierim, 'On Gabler', in *idem*, *The Task of Old Testament Theology: Substance, Method, and Cases* (Grand Rapids: Eerdmans, 1995), pp. 495-556.

5. J. Wellhausen, *Prolegomena to the History of Israel* (ET; Edinburgh: A. & C. Black, 1885).

hypothesis, for which Wellhausen is widely credited and blamed, is a preparation for doing *history*.

Historical criticism, perhaps inevitably, focused upon the history of Israelite religion, thus situating each religious practice and implied theological claim in a specific context, understanding each practice and claim as context specific. The outcome was to relativize every practice and claim, to permit a developmental scheme by which every practice and claim was eventually displaced (superseded!) by another. As a consequence, every practice and claim is pertinent only to its immediate historical context. In that enterprise that stretches, as we conveniently put it, from Gabler to Wellhausen, the study of the history of Israelite religion almost completely displaced Old Testament theology, and the latter continued only in a subdued way as a rearguard action to maintain the 'constancies' of 'orthodoxy'. It is of particular interest that whereas 'biblical theology' in the Reformation period was emancipatory, in the period of high Enlightenment it was, where it was undertaken at all, not so much emancipatory as conserving and consolidating, an attempt to resist the vigorous enterprise of relativizing historicism. Such an approach to the text was distinctly against 'the spirit of the times'.

3. *The Barthian Alternative*
The dominance of a history-of-religions approach, with its relativizing consequences, inevitably evoked a response. But no one could have imagined that the response would be as forceful, bold, and demanding as that offered by Karl Barth in his *Römerbrief* in 1919.[6] Barth's effort was to interpret the text in a boldly and unembarrassedly theological, normative way, without yielding anything to historical relativism and without reducing faithful practice and theological claim to contextual explanation.

It is difficult to overstate the decisive contribution of Barth in turning the interpretive enterprise and in freshly legitimating theological interpretation that dared to treat theological claim in the text as constant and normative. Barth enlivened and legitimated nearly a century of theological interpretation, including the most important work in Old Testament theology; but of course from the perspective of scholars who, for personal or intellectual reasons, fear and resist such claims of

6. It was presented in English translation by E.C. Hoskyns as *The Epistle to the Romans* (London: Oxford University Press, 1933).

the 'normative', Barth is to be regarded as an unfortunate digression in the discipline.

While Barth's theological eruption already in 1919 is taken as a decisive break in Enlightenment historicism, it is not possible to appreciate the impact of Barth apart from the later context of his work, with particular reference to the challenge of National Socialism in Germany and the articulation of the Barmen Declaration in 1934. The mood and tenor of the work is profoundly *confessional*, an assertion of *normative* truth that had practical consequences and that implied personal and concrete risk. That mood and tenor of confession did not bother to make itself persuasive to 'cultural despisers', who, by historical criticism, managed to tone down 'evangelical claims' for God, to make matters compatible with Enlightenment reason. The daring claims made in a Barthian posture stand in deep contrast with the consolidating, even reactionary function of biblical theology in the earlier period of historicism. Barth's dominance is a primal example of the ways in which context presents questions and challenges that push biblical theology in one direction rather than another. It is unmistakable that the crisis of the twentieth century both required and permitted biblical theology in ways neither permitted nor required in the earlier period of high historicism.

The legacy of Barth may be said to have dominated the field of biblical theology until about 1970. In the center of that period is the magisterial work of Walther Eichrodt who took *covenant* as his mode of normativeness, and the even more influential work of Gerhard von Rad, whose definitive essay of 1938 surely echoes the credo-orientation of Barmen.[7] While the normativeness and constancy of Barth's perspective can take different forms, both Eichrodt and von Rad sought to provide a place of normativeness in which to stand in the face of the huge barbarisms of the twentieth century, for it was clear that the domestications of historical criticism provided no standing ground at all. More than Eichrodt, von Rad continued to attend to and be puzzled by the unmistakable dynamic of historical change reflected in the faith

---

7. The pivotal essay for von Rad, surely reflecting the confessional crisis of Barmen, is 'The Form-Critical Problem of the Hexateuch', in *idem, The Problem of the Hexateuch and Other Essays* (ET; New York: McGraw-Hill, 1966), pp. 1-78. The belated English translations of the more comprehensive works are W. Eichrodt, *Theology of the Old Testament* (2 vols.; Philadelphia: Westminster Press, 1961, 1967); G. von Rad, *Old Testament Theology* (2 vols.; New York: Harper and Brothers, 1962, 1965).

of Israel, but he finally does not yield to it. In the United States, moreover, the odd juxtaposition of normative theological claim and historical vagary was handled with remarkable finesse and, for the moment, in
a compelling way by G. Ernest Wright in his influential *God Who Acts*.[8]

It is to be noticed that while this essentially Barthian enterprise of
'the Short Century' might provide credible ground for faith midst the
brutalities of history, it is also the case that the interpretive movement
out of Barth was vigorously hegemonic, providing in various ways a
summary account of the faith of ancient Israel that was exclusionary in
its claims and allowing little room for alternative reading.[9] While such
an assertiveness can well be understood in the context of brutality
whereby interpretation was an emergency activity, it is also important
to recognize that such a hegemonic posture evokes an inescapable
response at the end of its domination, a response of considerable force
and authority.

4. *The Coming of Post-Modernity*
It is now common to cite 1970 as the break point of what came to be
called (pejoratively) 'the Biblical Theology Movement', that interpretive enterprise propelled by Barth and especially voiced by von Rad and
Wright. The 'ending' of that monopolistic interpretive effort was occasioned by many factors. It is conventional to cite the work of Brevard
Childs and James Barr as the decisive voices of the ending, even though
it is clear that Barr and Childs come from very different directions and
agree on almost nothing except their critique.[10] Also to be fully appre-

8.   G.E. Wright, *God Who Acts: Biblical Theology as Recital* (SBT; London:
SCM Press, 1952). See also G.E. Wright, *The Old Testament against its Environment* (SBT; London: SCM Press, 1950).

9.   On the 'short century' see E. Hobsbawm, *The Age of Extremes: A History of
the World, 1914–1991* (New York: Pantheon Books, 1994). The 'short century'
refers to the time from the outbreak of World War I to the fall of the Soviet Union.
The nomenclature is pertinent for our topic that was dominated by a certain set of
assumptions growing from Barth. The exclusion practiced by what became 'the
Biblical Theology Movement' is easy to spot in retrospect. On the positivism related to the enterprise, see now B. O. Long, *Planting and Reaping Albright: Politics,
Ideology, and Interpreting the Bible* (University Park, PA: Pennsylvania State University Press, 1997).

10.   See especially B.S. Childs, *Biblical Theology in Crisis* (Philadelphia: Westminster Press, 1970), and J. Barr, 'Revelation Through History in the Old Testament and Modern Theology', *Interpretation* 17 (1963), pp. 193-205; *idem*, 'The

ciated, from inside the movement itself, are the insistence of Frank Moore Cross (a colleague of Wright) that Israel is enmeshed in ancient Eastern culture and is not as distinctive as had been urged, and Claus Westermann's (a colleague of von Rad) urging that the horizon of creation was as important as the 'historical recital' for the faith of Israel.[11]

More broadly the rise of feminist and liberation hermeneutics and the failure of mono-interpretation have produced, since 1970, an interpretive context that is by many styled 'postmodern', that is, after the hegemony that had dominated the twentieth century.[12] Coming to the more important features of this development of scholarship that has put the work of Old Testament theology in some disarray, we may notice three:

Pluralism. Von Rad has already taken seriously the pluralism of the theological claims of the Old Testament text. But now the awareness of pluralism is much deeper and more seriously noticed, so that the text seems to admit of no single, grand formulation. Indeed the text not only offers a plurality of God-claims, but when read closely, the several texts themselves are plurivocal, open to a variety of readings. The quality and character of the text, moreover, is matched increasingly by a plurality of readers, reflecting a diverse community of interests, so that no single synthetic reading is any longer possible.[13]

Ideology. It follows from a full-faced acknowledgment of pluralism,

Old Testament and the New Crisis of Biblical Authority', *Interpretation* 25 (1971), pp. 24-40; *idem, The Bible in the Modern World* (London: SCM Press, 1973); and *idem, Holy Scripture: Canon, Authority, Criticism* (Philadelphia: Westminster Press, 1983). In addition it is important to mention L. Gilkey, 'Cosmology, Ontology, and the Travail of Biblical Language', *Journal of Religion* 41 (1961), pp. 194-205.

11. See W. Brueggemann, 'The Loss and Recovery of Creation in Old Testament Theology', *TTod* 53 (1996), pp. 177-90, and the references there to F.M. Cross, C. Westermann and H.H. Schmid.

12. I have no special concern for the label 'postmodern', except that it is a convenient way to reference the quite new interpretive context in which we are now placed. See W. Brueggemann, *Texts Under Negotiation: The Bible and Postmodern Imagination* (Minneapolis: Fortress Press, 1993). For a vigorous and important resistance to postmodernity, see F. Watson, *Text and Truth: Redefining Biblical Theology* (Grand Rapids: Eerdmans, 1997).

13. For an insistence upon a unified reading that resists pluralism in faithful reading, see Watson, *Text and Truth*, and his earlier *Text, Church and World* (Grand Rapids: Eerdmans, 1994).

that one can readily see that every offer of normativeness is in some sense ideology. Most benignly this means it is an advocacy for a certain perspective and not a given. Thus, even the hegemonic approach held in common by Barth, Eichrodt, von Rad and Wright is seen to be not a stable foundation, but rather an advocacy on offer to the larger interpretive community that must be received and adjudicated by interpreters who occupy other ideological perspectives.[14] Behind this collage of interpretive adjudications among advocacies, we are able to see more clearly that the pluralism in the text itself concerns the things of God, a collage of competing advocacies that made it into the text, advocacies that are not done (we may assume) in bad faith, but that are not easily or quietly compatible.

Speech as Constitutive. Emphasis upon the power of rhetoric, when considered in the context of pluralism and ideology, makes clear that speech about God is not simply reportage on 'what happened' in history or 'what is' in ontology, but the speech itself is powerfully constitutive of theological claim as it is of historical 'past'.[15] Thus the new, postmodern world of theological interpretation is powerfully focused on utterance, a concrete utterance offered in the text, and on *interpretive utterance* offered in contemporary conversation. Insofar as utterance is taken as mere utterance, it may indeed be shaped either by the dogmatic claims of the ecclesial community or by the requirements of Enlightenment reason. But it is also in the very character of utterance that it may be a *novum*, that can be recognized in some quarters as a claim of truth beyond the fetters of church or academy.[16] Thus it is the *appropriation and reception of utterance* and *the critique of utterance* that I take to be the work of Old Testament theology. In our present context,

14. It seems evident that long-standing theological *hegemony* turns out to be ideological advocacy, as does *skepticism* that assumes the ideological claims of Enlightenment rationality. None is immune from an ideological insistence, so that we must work midst our competing advocacies.

15. On the constitutive power of public speech, see W. Brueggemann, *Israel's Praise: Doxology agaist Idolatry and Ideology* (Philadelphia: Fortress Press, 1988), pp. 1-28. A more rigorous discussion of mine would appeal to the work of Foucault.

16. G. Steiner, 'A Preface to the Hebrew Bible', in *idem, No Passion Spent: Essays 1978–1995* (New Haven: Yale University Press, 1996), pp. 40-87, luminously makes the case for the ways in which the discourse of the Bible is originary. See also W.A. Kort, *'Take, Read': Scripture, Textuality, and Cultural Practice* (University Park, PA: Pennsylvania State University Press, 1996).

this reception, appreciation and critique of utterance takes place in the loud and dissonant presence of many voices. But this accent on utterance as the offer of new truth also has important continuities with the Reformation accent upon the word, and with the insistence of Barth, even though that appreciation, reception and critique must now be done in a quite different form.

II

The location of Old Testament theology in a postmodern situation sets some severe limits on what is possible, but also yields some legitimate place for such demanding, important work. Both the severe limits and the legitimate place, however, are freshly situated in a new cultural, interpretive context in which old practices must indeed be relinquished. Indeed, the case is readily made that from our present vantage point (that also must not be absolutized, as has been a recurring temptation for every vantage point), Old Testament theology has been much too often imperialistically Christian, coercively moralistic and vigorously anti-Semitic.[17] These critiques of past work must be taken seriously and count much more, in my judgment, than the easier contention that theological interpretation does not honor Enlightenment rationality and is therefore fideistic.

Old Testament theology in such a context, I propose, may have the following marks.[18]

1. *'Theo-logy'* is 'speech about God'. That is, it does not concern, in any primary sense, all that might be said of Israel's religion, but it is an attempt to pay attention to the God who emerges in the utterance of these texts, a God marked by some constancy, but a God given in a peculiar, even scandalous characterization. What ever else may be said of this God, it is clear that the God of the Old Testament conforms neither to conventional monotheism nor to flat dogmatic categories, nor to usual philosophical Enlightenment assumptions of the West, though it

17. See J.D. Levenson, 'Why Jews are Not Interested in Biblical Theology', in *idem, The Hebrew Bible: The Old Testament, and Historical Criticism* (Louisville: Westminster John Knox Press, 1993), pp. 33-61.

18. For what follows, my more extended treatment is given in F.M. Cross *et al.* (eds.), *Theology of the Old Testament: Testimony, Dispute, Advocacy* (Minneapolis: Fortress Press, 1997).

is equally clear that a monotheizing tendency is at work.[19]

2. *Speech about God* is given by human persons, reflected in human institutions, in human contexts, serving human, political agendas. This is no new insight and no threat to the enterprise. All the efforts to minimize 'the historical', moreover, cannot eliminate the fact that human persons have made these utterances. Thus the God of Israel is given us *on the lips of Israel*, constituted through utterance, utterance no doubt deeply driven and informed by lived experience but in the end shaped by artistic, imaginative utterance.

3. Such speech about God is not idle chatter but is characteristically *intentional speech* and is so treated in the canonizing process. More specifically, we may say that *intentional human speech about* God is *testimony*, an attempt to give a particular account of reality with this God as agent and as character at its center.[20] And while we may notice the great pluralism in the text in God-utterances, we may also, perhaps more importantly, observe a family kinship of all these utterances when set over against alternative accounts of reality, ancient or modern. While close theological reading will attend to the differences in utterance, Old Testament theology in the end has a propensity toward that shared kinship, to see what is recurring midst the vagaries of testimony.

4. Old Testament theology treats of the *text of canon* and so takes human testimony as *revelation*.[21] One need not so take it, and many scholars preoccupied with 'historical questions' would not make that move, even though what is claimed to be 'history' turns out almost every time to be advocacy. Be that as it may, Old Testament theology, in its attention to what is recurring and constant in Israel's God-utterance, takes that God-utterance to be disclosing. I understand, of course, that the history of Christian revelation, with its deposit of dogmatic

19. See J.A. Sanders, 'Adaptable for Life: The Nature and Function of Canon', in F.M. Cross *et al.* (eds.), *Magnalia Dei: The Mighty Acts of God: Essays on the Bible and Archaeology in Memory of G. Ernest Wright* (Garden City: Doubleday, 1976), pp. 531-60.

20. On 'testimony' as the decisive genre for biblical theology, see Brueggemann, *Theology*, pp. 117-44.

21. It is especially Brevard Childs who has insisted that when the text is studied as 'Scripture', as the holy book of the ecclesial community, the shape and claims of canon are decisive for interpretation. Childs has rightly linked 'Scripture' to theological intentionality of a quite specific kind. But whereas Childs's notion of Scripture tends to be stable and consolidating, Kort, *Take, Read*, offers a much more radical, lively and serious notion of the reading of Scripture.

truth, has been profoundly coercive; here I use 'revelatory' and 'disclosing' to mean that the God-utterance of Israel seeks to *un-close* lived reality that without the generative force of Yahweh as character and agent is characteristically *closed* in ways of denial, despair, and/or oppression.

5. To take Israel's God-speech as revelatory means that it is utterance that seeks to speak about a *mystery* that attends to and indwells the world in which Israel lives. That mystery, according to Israel's utterance, is on the loose, wild and dangerous, often crude, inaccessible, unattractive, capable of violence, equally capable of positive transformation.[22] In its God-speech Israel does not set out everywhere to give us an attractive or appealing God, the stable God of church catechism or the winsome God of therapeutic culture. But it does seek to give an account of an agency of otherness who operates with intentional purpose and who refuses to be captive either to slogans of self-sufficiency or in the terminology of despair.[23] Israel's God-speech seeks to give an account of restless holiness that decisively redefines and resituates everything else about life.

6. Israel's God-speech, moreover, in a rich variety of ways, offers that this Other is—*provisionally identifiable*. 'God' in the Old Testament is identifiable, known by characteristic actions that are recognizable from one context to another, known by direct utterance treasured and passed on, known by moves that can be placed in the text and on the lips of the witnesses. Because that Other is genuinely *other*, however, Israel itself knows that all such identification is provisional and not final or certain.[24] And so there are 'many names', many metaphors

22. On the defining dimensions of violence in the text that is assigned to God, see D.R. Blumenthal, *Facing the Abusing God: A Theology of Protest* (Louisville: Westminster John Knox Press, 1993) and R.M. Schwarz, *The Curse of Cain: the Violent Legacy of Monotheism* (Chicago: University of Chicago Press, 1997).

23. It was, of course, Barth who focused on the 'Wholly Other'. The notion of *alterity* has been more fully and helpfully developed in Jewish interpretation, stemming from Martin Buber and given classic formulation by E. Levinas, *Totality and Infinity: An Essay on Exteriority* (Pittsburgh: Duquesne University Press, 1969). See also G. Steiner, *Real Presences* (Chicago: University of Chicago Press, 1989).

24. On the problematic of God's name, see the representative, rather conventional discussion in C.E. Braaten (ed.), *Our Naming of God: Problems and Prospects of God-Talk Today* (Minneapolis: Fortress Press, 1989). Kort, *Take, Read*, pp. 133-38, has important suggestions about the *scriptural* deconstruction of patriarchy that dominates Scripture.

and images, many songs, poems and narratives, all of which attest differently.[25] There are crises of naming when the name is displaced (Exod. 3.14; 6.2), and there is a withholding of the name (Gen. 32.29).[26] In the end, moreover, there is the inscrutability of the Tetragrammaton (YHWH), Israel's final resistance to idolatry and Israel's defiant notice to check both church theologians who know too much about this Other and academic theologians who work apart from this Other.

7. In a postmodern context, it is important to accept that these voices of God-talk are all advocates in the debate about how to voice provisional identity of the undoubted, unaccommodating Other. Thus 'J', Second Isaiah, Job and Ezra each advocate differently. At the most they advocate but they do not finally know. They are witnesses and neither judge nor jury.[27] They propose and offer, but do not finally comprehend. Insofar as all these witnesses agree (which is not very far), their shared utterance is also advocacy and not certitude. In our postmodern context, it can hardly be more than advocacy.

I am, however, quick to insist that there are many scholars who discount the God-speech of Israel in the name of 'disinterested' scholarship, who refuse theological questions on the ground of 'history', who are themselves advocates and not more than advocates.[28] We have arrived at the odd situation in which the *resisters* to the God-utterances of Israel posture themselves as more certain than the *practitioners* of Old Testament theology dare to be; but in fact the resisters also are only advocates of Enlightenment rationality, bespeaking old and long wounds from ancient theological coerciveness, preferring a self-contained, self-explanatory world to one of hurt-producing theological authoritarianism. A postmodern Old Testament theology, so it seems to me, dare not be coercive and need not be coercive. For in our present context, Old

25. See B. Wren, *What Language Shall I Borrow? God-Talk in Worship: A Male Response to Feminist Theology* (New York: Crossroads, 1989), especially chapter 6.

26. As is often remarked, it is important that the name of YHWH is withheld in the long poetic exchange of the book of Job until ch. 38. Such a withholding is surely intentional and strategic for the book.

27. On the witness and counter-witness, see W. Brueggemann, 'Life-Or-Death: De-Privileged Communication', *Journal for Preachers* 21.4 (1998), pp. 22-29.

28. Skepticism is not particularly high ground in intellectual activity. It simply advocates Enlightenment rationality, an increasingly doubtful stance for interpretation. See, e.g., the odd use of the term 'disinterested' by P.R. Davies, *Whose Bible is is Anyway?* (JSOTSup, 204; Sheffield, Sheffield Academic Press, 1995), p. 1.

Testament theology is proposal and not conclusion, offer and not certainty. Interpretation stands always in front of our deciding and not after. For the *otherness* of reality given us on the lips of Israel makes our deciding always penultimate and provisional, always yet again unsettled by new disclosings.

III

Given the history of the discipline, and given a postmodern situation with no agreed-upon 'meta-narrative',[29] we may now consider the role of Old Testament theology in the discipline, a role that must respect both the critical foundations of the discipline and the postmodern options that at the same time limit and permit.

I purpose that the primal role of Old Testament theology is to attend to the testimony out of which lived reality was then and may now be reimagined with reference to a Holy Character who is given us on the lips of Israel, who exhibits some constancy, but whose constancy is regularly marked by disjunction and tension.[30] The act of imagining alternatively is what these witnesses are doing in the text-world itself, and the ongoing option of imagining alternatively is kept alive by continual attentiveness to this testimony.[31] That Holy Character on the lips of the witnesses through whom lived reality is construed differently is

29. On this characterization of postmodernity, see J.-F. Lyotard, *The Postmodern Condition: A Report on Knowledge* (Minneapolis: University of Minnesota Press, 1984).

30. On such a characterization of God, see D. Patrick, *The Rendering of God in the Old Testament* (OBT; Philadelphia: Fortress Press, 1981).

31. To *imagine alternatively* seems to me a fair notion of what biblical theology is about. Brevard Childs is frequently worried that my emphasis on imagination is to assign too much to human initiative. It is surely the case, however, that any fruitful, faithful interpretation is indeed an act of imagination. See J.W.H. van Wijk-Bos, *Reimagining God: The Case for Scriptural Diversity* (Louisville: Westminster John Knox Press, 1995); E.F. Davis, *Imagination Shaped: Old Testament Preaching in the Anglican Tradition* (Valley Forge, PA: Trinity Press International, 1995); and G. Green, *Imaging God: Theology and the Religious Imagination* (San Francisco: Harper and Row, 1989). And even such a conservative perspective as that of Watson, *Text and Truth*, p. 325, yields the verdict: 'At the very least, the interpretative tradition that is here in process of formation is an expression of a *creative theological imgination* that has learned to see the scriptural texts in the light of Christ, and Christ in the light of the scriptural texts' (my emphasis). One must of course make differentiations, but to resist imagination in principle is impossible.

In Search of True Wisdom

often given as a characteristic assurance; but on many other occasions this same Character is rather a deconstructive force who moves against every settlement, every certitude and every assurance. Or, as Jürgen Moltmann has said of more belated, Christian claims for faith, the God given on the lips of witnesses is both 'foundation' and 'criticism', both the *power for life* who is profoundly generative and authorizing, as well as summoning and dispatching, but who is also a *critical principle* who stands as a check upon what these witnesses may say against this Character.[32] Or more summarily, this testimony to God is a claim that at the core of lived reality there is a mystery invested with transformative energy and with durable purposiveness. The witnessing community endlessly relearns, however, that embrace of that transformative energy and durable purposiveness does nothing to minimize the inscrutable Otherness of the Character who inhabits such mystery.

The role of Old Testament theology as attendance upon the testimony concerning this Character varies as we consider the various 'publics' addressed by such study. We may be guided by David Tracy's identification of three publics that concern us—the academic, the ecclesial and the civic.[33] Of any work in Old Testament studies, it may be especially Old Testament theology that reaches beyond the limits of the discipline of Old Testament study itself to address those other publics.

1. *Old Testament Theology within the Academic Community*[34]
There is no doubt that Old Testament theology is related to and much informed by many different kinds of critical study, literary and historical.[35] It no longer pertains, moreover, that these several modes of critical study are conducted in the service of theology, as might have been the case when theology could claim to be the 'queen of the sciences'. In a postmodern setting, it is clear that very much critical study is taken as

32. The subtitle of J. Moltmann, *The Crucified God* (ET; San Francisco: Harper and Row, 1974) is *The Cross of Christ as the Foundation and Criticism of Christian Theology*.

33. D. Tracy, *The Analogical Imgination: Christian Theology and the Culture of Pluralism* (New York: Crossroad, 1981), pp. 3-46.

34. I am aware that by 'The Public of the Academy' Tracy refers to the entire university community. Here, because of my particular topic, I refer more explicitly to the guild of Old Testament studies.

35. I take 'historical' here broadly to include more recent developments of 'social-scientific' methods.

an end in itself, without any reference to theological issues, or in some quarters critical study is undertaken precisely to defeat theological interpretation and eliminate the questions it purports to address.

Old Testament theology, in the present context of scholarship, has no leverage or need to be taken seriously by the guild of scholarship, and has no mandate to insist upon its own claims. Nonetheless, those of us in the field who take up the work of theological interpretation sense that critical study that is singularly preoccupied with historical or literary questions, or that proceeds according to positivistic rationality that in principle nullifies Israel's testimony to God, has in fact failed to pay attention to the text or to the claims that are expressed and that invite the hearer's engagement. In the end, it seems clear that the Old Testament text is not preoccupied with historical questions nor even with literary finesse—though both historical and literary issues are fully present—but with the strange, sometimes violent, sometimes hidden, often unwelcome ways of this Holy Agent in the midst of life.

Very much historical and literary study, taken in and of itself, while perfectly legitimate, is conducted in a way that is 'tone deaf' to the voice of the text. Thus Old Testament theology, if conducted in a way that is not reductive or coercive, may be an invitation that could keep the academic discipline from being turned in upon itself, preoccupied with greater and greater intensity on issues that matter less and less. In the end, so it seems to me, the history of ancient Israel that can be recovered by positivistic categories does not seem to go anywhere that would interest the witnesses themselves, for when the Holy Character is deleted from the calculus of meaning, not much that matters remains.[36] In the same way, attentiveness to literary and rhetorical elements of the text seems to indicate the artistry of the sort of folk who are always pointing beyond the artistry itself to the true Subject of the artistry who defies critical decoding. It seems to me inevitable that the core claim of Old Testament theology, witness to the Character, will continue to live in discomfort with a kind of positivistic criticism that resists its very

36. On the limits and inadequacy of positivistic history for our purposes, see Y.H. Yerushalmi, *ZAKHOR: Jewish History and Jewish Memory* (Seattle: University of Washington Press, 1982). Said another way, what concerns Old Testament theology must to some extent be concerned with an 'emic' approach to the text in distinction from a more conventional 'etic' approach. On the distinction, see briefly N.K. Gottwald, *The Tribes of Yahweh: A Sociology of the Religion of Liberated Israel, 1250–1050 B.C.E.* (Maryknoll, NY: Orbis Books, 1979), p. 785 n. 558.

subject. Nonetheless, its work is to keep before the more general discipline the central Character without whom much of the rest of our study
ends up being trivial.

2. *Old Testament Theology in the Context of Ecclesial Communities*[37]
Because Old Testament theology is here defined as speech about God, it
is inevitable that reference will be made to those communities that
intentionally engage in and attend to serious speech about God. There
is, I take it, an unresolvable tension between academic study and ecclesial study, if the former is defined in positivistic categories. But to
define academic study in positivistic categories is itself an advocacy of
special pleading and is not a necessary assumption. How the interplay
of academic and ecclesial references is adjudicated seems largely to
depend upon the interpreter, but to begin with an assumption of total
separation is a premise that in my judgment is not readily persuasive.[38]

But the more important ecclesial question concerns the tension and
interplay between faith communities, Jewish and Christian, both of
which look to these texts as Scripture.[39] It is now completely clear,
especially through the work of Jon Levenson, that Old Testament theology historically has been an unashamedly Christian enterprise, or
even more specifically, a Protestant enterprise. Such study, moreover,
has been deeply marked by unthinking anti-Jewish interpretation, an
outcome that is inescapable, I suggest, as long as work is done in isolation.

Moreover, Brevard Childs has made a powerful case that Jews and
Christians read different Bibles, so that the theological interpretation
among Christians and among Jews is different from the ground up.[40]

37. By speaking of such communities in the plural, I refer to both synagogue
and church. It is evident that my way of speaking concerns the church; but, *mutatis
mutandis*, the same issues pertain to the synagogue.

38. This large and important point is well urged by G.M. Marsden, *The Soul of
the American University: From Protestant Establishment to Established Non-Belief*
(Oxford: Oxford University Press, 1994).

39. The interplay of Jews and Christians concerning Scripture is as important as
it is vexed. The problematic is already reflected in the different nomenclature for
the texts, names that bespeak important issues. See R. Brooks and J.J. Collins
(eds.), *Hebrew Bible or Old Testament?: Studying the Bible in Judaism and Christianity* (Notre Dame: University of Notre Dame Press, 1990).

40. B.S. Childs, *Biblical Theology of the Old and New Testaments: Theological
Reflection on the Christian Bible* (Minneapolis: Fortress Press, 1992). Clearly Wat-

This same view is reiterated from the Jewish side by Jon Levenson.[41] While the argument has much to commend it, it is not one by which I am persuaded. It is my judgment, rather, that theological interpretation of these Scriptures can be and is better done by Jews and Christians together, who may part company in their reading only late, if at all. The ground for common reading is partly moral and historical, that Christian supersessionism and its consequent brutality require an alternative approach.[42] Beyond that and more important, however, is the generative, evocative character of the text and the Character dominant within it. It is evident that the Old Testament imagines toward the New, but it manifestly does not imagine exclusively toward the New. It is evident that Hebrew Scripture imagines toward the Talmud, but it does not imagine exclusively toward the Talmud.[43]

Rather the Old Testament/Hebrew Scriptures imagine vigorously, in pronouncedly polyvalent ways, an offer addressed to and received by both Jewish and Christian faith communities as authoritative for a life faith. But because the imaginative thrust of the text is richly generative beyond every interpretive domestication, it will not do for a subsequent faith community to construe itself as the exclusive receiver of that generativity. Thus it seems to me that it is not a mistake to see this text toward the New Testament, but it is a deep, substantive mistake to see this text *exclusively* toward the New Testament (and mistaken in a similar way to see it only toward the synagogue).[44]

The truth is that the ecclesial communities are summoned precisely to host this Character marked, on the lips of the witnesses, by inscrutable

son, *Text and Truth*, agrees with Childs on this point. See Watson, *Text and Truth*, pp. 209-19, for a reflection on the work of Childs.

41. Levenson, *The Hebrew Bible*, pp. 80-81 and *passim*. He concludes: 'There is no non-particularistic access to these larger contexts' (p. 80).

42. See R.K. Soulen, *The God of Israel and Christian Theology* (Minneapolis: Fortress Press, 1996).

43. F. Holmgren, *The Old Testament and the Significance of Jesus: Embracing Change—Maintaining Christian Identity* (Grand Rapids, MI: Eerdmans, 1999) has shown how the communities of Judaism, Christianity and Qumran all engaged in the same 'creative/ depth' interpretation of scriptural texts.

44. Clearly to move from the normative text to any of the emergent texts requires an immense act of imagination, surely imagination that is informed by the canonical community. On this kind of freedom and discipline in interpretation, see C.L. Campbell, *Preaching Jesus: New Directions for Homiletics in Hans Frei's Postliberal Theology* (Grand Rapids: Eerdmans, 1997).

mystery, assertive will and energy, and inviolable purpose. And while that mystery, will, energy, and purpose may be provisionally linked to the Jewish community (in the claims of election and covenant) or to the Christian community (in the claims of Christology), the linkages are indeed provisional and contingent. As Old Testament theology may have as its work to summon academic scholarship away from trivialization and preoccupation with marginal matters, so Old Testament theology may summon ecclesial communities from certitudes that are excessive and exclusions that are idolatrous, by witnessing to the elusive but insistent reality of this Holy Character.

3. *Old Testament Theology in Public Discourse*
If Old Testament theology is *a practice of reimagining lived reality with reference to this odd core Character*, then Old Testament theology, in its furthest stretch, may speak past academic and ecclesial communities to be concerned for public discourse.

I do not imagine that Old Testament theology can contribute specifically and concretely to questions of public policy and public morality, as interfaces between old text and public issues are exceedingly complicated. But if the emerging dominant construal of reality in the global economy is the unfettered pursuit of private power by the manipulation of the 'money government', then Old Testament theology as a witness to this Holy Character can indeed provide materials for an alternative imagination.[45] It seems evident that the more recent construal of the world in terms of privatized global economy is not one that will enhance our common life. Such a construal of the world, so it appears, ends either in self-sufficiency or in despair. In either case it offers a huge potential for brutality, either to fend off in active ways those who impinge and threaten, or simply by neglect to allow the disappearance of the non-competitive.

It may be that from some other source can come an alternative to this dominant construal of reality, perhaps from what Robert Bellah terms

45. The phrase 'money government' is from C.A. Reich, *Opposing the System* (New York: Crown Publishing Group, 1995). See also H.F. Daly and J.B. Cobb, Jr, *For the Common Good: Redirecting the Economy toward Community, the Environment, and a Sustainable Future* (Boston: Beacon Press, 1994); W. Greider, *One World: Ready or Not* (New York: S. and S. Trade, 1997); and R. Kuttner, *Everything for Sale* (New York: Knopf, 1997).

the 'republican' tradition.[46] It can hardly be doubted that some alternative construal of social reality is urgent among us. And if we work from the ground up, it is entirely plausible that *lived reality reimagined out from this Character who lives on the lips of these witnesses* could offer such a wholesale and compelling alternative.

IV

There is no doubt that Old Testament theology, in converstaion with any of these three publics, proceeds with something of a 'naive realism', prepared to take the utterance of the witnessing text as a serious offer.[47] Such 'naiveté' may be only provisional and instrumental, as the interpreter withholds a serious personal commitment, or that 'naive realism' may reflect (as in my case) the primal inclination of the practitioner. Either way, so it seems to me, the practitioner of Old Testament theology must move between a credulous fideism and a knowing, suspicious skepticism, wherein the former does not pay sufficient attention to the *problematic* of the witness, and the latter is *tone deaf* to the core claim of the witnesses.

At the moment and perhaps for the foreseeable future, Old Testament theology must work its way between two determined challenges. On the one hand are those whom I would term 'children of innocence', who are excessively credulous but who do not remain long with the elusive quality of the text, but immediately push the testimony along to the more reified claims of the ecclesial community—for example, in Christian parlance, to reduce the testimony to doctrinal categories. It appears to me that such innocence is so much powered by *anxiety* that old truths are in jeopardy and the world does not hold. The reduction of the testimony turns out to be a strategy for the recovery of a 'lost coherence'.

On the other hand, there are those whom I would term 'children of coercion', who are exceedingly skeptical, but who do not linger long enough with the playful disjunctive quality of the Character, but immediately push the testimony to reified formulation which they then immediately are obligated to combat. It appears to me that such skepti-

---

46. R.N. Bellah *et al.*, *Habits of the Heart: Individualism and Commitment in American Life* (Berkeley: University of California Press, 1985).

47. It is, to be sure, a 'second naiveté': see M.I. Wallace, *The Second Naiveté: Barth, Ricoeur, and the New Yale Theology* (Studies in American Biblical Hermeneutics, 6; Macon: Mercer University Press, 1990).

cism is rooted in *great rage*, not really rage at the text or even its claims, but rage rooted in old, hidden histories of coerciveness whose wounds remain endlessly painful.

Both such anxiety-rooted-in-innocence and such rage-rooted-in-coercion are serious, endlessly powerful postures that are not easily overcome. It seems equally clear, however, that neither *anxiety* over a world that is passing nor *rage* about a world that has injured is an adequate place from which to engage the Character who lives on the lips of the witnesses.

In a postmodern context where hegemonic claims of any sort are doubtful, Old Testament theology must play a modest role, not claim too much for itself, but stand in some interpretive continuity with ancient witnesses who imagined and uttered with radical difference. While embracing an appropriate modesty, however, Old Testament theology must have its own say, voice its own offer that claims no privilege but is not to be confused with any other claim. It could be that, if done with authority but without any streak of arrogance, Old Testament theology could invite

- *the academic community* away from self-preoccupied triviality that is such a waste;
- *the ecclesial communities* away from excessive certitude that is idolatry; and
- *the civic community* away from brutality rooted in autonomy long enough to engage this summoning mystery.

Anxiety and rage are real and legitimate. It remains to see if reading through them and past them is possible. The offer of these witnesses is sometimes as definite as 'a God so near and a Torah so just' (Deut. 4.7-8). Sometimes the witness is as open and inviting as a question, 'Where shall wisdom be found?' (Job 28.12). Either way, the witnesses invite beyond anxiety and beyond rage to a mystery whose name we know provisionally.

HERMENEUTICAL REFLECTIONS ON C. VITRINGA, EIGHTEENTH-CENTURY INTERPRETER OF ISAIAH

Brevard S. Childs

I

It is a common feature of biblical manuals when reviewing the history of the interpretation of the book of Isaiah to mention certain commentaries of special importance. Usually Calvin is singled out for the sixteenth century, Vitringa for the eighteenth, often Delitzsch for the mid-nineteenth, and Duhm for the transition to the twentieth. Of these great scholars the least attention has been paid to Vitringa, who dominated the field for a century.

Before attempting to make a case for a fresh assessment of him, it is necessary briefly to recall his career. Campegius Vitringa was born in 1659 in Leeuwarden, Frisia, a province in the northern Netherlands.[1] He was educated at the universities of Franeker and Leiden, and became Professor of Oriental Languages at Franeker in 1681. Shortly thereafter he moved to the theological faculty where he stayed until his death in 1722. He remained an avowed Reformed theologian of orthodox persuasion, and throughout his life engaged in the many heated doctrinal disputations of the period with numerous publications. By far his most important work was his commentary on the book of Isaiah.[2]

II

There are many reasons for the modern neglect of Vitringa. He wrote his huge commentary not only in Latin, but with such thoroughness and

---

1. An excellent portrait of Vitringa has been reproduced by R.E.C. Ekkart, *Franeker Professorenportretten* (Franeker: T. Wever, 1977), p. 227.

2. *Commentarius in librum prophetiarum Jesajae* (2 folio vols.; Leeuwarden: F. Halma, 1714, 1720).

prolixity as to encompass two massive folio volumes of almost seventeen hundred pages. Then again, he has long been tainted from his association with Johannes Cocceius, the famous federal theologian of Bremen, Franeker and Leiden, whose exegesis represented an extreme form of *Heilsgeschichte* and allegorical speculation. Finally, many modern commentators have assumed that any good observations which Vitringa might have made have long since been appropriated by others, thus eliminating the need for further study of his commentary.

Nevertheless, in spite of these initial obstacles, there are many serious reasons for resisting the temptation to relegate him to oblivion. First, even a casual perusal of his commentary reveals a remarkable learning in which he stands head-and-shoulders above his contemporaries. Such an acerbic and demanding grammarian as Gesenius spoke of Vitringa with great respect and even awe regarding his philological and historical prowess.[3] Moreover, throughout much of the nineteenth century he continued to be cited with approval by Rosenmüller, Delitzsch and Dillmann. Indeed among a small, but elite group of modern European scholars Vitringa has not been entirely forgotten, as shown by the most recent Isaiah commentary of Beuken.[4]

Secondly, there is a remarkable theological intensity evidenced in Vitringa which is rare in modern commentaries. He understood himself, above all, as a theologian of the church—a late seventeenth-century Dutch Reformed theologian to be sure—who viewed his work as a divine vocation. Yet because he was also a rigorous and superbly trained technical scholar, he wrestled to hold together these two dimensions of his work, throughout the entire commentary. As a theologian and exegete he engaged in constant debate with Grotius for historicizing the Old Testament to such an extent that the New Testament's understanding of Isaiah became an arbitrary and mystical appendage. Conversely, he remained critical of his mentor, Cocceius, for his uncontrolled and fanciful allegory which he thought denigrated the literal sense of the Old Testament.

Thirdly, there are numerous examples, often buried in details, that reveal his remarkable exegetical skill in trying to resolve perplexing exegetical problems. Even though his results cannot often be directly

---

3. W. Gesenius, *Commentar über Jesaia*, I (Leipzig: F.C.W. Vogel, 1821), pp. 132-33.

4. W.A.M. Beuken, *Jesaja*, IIA-B, IIIA-B (De Prediking van het Oude Testament; Nijkerk: Callenbach, 1979–89).

appropriated, the modern interpreter can still learn much from the reflections of a master. For example, he struggled long and hard with that most difficult of all passages, Isa. 7.10-17. At the outset he was critical of the traditional Christian interpretation of the Church Fathers that would identify Immanuel directly with Jesus Christ by using Mt. 1.23 as a warrant. He also rejected Calvin's attempt to overcome the difficulty of the prophecy's having an obvious eighth-century reference as well as a putative messianic one. Calvin was forced to distinguish between two different children, namely, Immanuel in vv.14 and 15 who referred to Jesus Christ, and a child in v.16, who did not refer to Christ but to all children in general. Instead Vitringa argued that the specific historical terminus designating the child's coming of age in v. 15 served as a temporal analogy. Thus, no more time would elapse from the announcement of the prophetic word to Ahaz and the destruction of the two threatening kings than the time involved in the conception and birth of Immanuel, whom the prophet envisioned as already present.[5] It is interesting to note that this ingenious interpretation has occasionally been adopted without any memory of the one from whom it derived.[6]

III

Perhaps the place to begin assessing the significance of Vitringa is to examine the preface of his Isaiah commentary. In contrast to his usual tendency to expound with exhaustive thoroughness, he succeeds in summarizing his main exegetical approach in a few succinct pages.

First, he stresses the need to explain the exact meaning of the prophet's words by the use of philological tools in order to reveal the *sensus genuinus*. Although focusing on the literal sense, he does make room eventually for an applied sense (*mystice*). He expresses his preference for the MT over the LXX, and also acknowledges the value of the early Greek translations and the role of rabbinic interpretation.

Next, he seeks to determine the subject matter of the oracle (*sensus realis*) and to penetrate to the object of which the words speak (*objectum vaticinii*). He continues to describe his approach by contrasting it

5. 'non esse plus lapsurus temporis inde a quo haec loquutus est verba, usque ad terram, cuius duo Reges Judaeos vexabant, spoliatam ac desertam, quam elaberetur a tempore concipiendi et nascituri Immanuëlis usque ad illud eiusdem tempus...' (*Commentarius*, I, p. 289).
6. E.J. Young, *The Book of Isaiah*, I (Grand Rapids: Eerdmans, 1965), p. 286.

with both Grotius and Cocceius, and sets forth his basic preference for seeing the nearest historical period as providing the prophecy's fulfillment rather than the distant future.

Finally, he states that the fulfillment of each prophecy must be carefully determined and compared with its historical reference, chiefly by means of a critical analysis of the classical Greek, Roman and rabbinical sources. Thus there are frequent references to the *implementum prophetiae literale* and the *themata collecta comparanda cum historia.*

For commentators like Gesenius this last concern of Vitringa's was of little interest and dismissed as irrelevant. However, it can be argued that attention to this issue is crucial for understanding Vitringa's major hermeneutical focus. A close study of his commentary makes very clear that the fulfillment of prophecy, and particularly its historical verification, form a central component of his interpretation.

IV

When one now turns to his handling of Isaiah 1–12, one is initially surprised that the development of his emphasis on the historical verification of Isaiah's prophecies is somewhat muted. This is to say, Vitringa follows largely the lines of traditional Christian interpretation with the effect that his particular stress on the verification of prophecy appears restrained. For example, Isa. 2.1-4 is interpreted as a picture of the coming of God's reign and the victory of true faith over the heathen gods. Following Christian interpretation, the portrayal of transformed Mt Zion is consciously set over against Mt Sinai which was the symbol of the old covenant of law. He does, however, argue that this eschatological prophecy received its first fulfillment (*implementum prophetiae primum*) in the early history of the Christian church for which he uses Acts 21.16-19 as a proof-text. The ultimate fulfillment is identified with the reign of Christ.

In ch. 4 he understands the prophecy to be describing the persecution of the church by hostile rulers, and he does identify a first fulfillment in the destruction of the evil rule of Herod Agrippa according to Acts 12.23. Chapter 6 is interpreted again as pointing to the kingship of Christ, and as announcing the harsh judgment against the Jews. Although he takes his main cue from Jn 12.41, he does try to retain some reference to Isaiah's mission as a prolepsis of future judgment. The prophecies of chs. 9 and 11.1-9 are seen as references to the messianic rule of Christ, but in the last verses of ch. 11 he finds a direct fulfillment of the promised destruction of Egypt, Arabia and Mesopotamia. He is, of course, forced to see the terms Egypt and Assyria as symbols for the post-Alexandrian Greek kingdoms. In sum, the traditional Christian reading of Isaiah's prophecies as fulfilled in Christ remains so strong that Vitringa's interpretation of these early chapters fits largely within this pattern. Only occasionally does he insist on seeing a multiple fulfillment of prophecies in earlier events of history.

A similar observation can be made in general regarding his interpretation of chs. 40–48 and 49–66. The first group of chapters is a revelation of the kingship of God and the exercise of his power, wisdom and might against all false deities. They speak of the restoration of true faith. Vitringa explicitly rejects the view that these chapters describe the conditions of the Jews exiled in Babylon awaiting deliverance. The prophecies were written by the prophet Isaiah soon after the deliverance from Sennacherib's attack on Jerusalem. The reference to the coming of Cyrus is understood as an accurate prediction spoken 170 years before his appearance. Chapters 49–66 are regarded as the most important section of the book. The ecstatic prophet (*propheta hic extra se raptus*) reports both what God and the Son speak and their words comfort the church with the promise of the coming messiah. The earlier format used in the commentary that succinctly summarized the verification of each prophetic fulfillment at the end of each section has usually been omitted because all the prophecies are seen as directed to the rule of Christ.

In striking contrast, only when one comes to the oracles against the nations in chs. 13–23 does one find a concerted effort made to demonstrate in the greatest of detail the historical fulfillment of these prophecies. Vitringa begins his analysis of ch. 13 by seeking to prove from history the literal fulfillment of Isaiah's prediction of Babylon's destruction. Accordingly, Babylon would be destroyed completely, forever and by the Medes. In attempting first to establish an exact date for the destruction, he refutes Grotius's contention that the fall of Babylon occurred in the period between Sennacherib and Nebuchadnezzar. He argues that parallels from Jeremiah 50 prove conclusively its Persian dating and can only be understood in relation to Cyrus's campaign. Then, pursuing many minutiae, Vitringa engages in harmonizing the accounts of Xenophon and Herodotus regarding Cyrus's relation to both the Medes and the Persians.

Vitringa encounters a problem when it appears that the city was indeed captured, but not fully destroyed, by Cyrus. He counters by arguing that Cyrus's victory was only the first fulfillment of the prophecy and that its complete fulfillment took place through various stages. The destruction that Cyrus began was continued by Darius Hystaspes, and again by Xerxes who tore down the pagan temple. But certainly by the fifth century CE the complete destruction of Babylon was attested to by Jerome. He concludes that Isaiah had predicted exactly the fall of Babylon some 200 years before the fulfillment had started to unfold. Vitringa also lists as an important feature of the prophecies of ch. 13 against Babylon that the announced destruction was near. Does not v. 22 say that 'its time is close at hand'? However, this element of the prophecy does not become a serious problem for him. In view of the speed of human history and viewed from the perspective of God, the time of fulfillment is indeed near!

In his treatment of the oracles against Moab (chs. 15 and 16) he again begins by refuting Cocceius's 'mystical' interpretation that Moab was only a cipher for the Jews at the time of Jesus Christ. He offers evidence from his usual list of historians, Josephus, Strabo and Diodorus Siculus, to show that Moab suffered destruction, first from Assyria and then from Babylon. Yet once he has established a historical fulfillment, Vitringa remains somewhat open to an allegorical interpretation when this is not used to challenge the literal fulfillment. Again, in ch. 19, concerning the oracles against Egypt, he rejects the attempts of the Church Fathers to see Egypt only as a symbol for the enemy of Christ in the New Testament. Rather he concludes that the fulfillment began in the period of Alexander the Great and Ptolemy Lagi. At that time a great number of Jews migrated to Egypt, built synagogues and flourished. Moreover, they succeeded in converting some Egyptians from idolatry, thus fulfilling another side of the Isaianic prophecy.

Finally, Vitringa's attempt to establish the historical verification of the prophecy of the fall of Tyre in ch. 23 is one of his most elaborate and complex discussions. He begins by showing from his classical historical sources that both Grotius and Abarbanel are wrong in arguing that Tyre was destroyed before Nebuchadnezzar's attack. Rather the evidence is clear that the fulfillment of the prophecy refers either to the Babylonian destruction of Tyre or to the destruction of the city by Alexander. The initial difficulty is that there is no conclusive extra-biblical evidence to prove the case for Nebuchadnezzar, even though Isa. 23.13 links the destruction to the Chaldeans, as does Ezekiel 26.

There is a further difficulty. Isaiah 23.15 speaks of the destruction of the city lasting only 70 years, whereas Ezek. 26.14, 19-21 announces unequivocally that the destruction will endure forever. 'I will bring you to a dreadful end...you will never be found again' (v. 21). How is this contradiction to be explained? For a time Vitringa toys with a clever distinction which had previously entered into the debate, namely, between the ancient land-based city of Tyre and the more recently constructed island city of Tyre. Could it be that Ezekiel was prophesying about the ancient city which was indeed destroyed forever, whereas Isaiah 23 was speaking of the island city? This latter fortification had been captured by Alexander, who built a dam in order to take the city, but then this city had later revived. However, Vitringa was too careful a historian to accept uncritically this way out of the dilemma. He remains convinced that the imagery of Isaiah 23 refers to Nebuchadnezzar's attack on the ancient, land-based city. Then Vitringa gets further involved in elaborate calculations as to when Nebuchadnezzar first assaulted Tyre. He sets the date five years after the destruction of Jerusalem, but then this dating calls for further adjustment with the complex rise of Persian hegemony. Vitringa's theory certainly reflects a whole series of very careful calculations, but in the end his reconstruction depends on a host of historical projections which may or may not be true. In a word, the biblical category of prophecy and fulfillment has been translated into a very different genre of complex historical speculation. In addition, there is the final problem that Isa. 23.18 speaks of Tyre's merchandise being 'dedicated to the Lord'. Vitringa finds this prophecy's fulfillment in the New Testament with reference to Mt. 15.22; Mk 7.26; and Acts 21.3-8. He concludes with a 'mystical' interpretation of Tyre which finds a proof-text in Rev. 18.23, and sees a similarity between the proud merchants of Tyre and papal Rome.

If one were to attempt a summary of Vitringa's view of prophecy and fulfillment, it appears clear that for him prophecy is the prediction of any future contingent occurrence disclosed through divine revelation. Therefore he is continually at pains to establish its exact, literal fulfillment. Vitringa remains under the influence of Cocceius to the extent that he strives to see a history of prophecies unfolding which he links in seemingly arbitrary stages ('haec pertinent ad implementum prophetiae primum'). Although he steadily resists redefining history in such a way as to distinguish between secular and sacred components, he does allow

In Search of True Wisdom

some elements of a typological sense to enter at the edges of his historical verification.

V

One of the major concerns of this analysis of Vitringa's commentary on Isaiah has been to assess his place within the history of biblical interpretation. Although he has obviously left an impact because of his enormous learning in the fields of philology, history and exegesis, the interest in this essay lies primarily in assessing his hermeneutical contribution, which has not been adequately studied in recent years.

In his well-known book,[7] Hans Frei has attempted to understand the history of modern biblical interpretation by focusing on the theological problem of truth as reference. He argued that the Reformers worked on the assumption of the coherence of historical meaning and ostensive reference. He then sought to characterize the crisis in biblical interpretation as an 'eclipse' when the various solutions for overcoming the growing polarity between text and reference which emerged in the wake of the Enlightenment only served to block access to the biblical narrative and its history-like depiction of reality.

One trajectory which Frei traced was the attempt to separate history into sacred and secular components and to project a special form of sacred history (*Heilsgeschichte*) which resulted in a fragmenting of the one unified biblical story of the creation and redemption of the world. Certainly in Cocceius one has a classic example of this blurring of vision. Another model proposed for resolving the hermeneutical problem was a philosophical, idealistic solution, most clearly formulated by Schleiermacher,[8] of distinguishing between 'prediction', which varied in accuracy, and 'Messianic prophecy' which dealt only in universals and thus achieved absolute value. Even Hengstenberg,[9] the champion of Lutheran orthodoxy, distinguished between 'incidental particulars' and 'general truth', the latter being the prophets' chief concern.

It is within this hermeneutical context that one sees another clear

---

7.   H.W. Frei, *The Eclipse of Biblical Narrative* (New Haven: Yale University Press, 1974).

8.   F. Schleiermacher, *The Christian Faith* (ET; Edinburgh: T. & T. Clark, 1928), §103.3.

9.   E.W. Hengstenberg, *Christology of the Old Testament*, IV (ET; Edinburgh: T. & T. Clark, 1871), p. 425.

option formulated by Vitringa. Although on the periphery of his interpretation he shared some features with Cocceius, his major contribution was in attempting a massive apologetic defense of the literal and rational coherence between text and historical reference in Scripture. He did not seek to redefine biblical history in any way, but employed a common-sense understanding as the occurrence of events in time and space which could be ascertained by anyone who applied rational analysis to historical sources.

It is also fully evident that Vitringa's approach became widespread by the early eighteenth century, especially in England, Scotland and North America. A multitude of books in the genre of Thomas Sherlock, Thomas Newton, and Alexander Keith flooded the British market.[10] In North America Vitringa's approach was most systematically developed by the old Princeton School, emerging in full form already in one of its founders, A.A. Alexander.[11]

As one might have expected, the approach that was represented by Vitringa called forth the exactly opposite reaction, first adumbrated in Spinoza, but shortly pursued by the English Deists. In his famous book Anthony Collins sought to demonstrate rationally the radical incoherence of Old Testament prophecy in relation to its alleged New Testament fulfillment.[12] Then again, in 1875 A. Kuenen wrote his exhaustive study of prophecy which included three lengthy chapters directed toward exploring 'the unfulfilled prophecies'.[13] Ironically he offered almost a mirror image of Vitringa's arguments before reaching the exactly opposite conclusions.

I think one can mount a convincing case that the present study of biblical prophecy from a hermeneutical perspective still falls roughly within these same options, namely, the rationalistic orthodoxy of Vitringa, the rationalistic agnosticism of Anthony Collins, the allegorical/typological *Heilsgeschichte* of Cocceius, and the romantic/idealistic

10. T. Sherlock, *Discourses on the Use and Interpretation of Prophecy* (London, 4th edn, 1744); T. Newton, *Dissertations on the Prophecies which have remarkably been fulfilled and are fulfilling* (London: W. Tegg, 10th edn, 1804 [1759]); A. Keith, *Evidences of the Truth of the Christian Religion derived from the Literal Fulfilment of Prophecy* (Edinburgh: W. Whyte, 31st edn, 1844).

11. A.A. Alexander, *Evidences of Christianity* (Philadelphia, 1825).

12. A. Collins, *The Scheme of Literal Prophecy Considered* (London, 1727).

13. A. Kuenen, *The Prophets and Prophecy in Israel: An Historical and Critical Enquiry* (ET; London: Longmans, Green, 1877).

approach of Schleiermacher. That the latter two categories have often been combined is equally clear. When in a recent monograph J.H. Sailhamer argues that modern Evangelicals share virtually the same 'precritical' view of Scripture as did the Reformers, he has failed to understand one of Frei's major points.[14] The Reformers in the 'pre-critical' era were still able to *assume* the coherence of text and historical reference. Following the challenge of the Enlightenment, this *assumption* was no longer possible. Thereafter, the biblical interpreter was forced either to be critical, anti-critical, or postcritical, but the pre-critical option has been forever lost.

There is one final observation to make on this history of interpretation. Although it would be completely arrogant for anyone to claim to have resolved this complex hermeneutical issue once and for all, it is important to note that the modern debate regarding Scripture as canon can only be correctly understood if it is placed within this larger hermeneutical context. The effort to understand and recover the significance of canon for biblical interpretation seeks to overcome the inherent problems involved in rationalism, whether on the left or right of the theological spectrum, by repudiating the assumptions of philosophical foundationalism. Moreover, it strives to retain the sense of a unified, concrete narrative testimony to the one purpose of God testified to by both synagogue and church, in both Old and New Testaments. Then again, it defines biblical factuality in terms of the subject matter of its Scriptural witness, which is available to critical scrutiny outside the context of faith only in varying degrees. Finally, it seeks to emphasize the primary theological focus on God's will confronting the world with power in word and deed, and thus to resist all pious human obfuscations and romantic appeals to human imagination as the key to the future. In sum, attention to the theological implications of Scripture understood as canon opens up a fresh avenue into the church's understanding of 'canonical history' in all its multiple dimensions.

---

14. J.H. Sailhamer, *Introduction to Old Testament Theology: A Canonical Approach* (Grand Rapids: Zondervan, 1995), p. 37.

WALKING IN GOD'S WAYS: THE CONCEPT OF *IMITATIO DEI*
IN THE OLD TESTAMENT

Eryl W. Davies

Recent years have witnessed an increasing interest in the ethics of the
Old Testament, and one aspect of the subject which continues to excite
scholarly debate is the basis on which its ethical teaching is founded.
Older studies in this area tended to focus on the law, and were content
to view Israelite ethics primarily in terms of obedience to God's commands.[1] Latterly, however, there has been an increasing awareness that
other models, such as 'natural law' and 'imitation of God', may have
served as the basis on which the ethics of the Old Testament has been
predicated. The presence of the phenomenon of 'natural law' in the
Bible has been the subject of much recent discussion, most notably in
the writings of James Barr,[2] but the concept of *imitatio Dei* has not
received such widespread attention. It is true that Martin Buber gave

1.   Cf., e.g., J. Hempel, *Das Ethos des Alten Testaments* (BZAW, 67; Berlin:
A. Töpelmann, 1938).
2.   *Biblical Faith and Natural Theology: The Gifford Lectures for 1991 deliv-
ered in the University of Edinburgh* (Oxford: Clarendon Press, 1993); *idem*, 'Bib-
lical Law and the Question of Natural Theology', in T. Veijola (ed.), *The Law in the
Bible and in its Environment* (Publications of the Finnish Exegetical Society, 51;
Helsinki: Finnish Exegetical Society, 1990), pp. 1-22. See also J. Barton, 'Natural
Law and Poetic Justice in the Old Testament', *JTS* NS 30 (1979), pp. 1-14; H.S.
Gehman, 'Natural Law and the Old Testament', in J.M. Myers, O. Reimherr, H.N.
Bream (eds.), *Biblical Studies in Memory of H.C. Alleman* (Locust Valley, NY: J.J.
Augustin, 1960), pp. 109-22; E.W. Davies, 'Ethics of the Hebrew Bible: The
Problem of Methodology', in D.A. Knight (ed.), *Ethics and Politics in the Hebrew
Bible* (Semeia, 66; Atlanta, GA: Scholars Press, 1995), pp. 43-53 (48-51). The idea
that 'natural law' might be present in the Old Testament was, in fact, mooted nearly
50 years ago by F. Horst ('Naturrecht und Altes Testament', *EvT* 10 [1950/1],
pp. 253-73 [reprinted in Horst, *Gottes Recht: Gesammelte Studien zum Recht im
Alten Testament* (ed. H.W.Wolff; Munich: C. Kaiser, 1961), pp. 235-59]).

some prominence to the idea in an essay published as long ago as 1926,[3] but, on the whole, the concept has been regarded as of only marginal significance in the Old Testament, and one which has hardly been worthy of serious consideration in any discussion of biblical ethics.[4]

There are some indications, however, that the pendulum is now beginning to swing in the opposite direction and that, far from being ignored or sidelined, the idea of 'imitating God' is being elevated to a more prominent place in the study of Old Testament ethics. Thus, in an article published in 1991, Eckart Otto suggested that this concept may well lie 'at the core of Old Testament ethics',[5] and in a paper read at the International Meeting of the Society of Biblical Literature in Münster in 1993, John Barton conceded that the theme was more central to the ethical thought of the Old Testament than he had previously supposed.[6] In view of the prevalence of this phenomenon in later Jewish[7] and

---

3. 'Nachahmung Gottes', *Morgen* 1 (1926), pp. 638-47 (reprinted in Buber, *Kampf um Israel: Reden und Schriften [1921–1932]* [Berlin: Schocken Books, 1933], pp. 68-83 [ET by G. Hort, 'Imitatio Dei', in *Israel and the World: Essays in a Time of Crisis* (New York: Schocken Books, 1948), pp. 66-77]). The citations of Buber's article in the present study are based on the English translation.

4. Cf. B. Lindars, 'Imitation of God and Imitation of Christ', *Theology* 76 (1973), pp. 394-402, who argued that it is not really until New Testament times that 'imitation of God' becomes a factor in Jewish ethical thought, and even then 'it remains peripheral' (p. 401). Consequently, with regard to biblical ethics, the concept should be treated 'with some reserve' (p. 402).

5. E. Otto, 'Forschungsgeschichte der Entwürfe einer Ethik im Alten Testament', *VF* 36 (1991), pp. 3-37 (esp. p. 20).

6. J. Barton, 'The Basis of Ethics in the Hebrew Bible', in Knight (ed.), *Ethics and Politics*, pp. 17-20. In an earlier article ('Understanding Old Testament Ethics', *JSOT* 9 [1978], pp. 44-64), Barton had only tentatively mentioned *imitatio Dei* as one possible model on which the ethical teaching of the Old Testament might be based.

7. The idea of 'imitating God' finds clear expression in the rabbinic literature, as, e.g., in the words of the third-generation Tannaite, Abba Saul. The words in Exod. 15.2, usually rendered 'This is my God and I will praise him' (Heb. *zeh 'ēlî wᵉ'anwēhû*) were read by him in a different sense, 'This is my God, I and He' (Heb. *zeh 'ēlî 'anî wāhû'*), which he expounded as follows: 'Be like him: just as he is merciful and gracious, you, too, must be merciful and gracious' (*Mek.*, Shirta 3 on Exod. 15.2). See also *Targum Pseudo-Jonathan* on Lev. 22.28: 'My people, children of Israel, as your Father is merciful in heaven, so you must be merciful on earth' (cf. Mt. 5.48; Lk. 6.36). For these texts, see G. Vermes, 'Jewish Literature and New Testament Exegesis', *JJS* 33 (1982), pp. 361-76 (371-72). Other rabbinic texts which allude to the notion of *imitatio Dei* include *y. Peah* 1.1 (15b); *b. Shabb.* 133b;

Greek[8] thought, and the importance of the corresponding notion of *imitatio Christi* in the New Testament,[9] it seems appropriate to review the evidence for the existence of the idea of *imitatio Dei* in the Old Testament. It will be my aim in the discussion that follows to consider the extent to which the concept is present in the legal and prophetic material, and in the Psalms and Old Testament narratives. Some factors which may have influenced the development of the concept will then be suggested and, finally, its hermeneutical implications will be explored.

It is generally agreed that the most clear and explicit expression of the principle of *imitatio Dei* in the Old Testament is to be found in Lev. 19.2, which forms part of the so-called Holiness Code: 'You shall be holy, for I the LORD your God am holy' (cf. Lev. 11.44; 20.7, 26; 21.8).[10] In this verse, the Israelites are commanded to comport themselves in a manner that reflects the very character of God himself. At first sight, it might appear that this command represents an abstract, utopian ideal, but it is clear from the verses that follow that the kind of holiness here envisaged was thoroughly practical in its orientation, for it entailed the fulfilment of specific social obligations, such as filial respect towards parents (19.3), generosity to the poor at harvest (19.9-10), compassion towards the infirm (19.14), integrity in the judicial process (19.15) and honesty in commercial transactions (19.35-36).[11] It is

Sifra on Lev. 19.2; *Sifre Deut.* 49. See further A. Marmorstein, 'The Imitation of God (*imitatio Dei*) in the Haggadah', in J. Rabbinowitz and M.S. Lew (eds.), *Studies in Jewish Theology* (Oxford: Clarendon Press, 1950), pp. 106-21; G.F. Moore, *Judaism in the First Centuries of the Christian Era* (3 vols.; Cambridge, MA: Harvard University Press, 1927), II, pp. 109-11; H.L. Strack and P. Billerbeck, *Kommentar zum Neuen Testament aus Talmud und Midrash* (4 vols. in 5 parts; Munich: O. Beck, 1922), I, pp. 372-73. I am grateful to my colleague Dr Catrin H. Williams for drawing my attention to much of the relevant rabbinic literature cited in this study.

8. The concept of *imitatio Dei* is found in Plato, Aristotle and Epictetus; for references see D.S. Shapiro, 'The Doctrine of the Image of God and Imitatio Dei', in M.M. Kellner (ed.), *Contemporary Jewish Ethics* (New York: Sanhedrin Press, 1978), pp. 127-51 (esp. pp. 139-41).

9. See O. Merk, 'Nachahmung Christi', in H. Merklein (ed.), *Neues Testament und Ethik: für Rudolf Schnackenburg* (Freiburg: Herder, 1989), pp. 172-206; E.J. Tinsley, *The Imitation of God in Christ* (London: SCM Press, 1960).

10. Cf. W.C. Kaiser, Jr, *Toward Old Testament Ethics* (Grand Rapids: Zondervan, 1983), pp. 139-244, who regards these words as forming the mainspring of the ethical values contained in the Old Testament.

11. Cf. Shapiro, 'Doctrine', p. 128, who notes that the holiness to which the

clear from these passages that the holiness demanded of the Israelites
was not limited to cultic or ceremonial duties (such as Sabbath observance and ritual cleanness); rather, it encompassed the kind of moral
behaviour expected of the people in their day-to-day activities.[12] The
concept of 'holiness' is here, therefore, brought firmly within the ethical
realm and is elevated into a guiding principle of human conduct.[13] In
Lev. 19.2 the Israelites are commanded to imitate a particular divine
attribute; in other passages, however, they are enjoined to imitate a particular divine *action*. In this regard, Israel's experience of the exodus
was to have a decisive impact on the kind of values and concerns which
the people were to embrace. In the first place, the activity of God in
redeeming his people from Egypt provided a rationale for some of
Israel's cultic duties. For example, the ritual requirement to sacrifice the
first-born of male beasts on the altar was intended to reflect Yahweh's
action in slaying the first-born male children among the Egyptians;
similarly, the redemption of Israel's first-born sons was intended to mirror the redemptive act of God in redeeming the Israelites from captivity
(Exod. 13.14-15). But it is in Israel's humanitarian, rather than cultic,
obligations that the requirement to emulate God's activity comes most
prominently to the fore. Thus, male and female slaves, and the resident
alien in Israel, were to be given rest on the Sabbath because God had
ceased from his own work on the seventh day (Exod. 20.8-11; cf.
31.12-17). Further, the divine partiality shown towards the poor and
needy was to provide an example for a similar concern to be exhibited
by the Israelites: 'He secures justice for the fatherless and the widow,
and he shows love towards the alien who lives among you...you too
must show love towards the alien, for you once lived as aliens in Egypt'
(Deut. 10.18-19). Moreover, as Yahweh had released his people from
their captivity in Egypt, so the Israelites must be prepared to release

Israelites were called was 'not so much a holiness of essence as a holiness of conduct'. See, too, C.J.H. Wright, *Living as the People of God* (Leicester: Inter-Varsity
Press, 1983), pp. 26-27.

12. Scholars who have found difficulty with the idea that God's holiness could
be viewed as providing an 'ethical modelling' for Israel (e.g. W. Janzen, *Old Testament Ethics: A Paradigmatic Approach* [Louisville: Westminster/John Knox Press,
1994], p. 115) have generally failed to appreciate that the divine holiness in such
contexts as these includes particular moral attributes.

13. Cf. J.G. Gammie, *Holiness in Israel* (OBT; Minneapolis: Fortress Press,
1989), pp. 32-34.

their enslaved brother, and on no account was the slave to be sent away empty-handed, for 'as the LORD your God blessed you, so shall you give to him' (Deut. 15.13-15). Having experienced God's justice and compassion themselves, the Israelites could only properly express their gratitude by showing a similar concern for the weak and underprivileged in their midst. In these passages, therefore, God's activity provided something of a blueprint or paradigm for a particular brand of ethical behaviour demanded of his people, a behaviour characterized above all by mercy and compassion.

The command to imitate God is also implied in the numerous exhortations encountered in Deuteronomy to 'walk in the ways of the Lord' (Deut. 8.6; 10.12; 11.22; 26.17; 28.9).[14] Such imagery implies that Israel was destined to travel on a journey in which God was to lead the way as a guide and example for the people to follow. It also suggests that the moral requirements demanded by God were those which he himself had evinced in an exemplary manner in his dealings with his people.[15] By mirroring the divine activity the people would become a visible exemplar to the nations as to the nature and character of the God whom they worshipped (Deut. 4.5-8). This was a God who had shown love (Deut. 7.7-8), mercy (Deut. 4.31), compassion (Deut. 30.3) and justice (Deut. 32.4) in abundance, and who expected these same qualities to be reflected in the conduct of his people (Deut. 6.5; 14.28-29; 16.19-20).Although it would clearly be something of an exaggeration to describe Deuteronomy as 'Israel's book of *imitatio Dei*',[16] its frequent

14. According to Shapiro, 'Doctrine', p. 129, the expression means 'nothing other than modelling one's life on the attributes of God'. Cf. also Tinsley, *Imitation*, p. 35. It is interesting to observe that this is the manner in which the phrase was interpreted by some of the rabbis, as is evident from the following comment by the second-generation Amora, Ḥama bar Ḥanina, on Deut. 13.5: 'How can man walk after God?... What is meant is that man should walk after the divine attributes. Just as the Lord clothes the naked, attends the sick, comforts the mourners and buries the dead, so you should do likewise' (*b. Soṭ.* 14a).

15. The reciprocal nature of the relationship between Yahweh and Israel in Deuteronomy may be implied in the way in which Israel's response to Yahweh in chs. 12-26 appears to mirror that of Yahweh's actions towards Israel in chs. 1-11. See J.G. McConville, *Law and Theology in Deuteronomy* (JSOTSup, 33; Sheffield: JSOT Press, 1984).

16. The phrase (quoted by Buber, *Israel and the World*, p. 75) is that of S. Schechter, *Some Aspects of Rabbinic Theology* (London: A. & C. Black, 1909), p. 119.

commands to follow in God's ways undoubtedly provided the Israelites with an indication of what was required of them in terms of moral behaviour.

The notion of *imitatio Dei* also underlies much of the prophetic preaching, for many of the characteristics postulated of God in the Old Testament are precisely those which were demanded by the prophets as the most noble expressions of human behaviour. The prophets conceived of God as possessing certain moral qualities, and they believed that these same qualities should be reflected in the behaviour of the Israelites towards one another. Thus, justice, truth and compassion were not simply abstract concepts but constituents of God's own character, and the prophets believed that those who worshipped Yahweh should exhibit in their everyday lives those virtues which inhered in him.

It follows that the message that the prophets proclaimed and the standard of conduct that they demanded of the people evolved, at least in part, from their overwhelming apprehension of God's character. The vision and call reports of the prophets show that they were able to enter into dialogue with Yahweh (cf. Amos 7.1–8.3; Isa. 6; Jer. 1.4-13), and on this basis they could lay claim to a direct intuition of divine truth. In this regard, the recent emphasis on the indebtedness of the prophets to tradition[17] has tended to eclipse the importance of their personal encounter with God, for it was through such experiences that they were able to discern the nature of God and the requirements which he demanded of his people. Indeed, their understanding of who Yahweh was conditioned, to a great extent, their understanding of what Israel as a nation was meant to be. Thus, for example, Isaiah, at the time of his call, encountered the holy God in the sanctuary (Isa. 6), and this encounter set the tone of much of his subsequent preaching and determined the way in which he was to interpret God's demands. God's holiness was the central standard by which Israel's life would be judged, and the iniquities that were present in Judah were largely due to the fact that the people had neglected the presence of the holy God in their midst (Isa. 1.4; 30.9-11; 31.1). Isaiah makes it abundantly clear that the divine holiness had ethical implications, for 'the Holy God

17. Cf. G. von Rad, *Old Testament Theology* (2 vols.; ET; Edinburgh: Oliver and Boyd, 1965), II, pp. 155-75; R.E. Clements, *Prophecy and Tradition* (Oxford: Basil Blackwell, 1975), pp. 8-40. For a discussion of some of the traditions that have been thought to have influenced Isaiah, see my *Prophecy and Ethics: Isaiah and the Ethical Traditions of Israel* (JSOTSup, 16; Sheffield: JSOT Press, 1981).

shows himself holy by righteousness' (Isa. 5.16). Perversion of justice (Isa. 10.1-2) and indulgence in magical and superstitious practices (Isa. 3.1-3) were not simply social evils but an affront to the very holiness of God himself. Significantly, the judgment which the prophet announced took the form of a purification of the people (Isa. 1.24-26), and it was quite in keeping with Isaiah's emphasis that a later editor should add that the survivors of Jerusalem would emulate the most sublime of Yahweh's characteristics—his holiness (Isa. 4.3).

The message of the prophets was largely based on the presupposition that the manner in which the God of Israel had acted towards his people should be mirrored in the way in which they were to act in their dealings with each other. If God demanded righteousness, it was because he himself was perceived as righteous; if God demanded mercy, it was because he himself was perceived as merciful (Jer. 9.24; 22.3). In this regard, it is not without significance that much of the prophetic preaching was concerned with Yahweh's activity in the arena of history (cf. Amos 2.10-11; 9.7; Mic. 6.3-8).The prophets regularly addressed Israel as a people who had experienced the merciful activity of God in the past, and many of their indictments were based on the fact that the people had not reflected the divine compassion in their own behaviour towards the weak and vulnerable in society. When the prophets condemned those who exploited the misfortunes of others by offering bribes (Isa. 1.23), perverting justice (Amos 5.7) and cheating in commercial transactions (Amos 8.5-6), their indictments were based on the presupposition that such acts were the very antithesis of the justice which God had shown in his past dealings with his people. To take up the cause of the widow and defend the fatherless (Isa. 1.17; Zech. 7.10) was merely to act as God had acted towards his people when they were defenceless slaves in Egypt. In many respects, therefore, the prophetic call was a summons for Israel to take seriously its special vocation as *imitator Dei*, for the prophets saw it as the duty of the people to embody in their daily lives the very character of the God whom they worshipped.[18]

It is clear that the type of response demanded of the people by the prophets involved far more than obedience to the commands of God as formulated in the law. Of course, the people were occasionally con-

18. On the role of Israel as *imitator Dei* see Tinsley, *Imitation*, pp. 50-64; S. Hauerwas, *The Peaceable Kingdom: A Primer in Christian Ethics* (London: SCM Press, 1984), pp. 76-81.

demned for violating particular commandments (cf. Hos. 4.1-2), and in such cases the prophets based their indictments firmly on the specific legal stipulations that were being infringed. But, on the whole, the prophets declared that God's will for his people was revealed as much through his character as through the law:

> He has showed you, O man, what is good;
>> and what does the LORD require of you?
> To act justly and to love mercy
>> and to walk humbly with your God (Mic. 6.8).

Since the ethical behaviour of the people was to flow naturally from their apprehension of God's character, it was clearly a matter of grave concern for the prophets that there appeared to be no 'knowledge of God' in the land (Hos. 4.1; 5.4; 6.6; Jer. 4.22; 5.4-5; 9.3, 6). It is sometimes suggested that the prophets were here alluding to a widespread neglect of the traditions of the law and covenant,[19] but it is probable that the phrase had a more personal connotation, and that the prophets were referring to the absence of a close and intimate association between Yahweh and his people. From the prophetic perspective, 'knowledge of God' did not involve an intellectual, cognitive process but, rather, an intuitive awareness of God's character and nature, and it was precisely because the people lacked such an awareness that they had failed in their social obligations. The significance of the prophets for the theme of the present study, therefore, may be seen to lie in their penetrating insights into the nature of God and in their insistence that the divine character be reflected in the conduct of the people.

In the Psalms, the requirement to imitate God is nowhere stated in clear and categorical terms but it is perhaps implied in the way in which God's character and deeds are presented as the basis on which the pious should model their lives. The frequent descriptions of God's justice, mercy and compassion in the Psalms (cf. 25.6; 33.5; 37.28; 119.156) were clearly designed to inculcate the same ethical values in the worshipper, for God's character was regarded as the foundation upon which the believer's life should be based.[20] The desire of the Psalmist was to 'walk before God' (56.13; cf. 119.3; 128.1), and it was God's own wish that Israel should 'walk in my ways' (81.13), for by following in the

19. Cf. R.E. Clements, *Prophecy and Covenant* (SBT; London: SCM Press, 1965), pp. 55-56, 96.
20. Cf. Wright, *Living*, p. 28.

divine footsteps the believer would live a life of 'integrity and upright-
ness' (25.21), and would reflect in his own character the very attributes
of God himself.

The extent to which the Psalmist viewed human virtues as a reflection
of the divine is nowhere better illustrated than in the twin acrostic
Psalms 111 and 112.[21] The attributes of God set forth in Psalm 111 are
regarded in Psalm 112 as being reflected in the life of the true believer.
Thus, just as the righteousness of God 'endures forever' (*'ōmedet lā'ad*,
111.3b), so the righteousness of the upright 'endures forever' (*'ōmedet
lā'ad*, 112.3, 9); just as God is 'gracious and merciful' (*ḥannûn
w*ᵉ*raḥûm*, 111.4b), so the pious is 'gracious, merciful and righteous'
(*ḥannûn w*ᵉ*raḥûm w*ᵉ*ṣaddîq*, 112.4b);[22] just as God 'gives' (*nātan*) food
for those who worship him (111.5), so the godly exhibit a similar generosity by 'giving' (*nātan*) freely of their possessions to those in need
(112.9); just as God acts with 'justice' (*mišpāṭ*) towards his people
(111.7a), so the pious will act 'with justice' (*b*ᵉ*mišpāṭ*) towards each
other (112.5b) and just as the works of God will always be remembered
(*zēker 'āśāh l*ᵉ*nipl*ᵉ*'ôtāyw*, 111.4a), so the righteous will never be
forgotten (*l*ᵉ*zēker 'ôlām yihyeh ṣaddîq*, 112.6b). In fact, Psalm 112 may
be understood as an elaborate way of saying that the characteristics of
the pious mirror those of God himself, and that an element of con-
formity exists between the acts of the faithful and those of the God
whom they worship.

The narratives of the Old Testament appear, at first sight, to offer
little relevant material for the subject under discussion, since the characters depicted therein are seldom portrayed as consciously imitating
God's character. It is true that David is presented as exhibiting magna-
nimity on a divine scale when he undertakes to show the *ḥesed* of the
Lord (1 Sam. 20.14) or the *ḥesed* of God (2 Sam. 9.3) in his dealings

---

21. The two psalms are generally regarded as forming a pair by virtue of both
form and content, and they may well be the product of a single author. For a dis-
cussion of them, see W. Zimmerli, 'Zwillingspsalmen', in J. Schreiner (ed.), *Wort,
Lied und Gottesspruch: Beiträge zu Psalmen und Propheten. Festschrift für Joseph
Ziegler* (2 vols; Würzburg: Echter Verlag, 1972), II, pp. 105-13; S. Holm-Nielsen, '
The Importance of Late Jewish Psalmody for the Understanding of Old Testament
Psalmodic Tradition', *ST* 14 (1960), pp. 35-39.

22. RSV takes the adjectives in Ps. 112.4b to refer to God (following LXX A and
Vulgate), but it seems preferable to take them to refer to the godfearing persons (so
NRSV; REB).

with the house of Saul, but such passing references are hardly sufficient to demonstrate that the king was being portrayed as deliberately mirroring the divine attributes. Some scholars suggest that a more promising line of inquiry might be to focus upon those characters who are described as having walked 'with' or 'before' God.[23] Thus Enoch, for example, is depicted as having 'walked with God' (Gen. 5.22-24), as is Noah, who is portrayed as a particularly righteous and blameless man in his generation (Gen. 6.9). Similarly, Abram was commanded by God to 'walk before me' (Gen. 17.1; cf. 48.15), and in 1 Kgs 3.6 David is said to have walked before God 'in faithfulness'. But, although such characters exhibit many admirable qualities, they are not portrayed as individuals who regularly reflected in their lives the divine attributes, nor are they regarded as normative models for the people to emulate.[24] On the contrary, the biblical narrators are only too aware of their moral defects, and no attempt is made to conceal their ethical shortcomings (cf. Gen. 9.20-27; 20.1-18; 2 Sam. 11-12).[25] That these characters are described as having walked 'with God', as opposed to 'in God's ways', may be significant, for the phrase was probably meant to imply only that they enjoyed a special relationship with God, not that they lived their lives in conscious imitation of his character. This is not to say that the Israelites could not learn from (and even identify with) such individuals, but the fact remains that nowhere are the people encouraged to imitate their behaviour, and nowhere are the characters themselves depicted as conscious imitators of God.

It must not be supposed, however, that the narrative portions of the Old Testament are thereby of no relevance to the present inquiry. On the contrary, the biblical stories assume a particular significance inasmuch as they serve to probe and explicate the nature of God's character. After all, if the Israelites were to emulate God, it was clearly important that they should have some knowledge of the divine nature and

23. Cf. J. Barton, 'Basis', p. 20, who observes that particular individuals in the Old Testament are singled out to be God's agents and, as such, are empowered to represent the Deity before the community at large.

24. Cf. R.R. Wilson, 'Approaches to Old Testament Ethics', in G.M. Tucker, D.L. Petersen, R.R. Wilson (eds.), *Canon, Theology, and Old Testament Interpretation: Essays in Honor of Brevard S. Childs* (Philadelphia: Fortress Press, 1988), p. 66.

25. Cf. R.H. Bainton, 'The Immoralities of the Patriarchs according to the Exegesis of the Late Middle Ages and of the Reformation', *HTR* 23 (1930), pp. 39-49.

attributes, and it was (at least in part) through stories relating Yahweh's encounters with his people that such knowledge was mediated to them. The manner in which God was portrayed in the narratives was thus of profound significance, for the depiction of the divine character was to become the basis for subsequent ethical reflection. If God could be shown to have acted with justice and compassion, it was surely incumbent upon his people to act likewise; if he had identified himself with the weak and oppressed, it was surely imperative that his people should do the same. Thus, the character and actions of God were not presented as morally neutral observations; rather, they were designed to inculcate a sense of duty and moral responsibility in the people and to provide them with a model of the type of behaviour that should be mirrored in their own lives.[26] Of course it was assumed that God was bound by the same ethical constraints as those which he had imposed upon his people, and that he was subject to the same moral laws as those which applied to them. It was thus a matter of some concern if God was believed to have acted in a way that was morally unacceptable, and in such circumstances the biblical narrators deemed it to be entirely appropriate to question God's behaviour and motives, and even to insist that he act in a manner that was considered to be right and proper. Such appears to be the upshot of the account of Abraham's intercession over Sodom (Gen. 18.22-33), for the narrator was clearly concerned to probe the ethical aspect of God's being, and to assure the readers that God would not ultimately act out of character or do anything that fell short of man's loftiest moral insights.[27]

Thus, although concrete examples of individuals imitating God are conspicuously lacking in the biblical narratives, such stories were nevertheless important, for it was through them that the basic character and identity of God were established. The Israelites had to have an adequate knowledge and understanding of God's attributes before they could model their lives on him, and it was through the stories relating Yahweh's encounters with his people that his character and nature were made known.

26. Cf. B.C. Birch, *Let Justice Roll Down: The Old Testament, Ethics, and Christian Life* (Louisville: Westminster/John Knox Press, 1991), p. 125.
27. Cf. C.S. Rodd, 'Shall not the judge of all the earth do what is just? (Gen 18.25)', *ExpTim* 83 (1971/2), pp. 137-39.

It is not clear how the concept of 'imitating God' originated in ancient Israel, but two factors may have proved significant for the development of the idea. The first is that the God of Israel was frequently depicted in human terms.[28] Far from entertaining an abstract, nebulous concept of God and regarding him as a deity who stood aloof from human emotions, the biblical writers preferred to view him as thinking and acting in a way with which humans could identify (cf. Gen. 3.8; Num. 11.1; Ps. 2.4). It is true that impersonal images (such as wind, fire, spirit) were occasionally deployed to depict God's holiness and transcendence, but there can be little doubt that the most striking portrayal of God which emerges from the Old Testament is that which views him as a person.[29] This was not, of course, intended in any way to impugn God's omnipotence or detract from his transcendence; on the contrary, it is constantly emphasized that he was wonderfully free of the constraints which normally circumscribe human existence (cf. 1 Sam. 15.29; Isa. 55.8-9). Nevertheless, by depicting God in such explicitly personal terms, the biblical writers effectively paved the way for the idea that God's character and actions could be mirrored in human behaviour.

The second factor which may have influenced the development of the notion of *imitatio Dei* is the doctrine that human beings were created in God's image.[30] It is true that there is no direct evidence in the Old Testament to support the idea of a link between the concept of *imitatio Dei* and that of the *imago Dei*, but it is not without significance that some of the passages which clearly presuppose the notion of imitating God (Exod. 20.8-11; 31.12-17) do so on the basis of the tradition of creation (cf. Gen. 2.2-3). The precise meaning of the phrase 'in our image, according to our likeness' in Gen. 1.26-27 has, of course, been much

---

28. Cf. I. Abrahams, *Studies in Pharisaism and the Gospels* (Second Series; Cambridge: Cambridge University Press, 1924), p. 139, who notes that the notion of *imitatio Dei* 'obviously needs as its basis an anthropomorphic conception of God'.

29. Cf. R.E. Clements, *Old Testament Theology: A Fresh Approach* (London: Marshall, Morgan and Scott, 1978), pp. 58-62.

30. This possibility should not be dismissed simply because the doctrine of the creation of humans in the divine image is encountered only in the late P source (Gen. 1.26-27; 5.1; 9.6), for it is quite probable that the idea existed in Israel long before the Priestly writer formulated it in such a fashion. Cf. D.J.A. Clines, 'The Image of God in Man', *TynBul* 19 (1968), pp. 53-103 (esp. pp. 78-79).

disputed,[31] but there can be little doubt that the expression implies at the very least that some similarity exists between human beings and their creator. It is probable, however, that the phrase also connotes the idea that humans were created as God's representatives,[32] just as in the ancient Near East the image was intended to embody the character of the god whom it depicted.[33] Understood in this way, the implication of Gen. 1.26-27 is that human beings were created as godlike creatures whose duty it was to deputize for God on earth. As representatives of God, it was incumbent upon them to reflect, in their own lives, the character of their creator, and this, in essence, is the idea behind the concept of the *imitatio Dei*.[34] Whether the doctrine of the forming of human nature after the pattern of the divine gave rise to the concept of 'imitating God' must remain uncertain,[35] but it seems not unlikely that the affinity of human nature with God presupposed in such passages as Gen. 1.26-27 provided one of the motives for imitating the divine attributes.[36]

The attraction of the concept of *imitatio Dei* for the biblical writers is not difficult to appreciate, for it implied a type of ethic that transcended the more mechanical 'rule/obedience' model of morality. One of the problems with an ethic based on obedience to the rule of law was that it tended to abstract the moral agent from direct communion with the deity; the concept of *imitatio Dei*, on the other hand, based the moral

31. A convenient overview of research on the topic is provided by G.A. Jóns-son, *The Image of God: Genesis 1.26-28 in a Century of Old Testament Research* (ConBOT, 26; Lund: Almqvist and Wiksell, 1988).

32. Cf. E. Jacob, 'Les bases théologiques de l'éthique de l'Ancien Testament', *Congress Volume Oxford 1959* (VTSup, 7; Leiden: E.J. Brill, 1960), pp. 39-51 (esp. pp. 48-49); Clines, 'Image', pp. 87-92.

33. Cf. P.A. Bird, '"Male and Female he created them": Gen 1.27b in the Context of the Priestly Account of Creation', *HTR* 74 (1981), pp. 129-59 (esp. pp. 141-43).

34. Cf. the comment by Buber, *Israel and the World*, p. 73: 'The fact that it has been revealed to us that we are made in his image gives us the incentive to unfold this image, and in doing so to imitate God'.

35. Cf. Shapiro, 'Doctrine', p. 128, who claims that the 'doctrine of man as created in the image of God is the ground for the mandate of *imitatio Dei*'.

36. It is interesting to observe that in rabbinic Judaism the notion of *imitatio Dei* was believed to be a consequence of God's having created humanity in his own image, and this was interpreted to mean that human destiny was to become like God. Cf. Buber, *Israel and the World*, pp. 73-74; Tinsley, *Imitation*, pp. 63-64.

life on a personal experience of God and afforded individuals with a source of immediate and direct guidance in their moral lives. Moreover, the law was often heavily tinctured by an appeal to self-interest, as is evidenced by the presence of the 'motive clause' attached to specific enactments.[37] The command to imitate God, on the other hand, was not based on any selfish desire to achieve a particular outcome; rather, it presupposed that treating others with justice and compassion was itself an outcome, namely, an outcome of the way in which the people themselves had been treated by God.[38] Further, the law was often very limited in its scope and application, for an ethic based exclusively on obedience to divine commands was never likely to induce individuals to achieve the highest reaches of human excellence. On the other hand, an ethic based on the notion of *imitatio Dei* was designed to inspire individuals to ever greater and nobler acts of compassion and love, for it spoke in the most eloquent terms of a morality of aspiration rather than a morality of duty, of what was intrinsically desirable rather than what was legally obligatory. Thus the importance of the concept of *imitatio Dei* for the biblical writers was that it led to a deepening of Israel's ethical understanding and to a more finely developed sense of social responsibility and obligation. It demanded far more of the individual than dutiful obedience to legal commands, for it required nothing less than an imitative response to the very character and activity of God himself.

Of course, the idea of imitating God was not without its potential dangers, for the concept was—perhaps inevitably—open to possible misunderstanding or misrepresentation. In the first place, there was a danger that an attempt to 'imitate God' might drift imperceptibly into a desire to become 'like God', and that individuals might be tempted to overstep the limits of their creatureliness and arrogate to themselves the divine prerogatives (cf. Gen. 3). It was in order to guard against such temptations that the biblical writers emphasized the uniqueness and incomparability of Yahweh (cf. Exod. 9.14; Deut. 33.26; 2 Sam. 7.22; Ps. 86.8)[39] and warned the people against all pretensions to divine

37. Cf. B. Gemser, 'The Importance of the Motive Clause in Old Testament Law', *Congress Volume Copenhagen 1953* (VTSup, 1; Leiden: E.J. Brill, 1953), pp. 50-66.

38. Cf. D. Harrington, *What is Morality?* (Dublin: Columba Press, 1996), p. 42.

39. For this aspect of the understanding of God, see C.J. Labuschagne, *The Incomparability of Yahweh in the Old Testament* (Pretoria Oriental Series, 5; Leiden: E.J. Brill, 1966). There is inevitably a tension between the view that God is

omnipotence (cf. Isa. 14.14; Ezek. 28.2). Further, it is clear that not all of God's attributes could be deemed worthy to serve as a model or paradigm for humans to emulate. There was obviously no problem with the concept of *imitatio Dei* while it was confined to such exemplary characteristics as God's mercy, justice and compassion, but when God's behaviour appeared as vindictive, tyrannical and capricious the command to imitate him would inevitably be seen as morally perverse.[40] The concept of imitating God was thus not without its drawbacks, and it had to be carefully nuanced in order to avoid the possible pitfalls inherent in its use.

It seems appropriate, given the emphasis of the present volume, to conclude this study with an examination of the hermeneutical implications of the concept of *imitatio Dei* in the Old Testament. The very idea of 'imitation' is, of course, one which is deeply rooted in the human psyche. The child learns to imitate parental attitudes and values and, in time, begins to appropriate them and accept them as his or her own.[41] This basic human instinct can, without undue difficulty, be applied to the religious realm. To believe that God acts in a particular way disposes the worshipper to behave in like manner. This mirroring of the divine character thus has implications for the social conduct of the believer, for by imitating God he allows God's actions towards him to inform—and transform—his own actions towards others. By reflecting upon God's character his own sense of moral obligation is deepened and enriched.

Further, the concept of *imitatio Dei* may cause us to reappraise the

unique and incomparable, on the one hand, and the notion that he is capable of being imitated, on the other. Buber, *Israel and the World*, p. 71, referred to this incongruity as 'the central paradox of Judaism'.

40. It is interesting to observe that the rabbis were careful to emphasize that humans should not seek to emulate *all* the attributes of God. It is clearly taught in one midrash that humans should not attempt to imitate God's jealousy (Exod. 20.5), revenge (Ps. 94.1), grandeur (Exod. 15.21) or deviousness (1 Sam. 2.3), for only he knew how to deploy such qualities for benevolent ends. See Schechter, *Some Aspects*, p. 204; S.S. Cohon, *Essays in Jewish Theology* (Cincinnati: Hebrew Union College Press, 1987), p. 211. Abrahams, *Studies*, p. 152, observes that 'the whole Rabbinic literature might...be searched in vain for a single instance of the sterner of the Old Testament attributes of God being set up as a model for man to copy'.

41. See R. Yando, V. Seitz and E. Zigler, *Imitation: A Developmental Perspective* (Hillsdale, NJ: Lawrence Erlbaum Associates, 1978).

way in which the ethical teaching of the Old Testament is commonly viewed. The popular perception of Old Testament morality is that it is framed in the language of command and obedience, and in an age which seems inherently suspicious of all forms of authoritarian control, it is hardly surprising that the Old Testament is often neglected as a source of moral guidance. The presence in the Old Testament of the concept of *imitatio Dei*, however, may serve as a salutary reminder that the moral requirements demanded of God's people are not always couched in the language of law, and that there is far more to Old Testament ethics than the mere observance of prescribed rules. The moral norms encountered in the Old Testament arise out of imitation of God's character as well as out of obedience to God's will, for he is presented not only as the source of ethical commands, but as the pattern of ethical behaviour. The importance of this insight has often been clouded by too narrow a concentration on the image of God as lawgiver who demands total obedience and loyalty from his people, and punishes or rewards them according to their deeds. Of course, it is not to be denied that the depiction of God as the supreme dispenser of justice does figure prominently in the Old Testament, but if due regard is given to the wide range of testimony concerning God's activity in Scripture, it may well emerge that the law is not such a dominant feature of Old Testament ethics as is often supposed.

Finally, the concept of *imitatio Dei* may serve as a reminder that morality is concerned with the capacity of individuals to grow and develop in their ethical perception. In this regard, the concept of 'walking in the ways of the Lord' may prove helpful, for, as has been noted, the phrase implies that the moral life is a journey or pilgrimage travelled continually in the presence of God. Such a journey obviously consists of particular ethical decisions made in particular circumstances, but it also consists of something infinitely more significant, namely, the gradual formation of the moral character.[42] An important aspect of character-formation is the recognition that the moral endeavour is never a static phenomenon, but involves a continual striving for perfection as individuals attempt to realize their fullest potential. It is, perhaps, in this

---

42. Recent ethicists have rightly recognized that the formation of character is a particularly important constituent of the moral life. See, e.g., S. Hauerwas, *Character and the Christian Life: A Study in Theological Ethics* (San Antonio: Trinity University Press, 1975); B.C. Birch and L.L. Rasmussen, *Bible and Ethics in the Christian Life* (Minneapolis: Augsburg Publishing House, 1976), pp. 79-94.

regard that the concept of *imitatio Dei* may prove particularly significant for hermeneutics, for it invites the believer to achieve a pattern of behaviour worthy of God himself, and it does so by providing him or her with a benevolent vision of a goal to which all may aspire though none will ever fully attain.

FRONTIERS AND BORDERS IN THE OLD TESTAMENT

J.W. Rogerson

I

In his book *The Nation-State and Violence* Anthony Giddens distinguishes between frontiers and borders. The latter are typical of modern nation-states. They are agreed boundaries that separate nation-states and within these boundaries nation-states claim and seek to establish sovereignty. Frontiers are typical of traditional states. They can be either primary settlement frontiers, marking the limits of the activity of a traditional state, or they can be secondary settlement frontiers, which means that they are sparsely inhabited areas within the state, usually characterized by infertile or inhospitable terrain.[1] In either case a frontier in a traditional state is a peripheral region in which the political power exercised by the centre is thinly spread or diffuse. Further, such frontiers do not necessarily separate one state from another. Giddens notes that even in the rare cases where the boundaries of traditional states are marked by installations such as Roman walls or the Chinese Great Wall, such boundaries do not mark the limits of national sovereignty in the modern sense. They are simply defensive systems in a state in which central political authority is weak. Giddens sums up the importance of the distinction between borders and frontiers for understanding how administrative and surveillance power is exercised:

> Traditional states depend upon the generating of authoritative and allocative resources, made possible by the intersecting relations between city and countryside... Traditional states are, however, fundamentally segmental in character, with only limited sustained administrative authority of the state apparatus. The fact that such states have frontiers...rather than boundaries is indicative of their relatively weak level of system

1.   A. Giddens, *A Contemporary Critique of Historical Marxism*. II. *The Nation-State and Violence* (Cambridge: Polity Press, 1985), pp. 49-53.

integration. It is essential to emphasize how different, as 'social systems', traditional states are from modern ones.[2]

Later in the book, when commenting on the acquisition of territory by feudal states, Giddens notes that the territories of mediaeval rulers were not necessarily continuous and that a ruler might claim or own a segment of land within the territory of another ruler.[3]

The aim of the present essay, offered in friendship and appreciation to Ronald Clements, is to ask whether, and if so how, Giddens's distinction between frontiers and borders can be applied to the Old Testament and ancient Israel.

At first sight, is seems as though Giddens's distinction does not apply to the Old Testament. The Hebrew dictionaries give, under the entry *g^ebul*, meanings such as 'border' and 'boundary'. BDB gives 'border' and 'boundary' for the most frequent occurrences of *g^ebul* and 'territory' for a smaller group of occurrences, defining territory as 'enclosed within boundary'.[4] The Sheffield Dictionary defines *g^ebul* as 'border...usu. in ref. to tribal, national, or more local borders, including borders of private property or of buildings and smaller structures (e.g. Ezk 40$_{12}$ 43$_{12. 17. 20}$. Pro 15$_{25}$) also to territory within borders'.[5] The translations of the Ezekiel passages offered differ considerably from what is found in recent translations. Whereas 'border' is used consistently by the dictionary for the Ezekiel passages, RSV and NRSV use English equivalents such as 'barrier' (Ezek. 40.12), 'territory' (43.12) and 'rim' (43.13, 17, 20). If one looks at passages such as Josh. 15.1-12 and 18.11-20 there are descriptions of what appears to be a continuous line defining the boundaries of Judah and Benjamin respectively. The renderings of *g^ebul* in these instances are interesting. AV and RV have 'border', RSV, NRSV and NIV have 'boundary' while REB has both 'border' and 'boundary'. The NJB has 'frontier', but it is difficult to know whether this rendering recognizes any sociological distinction between frontiers and borders. The German *Einheitsübersetzung* has *Grenze*.

As a first step in examing the matter I shall summarize part of Martin

2. Giddens, *Nation-State*, pp. 52-53.
3. Giddens, *Nation-State*, pp. 88-89.
4. F. Brown, S.R. Driver, C.A. Briggs, *A Hebrew and English Lexicon of the Old Testament* (Oxford: Clarendon Press, 1907), pp. 147-48.
5. D.J.A. Clines (ed.), *The Dictionary of Classical Hebrew* (4 vols. so far; Sheffield: Sheffield Academic Press, 1995), II, p. 300.

Noth's detailed examination of the descriptions of 'borders' in Joshua 15 and 18 in his 1935 article.[6] Noth deploys several arguments to support the view that the descriptions of borders/boundaries in Joshua 15 and 18 are literary creations, based upon sources that were originally simply lists of towns or cities. The arguments can be summarized as follows:

1. A comparison of Num. 34.3b-5 and Josh. 15.2-4 shows that they have place names in the same order but that these names have been connected together with differing verbs and expressions.

Numbers 34.3b-4:

והיה לכם גבול נגב מקצה ים־המלח קדמה:
ונסב לכם הגבול מנגב למעלה עקרבים ועבר צנה והיה
תוצאתיו מנגב לקדש ברנע ויצא חצר־אדר ועבר עצמנה:

Joshua 15.2-4:

ויהי להם גבול נגב מקצה ים המלח מן־הלשן הפנה נגבה:
ויצא אל־מנגב למעלה עקרבים ועבר צנה ועלה מנגב לקדש
ברנע ועבר חצרון ועלה אדרה ונסב הקרקעה:
ועבר עצמונה ויצא נחל מצרים והיה תצאות הגבול
ימה זה־יהיה לכם גבול נגב:

your *southern boundary* shall be from the *end of the Salt Sea* on the east; and your boundary shall turn *south of the ascent of Akrabbim*, and cross to *Zin*, and its end shall be *south of Kadesh-barnea*; then it shall go on to *Hazar-addar*, and pass along to Azmon; and the boundary shall turn from *Azmon* to the *Brook of Egypt*, and its termination shall be at the *sea*.

their *south boundary* ran from the *end of the Salt Sea*, from the bay that faces southward; it goes out *southward of the ascent of Akrabbim*, passes along to *Zin*, and goes up *south of Kadesh-barnea*, along by *Hezron*, up to *Addar*, turns about to *Karka*, passes along to *Azmon*, goes out by the *Brook of Egypt*, and comes to its end at the *sea*.

2. The difference between the two passages in Num. 34.4 and Josh. 15.3 can be explained as follows. In the common source the sequence of names was

---

6.   M. Noth, 'Studien zu den historisch-geographischen Dokumenten des Josua-Buches', *ZDPV* 58 (1935), pp. 185-255, reprinted in *Aufsätze zur biblischen Landes-und Altertumskunde* (2 vols.; Neukirchen–Vluyn: Neukirchener Verlag, 1971), I, pp. 229-80, to which reference will be made.

קדש ברנע—חצר־אדר—עצמנה

Azmon—Hazar-addar—Kadesh-barnea

The writer of Numbers reproduced the source correctly, while the writer of Joshua took Hazar-addar to be two place names and separated them thus: 'along by Hezron, up to Addar', adding a typical place-name ending to the now problematic 'Hazar'.

3. If the frontiers between Benjamin and Jospeh are compared, as set out in Josh. 16.1-3 and 18.12-13 it is possible, again, to reconstruct a common source.

Joshua 16.1-3:

ויצא הגורל לבני יוסף מירדן יריחו למי יריחו מזרחה המדבר
עלה מיריחו בהר בית־אל:
ויצא מבית־אל לוזה ועבר אל־גבול הארכי עטרות:
וירד־ימה אל־גבול היפלטי עד גבול בית־חורן תחתון ועד־גזר
והיו תצאתו ימה:

Joshua 18.12-13:

ויהי להם הגבול לפאת צפונה מן־הירדן ועלה הגבול אל־כתף
יריחו מצפון ועלה בהר ימה והיה תצאתיו מדברה בית און:
ועבר משם הגבול לוזה אל־כתף לוזה נגבה היא בית־אל
וירד הגבול עטרות אדר על־ההר אשר מנגב לבית־חרון תחתון:

The allotment...went from the *Jordan* by *Jericho*, east of the waters of Jericho, into the wilderness, going up from Jericho into the hill country to *Bethel*; then going from Bethel to *Luz*, it passes along to *Ataroth*, the territory of the Archites; then it goes down westward to the territory of the Japhletites, as far as the territory of *Lower Beth-horon*, then to Gezer, and it ends at the sea.

On the north side their boundary began at the *Jordan*; then the boundary goes up to the shoulder north of *Jericho*, then up through the hill country westward; and it ends at the wilderness of Beth-aven. From there the boundary passes along southward in the direction of *Luz*, to the shoulder of Luz (the same is Bethel), then the boundary goes down to *Ataroth*-addar, upon the mountain that lies south of *Lower Beth-horon*.

Noth reconstructs the common source as follows: 'der Jordan—Jericho—die Steppe—Bethel—Luz—das Gebiet der Arkiter [lacking in Jos. 18.13]—das Gebiet der Japhletiter [lacking in Jos. 18.13]—das untere Bethhoron'.[7]

7. Noth, 'Dokumente', p. 235.

Noth's arguments can be commented on as follows. The first and second points are more persuasive than the third, but the third point shows immediately that the translation of $g^e bul$ is far from straightforward. In Josh. 16.1-3 the allocated area is described in terms of a *gōrāl*; and even if the Septuagint *ta horia* is followed and $g^e bul$ is read, it has to be admitted that the text appears to make sense with *gōrāl*. Indeed where $g^e bul$ occurs in Josh. 16.5, in a position identical to that of *gōrāl* in 16.1 (and see also 17.1 where *gōrāl* is in the same position and the Septuagint has *ta horia*!), the NIV and NJB join the RSV and NRSV in translating it as 'territory'. Where $g^e bul$ appears in Josh. 16.3 in connection with the Archites and the Japhletites, it is translated as 'borders' and 'coast' by the AV, 'border' by the RV, 'territory' by the RSV, NRSV and NIV, 'border' and 'boundary' by the NEB and REB, and 'frontier' by the the the NJB. Noth and the *Einheitsübersetzung* have '*Gebiet*'.

If the point is now taken as reasonably established, that the materials in Num. 34.3-5 and Josh. 15.3-5; 16.1-3; 18.12-13 are literary creations in which lists of cities or towns have been formed into narratives by the use of appropriate verbs and the word $g^e bul$, what did the authors/ editors think that they were doing, and how did they understand $g^e bul$ (assuming that they were agreed, and if there was more than one author/ editor)? Albrecht Alt, whose researches in this field were fundamental and pioneering, had no doubt. He believed that the outer and inner territorial divisions of ancient Israel were fixed divisions grounded in tradition and retained when new outer or inner political arrangements were made.[8] It was such borders that were being described in Joshua. Noth agreed with Alt about the 'hohe Alter, das für das System der Grenzfixpunktreihen zu vermuten ist' ('the great age that can be assumed for the system of the fixed points of the border').[9] However, bearing in mind Giddens's distinction between frontiers and borders, it is legitimate to question whether Alt and Noth were reading back into

8. A. Alt, 'Israels Gaue unter Salomo', in *Alttestamentliche Studien Rudolf Kittel zum 60. Geburtstag dargebracht* (Leipzig: J.C. Hinrichs, 1913), pp. 11-12; reprinted in *Kleine Schriften zur Geschichte des Volkes Israel* (2 vols.; Munich: C.H. Beck, 3rd edn, 1963–64), II, p. 83; 'Judas Gaue unter Josia', *Palästinajahrbuch* 21 (1925), pp. 113-14; *Kleine Schriften*, II, p. 285; 'Das System der Stammesgrenzen im Buche Josua', in *Sellin-Festschrift: Beiträge zur Religionsgeschichte und Archäologie Palästinas* (Leipzig: A. Deichert, 1927), pp. 13-24; *Kleine Schriften*, I, pp. 193-202.

9. Noth, 'Dokumente', p. 244.

their analysis a view of borders and territoriality that derived from modern nation-states. Before this is pursued further, however, a comment is needed about attempts to translate g^ebul in the passages under consideration.

It can be asserted with reasonable probability that the rendering 'border' is misleading if for modern readers it suggests borders as understood by modern nation-states, that is, clearly-marked boundaries which, in some cases, are defended either by continuous physical obstacles or border guards or both and within which the nation-state exercises complete sovereignty. Ancient Israel did not have borders in the first sense, and it will be argued later that there was no claim or apprehension that complete sovereignty was or could be exercised within frontiers. 'Boundary' is less strong a word and perhaps nearer to what was understood by g^ebul, as are 'territory' and 'frontiers' as long as the point about exercising sovereignty within them is taken note of. An interesting modern illustration of the problems that arise when borders as understood by modern nation-states are imposed upon areas and peoples to whom such notions are alien is provided by the attempts of the government of Iraq and the British Royal Air Force to defend the border between Iraq and Saudi Arabia in the late 1920s. Not only did this border cut across traditional tribal rivalries but, once established, it became a target for violations from the Saudi side which were 'punished' by bombing sorties by the RAF.[10]

Returning to the fundamental work of Alt and Noth and their belief in a system of fixed border points, an understanding of 'border' as understood by modern nation-states can be ruled out; in which case, various questions arise. Who originally fixed the borders and by what mechanisms was the information stored and made available? What happened if the 'borders' were violated? Presumably, the answers to these questions are to be looked for in the twelve-tribe amphictyony which Noth sought to establish for ancient Israel and whose existence is no longer widely accepted.

It may be that a much more radical approach to the question of the 'borders' in Numbers 34 and Joshua 15–19 is required, an approach already hinted at by Alt and Noth. Both of these authors regarded some, at least, of the material in Joshua as literary creations of a much later

10. See T. Royle, *Glubb Pasha: The Life and Times of Sir John Bagot Glubb, Commander of the Arab Legion* (London: Abacus, 1993), chapters 4-5; J.B. Glubb, *War in the Desert* (London: Hodder and Stoughton, 1960).

period than that of the '*Landnahme*'[11] while Noth also argued that the Transjordanian '*Ortslisten*' in Joshua 13 and Numbers 34 were to be connected with an attempt by Josiah to extend his territory across the river Jordan.[12] Recently, Ulrike Schorn has argued that the notion of Israel as a twelve-tribe system based upon the idea of Jacob as the father of the eponymous ancestors of the tribes is a literary creation from a period between the eighth and the sixth centuries BCE when it was necessary to reformulate the identity of Israel following the loss of the northern kingdom. The possibility that part of this reformulation included designating land to 'tribes' by way of a literary process cannot be ruled out and deserves further investigation,[13] while Noth observed that the redactor/editor of Joshua had a firmer grasp of the geography of Judah than that of the northern regions.[14]

II

In the second part of this essay I shall examine the question of the relationship between 'borders' and sovereignty, and consider how this may affect the interpretation of some parts of the Old Testament. Hermann Niemann has examined the extent of central administrative control over the northern kingdom, Israel, by investigating the position of towns from which such control could be affected. His maps show large areas of the kingdom unaffected by central control, and his long conclusion is worthy of quotation (in my translation):

> If all the conjectured royal administrative centres, or sites where royal economic, cultic, and border defence interests were represented, are put together on a map, three things become apparent. There is a military securing of the border particularly in the north-east and south, less so in the north-west (because of good relations with Phoenicia) and the south-

11. Alt, 'System der Stammesgrenzen', pp. 200-202; Noth, 'Dokumente', *passim*.

12. Noth , 'Dokumente', pp. 262-80, especially 279-80.

13. U. Schorn, *Ruben and das System der Zwölf Stämme Israels: Redaktionsgeschichtliche Untersuchungen zur Bedeutung des Erstgeborenen Jakobs* (BZAW, 248; Berlin: W. de Gruyter, 1997), pp. 54-103.

14. Noth, 'Dokumente', p. 239: 'Wir werden den Schluß ziehen dürfen, daß er nicht in der Lage war, hier so sachgemäß zu arbeiten wie dort, weil ihm die geographischen Kenntnisse fehlten, die notwendig waren, um die Reihen der Grenzfixpunkte in einem zusammenhängenden Text umzusetzen. Wir können etwa annehmen, daß er Jerusalemer war und sich daher in Galiläa weit weniger gut auskannte als im Bereich der Stämme Juda und Benjamin.'

east. There is no internal military structure. Megiddo and Taanach can only be regarded as very limited examples of internal military arrangements since they were traditionally defensive points in the important Jezreel valley and at an important mountain pass along the Via Maris. The security of the border even in the most favourable time, that of Omri and Ahab, was sporadic and incomplete, even though the Omrides supported defence additionally through expansive politics. What is most striking is that apart from Megiddo (and Taanach), there was no internal administrative centre apart from the royal capital (Samaria) itself... The large areas that were free of royal administrative centres show that the northern kingdom possessed no organizational structures through which power was exercised. Two initial moves in that direction can be noted. There was an attempt to connect the local and ruling élite of the area immediately around Samaria with the royal power in Samaria, as indicated by the Samaria ostraca of the first half of the eighth century BCE. There was also the establishment of an apparent network of four military areas (*mdynwt*) for which, however, the evidence is significantly restricted to the time of the Omrides.[15]

Alongside this quotation it is worth placing another from Giddens. Writing about the centralization of power he comments:

Efforts at centralisation were normally consciously made by rulers, who attempted to produce homogeneous modes of administration and political allegiance within particular territories. But it would be a major error to suppose that the level of centralisation of power was usually anywhere near as great as in the industrialised societies. Before the arrival of capitalism there was no large-scale society in which the village community did not remain a basic unit, however strongly developed the urban areas in that society may have been... The persistence of localised communities, and of the modes of organisation of kinship and tradition that characterised them *are the chief foundations of the dialectic of control in non-capitalist societies*.[16]

The findings of Niemann agree with the general observations of Giddens, and are also in line with observations made by writers such as Hopkins and Lemche which stress the independence of villages and 'tribes' during the Israelite monarchy.[17] They indicate that it is neces-

15. H. Niemann, *Herrschaft, Königtum und Staat: Skizzen zur soziokulturellen Entwicklung im monarchischen Israel* (Forschungen zum Alten Testament, 6; Tübingen: Mohr/Siebeck, 1993), p. 148.

16. A. Giddens, *A Contemporary Critique of Historical Materialism* (Basingstoke: Macmillan, 2nd edn, 1995), pp. 102-103. The italics are those of Giddens.

17. D.C. Hopkins, *The Highlands of Canaan: Agricultural Life in the Early Iron*

sary to re-think the way in which sovereignty and the exercise of power within frontiers is approached in the Old Testament.

A recent example of what needs to be revised is found in the book by Walter Dietrich on the tenth century in ancient Israel.[18] This is an admirable work in many respects, but on page 164 it prints a map of David's 'Reich' ('empire') in which are represented 'Gebieten unter davidischer Oberherrschaft' ('areas under davidic rule') and 'Vasallen-staaten' ('vassal states'). Whether or not there was a Davidic empire which included southern Syria, Ammon, Moab and Edom is not the issue here. The point is that the map gives the impression, and no doubt makes the assumption, that David controlled large areas of land and that these areas of control can be indicated by drawing lines on a map and by shading the enclosed areas appropriately. This is how maps of modern nation-states indicate the boundaries within which sovereignty is exercised; but it is inappropriate to traditional societies in general and ancient Israel in particular, and a new way is needed of mapping the ancient world if one wishes to avoid either reading in modern notions of sovereignty or of misleading users of maps into imposing modern notions of sovereignty upon traditional societies.

The attempt will now be made to elaborate this point by discussing several biblical texts. The historical accuracy or otherwise of these texts will not be an issue. Rather, it will be assumed that, whenever the texts were composed, they implied a view of what it meant to 'control' an area, a view that would be understood alike by writers and readers.

Modern historians of ancient Israel reading the book of Joshua have been struck by the apparent contradiction between passages such as Josh. 10.40-41; 11.16-22 and the remainder of the book. In parts of chs. 10 and 11 the claim is made that Joshua took the whole land, from Kadesh-barnea (10.41) to the valley of Lebanon (11.17). In the book itself there is, famously, no account of the taking of the central hill country to the north of Judah. Instead, Joshua's campaigns are limited to the Jordan valley just north of the Dead Sea (6.1–8.29), various cities in Judah including Hebron, Lachish and Eglon, arguably frontier cities (10.1-39) and the undoubted frontier city of Hazor in the far north

Age (Social World of Biblical Antiquity Series, 3; Sheffield: Almond Press, 1985), Chapters 6, 9, 10; N.P. Lemche, *Ancient Israel: A New History of Israelite Society* (Biblical Seminar, 5; Sheffield: JSOT Press, 1988), pp. 137-54.

18. W. Dietrich, *Die frühe Königszeit in Israel, 10. Jahrhundert v. Chr.* (Biblische Enzyklopädie, 3; Stuttgart: W. Kohlhammer, 1997).

(11.10-14). Now it would be possible to regard the apparent discrepancy between what is claimed and what is described in detail, as the result of deuteronomistic editing of Joshua. But even if passages such as Josh. 10.40-41 are deuteronomistic summaries, do they necessarily introduce a discrepancy? What would 'taking the whole land' mean in practical terms for the deuteronomistic editors? If it meant taking possession of strategic frontier towns, the editor might think that there was sufficient evidence in the accounts of Joshua's campaigns to warrant the summaries claiming subjugation of the whole land, even if modern readers find these accounts insufficient.

Becoming more specific, there are several passages in the books of Kings which locate incidents at surprising places if one works with modern notions of borders and territory. In 1 Kgs 15.27-28 Baasha kills King Ahijah of Israel while the latter is besieging Gibbethon, which is said to belong to the Philistines. Whether Gibbethon is identified with Tell el-Melât south-west of Gezer, or less likely, with Ras Abu Hamid, six kilometres north-west of Gezer, it is an odd place for the army of the northern kingdom to be operating.[19] It may well have been close to the main international route from north to south,[20] in which case the aim of the operation might have been to establish a garrison there that could collect toll from passing travellers. It might also have been reckoned as a frontier settlement whose possession would theoretically enlarge the territory of its victor. Gibbethon reappears in the story of the accession of Omri, being the place where the besieging Israelite army made him king (1 Kgs 16.15-17). The operation can at least be regarded as an instance of a ruler trying to take possession of a town well outside his own territory.

We are on surer ground when the various battles for Ramoth-gilead in 1 Kings 22 and 2 Kgs 9.14. If Ramoth-gilead is to be identified as Tell-Ramith south of the Syrian border with Jordan, it can be regarded as a frontier settlement whose possession made possible a nominal claim to control territory between the Yarmuk and the Jabbok. Or perhaps there was no wider claim involved, and it was simply a matter of possessing what were regarded as frontier settlements (compare 1 Kgs 22.2: 'Do you know that Ramoth-gilead belongs to us and we…do not

19. For the identification see J.L. Peterson, 'Gibbethon', *ABD*, II, pp. 1006-1008.

20. *Student Map Manual: Historical Geography of the Bible Lands* (Jerusalem: Pictorial Archive, 1979), section 9-3.

take it out of the hand of the king of Syria?').

Other incidents can be read in the same way. Thus, David's conquest of the Ammonite capital Rabbah (2 Sam. 12.29-31) did not give him control over Ammon as a whole in spite of what is probably the gloss in 12.31, 'thus he did to all the cities of the Ammonites'. His was a thrust at a capital, as was that of Ben-hadad against Samaria in 2 Kgs 6.24–7.20. The capture of such glittering prizes did not lead to subjugation and control of the entire territories of which they were the king's seat. The view of Ulrich Hübner, that David's conquest of Rabbah was an indication of Israel's superior economic and administrative organization, and that there was a 'wirtschaftliche Ausplünderung und Ausbeutung' ('economic plundering and exploitation') of Ammon during the reigns of David and Solomon implies the methods and achievements of modern nation-states rather than the realities of very small traditional nations.[21] Of course, the advent of what were by comparison with Israel's armies the huge armies of Assyria and Babylon introduced a new factor: the exiling of populations and their replacement with people loyal to the conquerer. Yet even here it has to be asked how the villages were affected. Could new settlers from Mesopotamia or wherever they came from be expected to adapt to the harsh conditions of subsistence agriculture in the hill country of Judah or Samaria?

III

The aim of this essay has been more to raise questions than to answer them. Thus, if Noth was right to find behind the descriptions of territory in Numbers 34 and Joshua 15 a common source list of towns, the question is raised about the origin and purpose of such lists. But if some of the questions raised remain unanswered, it is to be hoped that a warning will have been sounded about the sociological assumptions that are commonly made when Old Testament texts are read and Israel's history is reconstructed. If only some of the points that have been made are correct, this will have implications for the way in which words such as g^ebul are translated and maps are drawn which reconstruct borders and posit spheres of control.

21. U. Hübner, *Die Ammoniter: Untersuchungen zur Geschichte, Kultur und Religion eines transjordanischen Volkes im 1. Jahrtausend v. Chr.* (Abhandlungen des Deutschen Palästinavereins, 16; Wiesbaden: Otto Harrassowitz, 1992), pp. 170-79.

NOAH, ABRAHAM AND MOSES: GOD'S COVENANT PARTNERS

Rolf Rendtorff

In the first chapter of his book *Old Testament Theology: A Fresh Approach* Ronald Clements deals with the topic 'The Old Testament as Canon'. He explains the fundamental relevance of the fact that 'the Old Testament forms a canon, and is not simply a collection of ancient near Eastern documents'. This insight includes the point that

> where, as is supremely the case in the Pentateuch, there is evidence that a great multitude of sources have been used to create the extant whole, then we are in a real way committed to trying to understand this whole, rather than to elucidating the separate parts.

Furthermore, 'the concern with canon forces us to realise that the Old Testament has a distinctive, and in many ways unexpected, shape'.[1]

The first and basic element of this shape is the Pentateuch, the *Torah*. None of the other parts of the canon contains so many fundamental elements of the religious identity of Israel. And none of them has been worked on and shaped in such an intensive way. Because of this history of its emergence the Pentateuch shows in a surprising way not only tensions and even contradictions but also an impressive unity and consistency. Obviously the Pentateuch was the earliest part of the canon to achieve its final shape. This shows the importance that was attached to the traditions contained in it. At the same time the Pentateuch is of major importance for the rest of the Hebrew Bible. Many other books would not be fully comprehensible without knowledge of the Pentateuch to which they often refer directly or indirectly.

---

1. R.E. Clements, *Old Testament Theology: A Fresh Approach* (London: Marshall, Morgan and Scott, 1978), p. 15.

I

The period the Pentateuch covers is a time with a very specific relevance. This is expressed in a quite simple but impressive way. God
says: 'My servant Moses is dead' (Josh. 1.2). These three words
(*mōsheh 'abdî mēt*) mark the turn of an era. Nothing is any longer as it
was before, and everything that follows will be considered according to
the criteria laid down in this foundational era. It is very important to
keep this in mind when looking at the canon as a whole. The Pentateuch
is not only the first of three parts of the original Hebrew canon, but it
essentially constitutes the canon as a whole. Everything that follows is
in one way or another dependent on and related to the Pentateuch.

The dominating figure in the Pentateuch is Moses. Four of the five
books of the Pentateuch deal with him. Yet he is not present in the book
of Genesis. There are two very important epochs prior to the appearance
of Moses. Gerhard von Rad emphasized this more than half a century
ago by explaining the traditio-historical emergence of the Pentateuch in
three steps. The basis was, according to von Rad's theory, the 'Credo'
of Israel's deliverance from Egypt. Then the first step was *Der Einbau
der Sinaitradition*, the second one *Der Ausbau der Vätergeschichte*, and
the third one *Der Vorbau der Urgeschichte*.[2] The last two, the patriarchal history and the primeval history, are the fundamental periods in
which Moses is not present.

It is not by chance that in each of these two periods there is one central human figure of great importance for the future of the story and for
the canon as well: Noah and Abraham. Noah represents humanity in
general, Abraham is the father of the people Moses later had to lead out
of Egypt. But there is one fundamental difference between Moses and
the other two. Noah and Abraham are portrayed as individual figures,
standing by themselves before God. Moses, however, stands from the
outset between God and Israel.[3] He is the leader of the people in all

---

2.   G. von Rad, *Das formgeschichtliche Problem des Hexateuchs* (BWANT, 4;
Stuttgart: W. Kohlhammer, 1938) (ET *The Problem of the Hexateuch and Other
Essays* [Edinburgh: Oliver and Boyd, 1966], pp. 1-78).

3.   There are also certain canonical relations between these figures. See
R. Rendtorff, 'Some Reflections on the Canonical Moses: Moses and Abraham', in
E.E. Carpenter (ed.), *A Biblical Itinerary: In Search of Method, Form and Content.
Essays in Honor of George W. Coats* (JSOTSup, 240; Sheffield: Sheffield Aca-
demic Press, 1997), pp. 11-19.

kinds of aspects, and he represents the people before God. In the overall conception of Israel's history in biblical times Moses is Israel's first leader. More than that: he is Israel's first ruler, a ruler without any institutional sovereignty, but precisely therefore without any restriction of his rulership. And that is why he is more than any ruler after him could ever be.

The precondition for Moses' leadership is the emergence of Israel as a people. This came about during the time of Israel's captivity in Egypt. The word *'am* is first used in respect of Israel in Exod. 1.9 (*'am bᵉnê yiśrā'ēl*). But it is obvious that this development could not have happened—and could not have been recorded—without the previous stories about Abraham and his family, culminating in the 70 persons of Jacob's descendants (Exod. 1.5). The narrative connections are clearly established when Jacob/Israel moved with his family from Canaan (Gen. 37.1) to Egypt (Gen. 46). When God spoke for the first time to Moses he identified himself as the 'God of the father(s)' (Exod. 3.6, 13-15). But the God of the fathers is now concerned with the misery of 'my people' (3.7) and entrusts Moses with the task of bringing the people out of Egypt.

Reading further back it is seen that the story of the liberation from Egypt had begun already when God first spoke to Abraham and promised to give the land he had just arrived in to Abraham's offspring (Gen. 12.7). In varying ways the land is a subject through the whole story of Abraham and his descendants (see, e.g., chs. 13; 15; 23). But they do not possess the land, so that the book of Genesis finishes open-ended. A continuation is necessary.

This is one of the points where the tension between the unity and the disunity of the Pentateuchal texts is clearly visible. At the beginning of the Moses story there is no hint either of the previous stories in the book of Genesis or of the following events. Moses grows up as a foundling at the Egyptian court (Exod. 2). His Israelite parents are not mentioned any more. And when Moses many years later went out to his 'brethren' (v. 11—why did he think that they were his brethren, and what did he know about them?) nothing is said about the land where they came from or the like. Then Moses has to flee, and he is taken by the Midianites as an Egyptian refugee who looks for a place to live and a new family; an outcome that will take years (vv. 16-22).[4]

---

4. See in more detail Rendtorff, 'Reflections', pp. 12-14.

The bridge is built not on the narrative level but by a brief remark of the final, 'canonical' author (Exod. 2.23-25). After a long time God heard the groaning of the Israelites, and he 'remembered'. Only now does God enter the scene, but at the same moment the theological commentator constructs a long arch back to the first mention of the decisive key word: 'covenant' ($b^e r\hat{\imath}t$). God remembers his covenant as he first promised to Noah in respect of the covenant with all humanity and all living creatures (Gen. 9.15-16), and as he will soon promise Moses with reference to the covenant with the fathers (Exod. 6.5).

From this point on Moses is brought back step by step into the story of his people. At first, when he heard a voice out of the miraculously burning bush he had no idea what kind of deity ($h\bar{a}'^e l\bar{o}h\hat{\imath}m$, 3.7) might be speaking to him. Then God identifies himself as 'the God of your father' (v. 6), and finally because of Moses' insistence he also reveals his name YHWH (v. 15). At this point Moses has reached the level of knowledge of God that was present in the patriarchal stories.

II

Back to Abraham. In Genesis many times the 'seed', the offspring of the patriarchs, is mentioned, to whom God will finally give the land (see, e.g., Gen. 12.7; 13.15; 15.5). The readers would understand this as referring to the Israelites now living in the promised land, including themselves. They are those who live in the land that God promised to Abraham and finally gave to a later generation. Because nowhere else in the Hebrew Bible is the land itself the focus in such a way, the reader can walk through it together with Abraham and Sarah, Isaac and Rebekah, Jacob, Leah and Rachel and their families. And because the figures in the patriarchal stories are human beings of flesh and blood with their often very human problems the reader can identify events and places of their lives, as the visitor to the country can still do today.

On the other hand, nowhere else are the events in such an immediate way influenced by God's words and by his own actions. Therefore the possibility of identification for the reader is limited. The figures of the patriarchal stories are examples in several ways, but at the same time they are very far from the real life of the reader. It is just this tension between their closeness and their remoteness that makes the patriarchal figures still so fascinating for the reader today.

But the promise of the land was only one element in God's first speaking to Abraham. The fact that God spoke to him at all singled him out from the majority of humankind: God 'elected' Abraham.[5] The reader has that in mind when he or she reaches the beginning of the Moses story. What God said to Moses out of the bush would not make any sense without the previous stories about God's dealing with the patriarchs. Notwithstanding the peculiar beginning of the Moses story, it is only understandable as a whole as the continuation of the patriarchal story. According to the Pentateuch it is not enough to say that God delivered Israel from slavery in Egypt without first saying what God did with the Patriarchs and also what he promised to do with their descendants. By the way: even von Rad's 'Credo' in its 'classic' version (Deut. 26.5-9) begins with the mention of the (Aramean) 'father'.

Abraham's election singled him out from the rest of the 'families of the earth' (Gen. 12.3). But it does not in any sense isolate him. The chronologies make it quite clear that Abraham is one of the descendants of Noah, in particular one of the descendants of Shem (Gen. 10; 11.10-30). He is not at all a particularly important figure in the framework of the world-wide Noachian humanity. His name appears only late in the chronologies (Gen. 11.26), and it could be said about Israel that it is 'the fewest of all peoples' (Deut. 7.7). On the other hand, God's new beginning with Abraham will be to the benefit of all the 'families of the earth' (Gen. 12.3). God singles out one person and through him one people in order to be in an immediate relation to one group of humans, to the benefit and blessing of the rest of humanity that will finally be enclosed in the world-wide family of those who praise the name of the one and only God (Mal. 1.11; Ps. 113.3).

Abraham's election is confirmed by the covenant that God establishes with him. This fundamental event is recorded in two different versions showing different aspects of the covenant. The first is concentrated on God's promise to give the land to Abraham's offspring (Gen. 15.18). The second has a much broader view of the covenant: not only will Abraham's offspring possess the land (17.8); Abraham himself will become the primogenitor of many nations (vv. 2, 4-6), and finally the covenant will be an 'everlasting covenant' (*b^erît 'ôlām*) as a solemn confirmation that God will be the God of Abraham and his descendants forever (v. 7). The establishing of the covenant includes also an obligation for Abraham as God's covenant partner: to circumcize every male member of Abraham's family and offspring throughout their genera-

---

5. The *terminus technicus bāḥar* is used of Abraham only in Neh. 9.7.

tions (vv. 9-14). All these aspects are referred to in later books of the Hebrew Bible and would remain obscure without a previous knowledge of the Pentateuch, and of Genesis in particular.

III

The history of humanity does not begin with Abraham, and neither does God's relation with humankind. The earlier relation as recorded in the 'Primeval History' is one of great dramatic complexity. The first pair of human beings created by God 'in the beginning' (Gen. 1.1, 26-28) violated God's commandments (ch. 3), and then sin grew and spread until God decided to destroy his own creation (6.5-8, 11-12). Only his own regret prevented him from destroying it totally, and finally he established a covenant with the only one who found favour in his sight, Noah. This covenant builds the basis and the precondition for any life on the earth. Human sinfulness continues to exist, but nevertheless God promised never to destroy his creation (ch. 9).

These dramatic events make us aware of a double fundamental precondition of human life on the earth: humans do not live in an uncorrupted creation; and they live only because of God's patience and grace. The sign of his grace is the covenant God established with Noah and through him with all humanity and also with all living creatures. Viewed from this angle it is Noah who is the primogenitor of all living humankind: Noah the reprieved. He is the archetype of all human beings: they all—*we* all—live only because we are reprieved. The sign of this is the covenant God established with Noah.

The worst thing that could happen would be for God to forget his covenant. This is impressively voiced in the book of Isaiah:

> For a brief moment I abandoned you,
> but with great compassion I will gather you.
> In overflowing wrath for a moment
> I hid my face from you,
> but with everlasting love
> I will have compassion on you
> says the LORD, your Redeemer.
> This is like in the days of Noah to me:
> Just as I swore that the waters of Noah
> would never again go over the earth,
> so I have sworn that I will not be angry with you
> and I will not rebuke you.
> For the mountains may depart

and the hills may be removed,
but my steadfast love shall not depart from you,
and my covenant of peace shall not be removed,
says the LORD, who has compassion on you (Isa. 54.7-10).

This quotation shows the fundamental relevance of the Pentateuchal traditions for the Hebrew Bible as a whole, and that means for Israelite thinking and faith as a whole. As fundamental as God's covenant with Noah is for the existence of the world in general, so is God's covenant of peace for Israel's existence.

IV

One remark on the term *b^erît*, 'covenant'. The concept of covenant 'stands as the most widely used of the concepts, or analogies, to express the nature of the relationship between' God and Israel.[6] It is mainly used with regard to the three points in God's history with humanity and with Israel in particular that are recorded in the Pentateuch: with Noah, with Abraham, and with Israel represented by Moses. But the Hebrew Bible is not strictly systematic in a modern sense in its use of terminology (as we are not either, in the use of certain theological terms!). The covenant with Israel is mainly connected with the events at Mt Sinai (Exod. 24 and 32). Yet sometimes the expression 'covenant with the fathers' is related to the Exodus from Egypt and even brought together with the Sinai ceremony (1 Kgs 8.21; cf. Deut. 29.24; Jer. 31.32). But it is important that the word *b^erît* is never used in the plural. There is only one covenant, even if in different contexts and different shapes.

The Moses story begins as the story of Israel's deliverance from Egyptian slavery. The final goal of the exodus is the 'land'. Surprisingly in this context it is not mentioned that Israel's forefathers had already lived in that land but it is introduced as 'a good and broad land, a land flowing with milk and honey' (Exod. 3.8). Yet there is another goal prior to the land: 'When you have brought the people out of Egypt, you shall worship God on this mountain' (v. 12). Later in the context of the installation of the sanctuary God says: 'And they shall know that I am the LORD their God, who brought them out of the land of Egypt that I might dwell among them' (Exod. 29.46). This is the first goal: Sinai, where God could live in the midst of Israel in his newly-erected sanctuary.

6. Clements, *Old Testament Theology*, p. 96.

At the foot of Mt Sinai there is also the place of the most important covenant scene. But it is much more than one scene. Rather it is a sequence of the most dramatic and most momentous events in the relationship between God and Israel. It is very important to read these texts in their given 'canonical' shape and not to separate the individual chapters and scenes from each other. The section begins with the declaration of the Ten Commandments as the summary of God's will (Exod. 20.1-17), followed by a collection of more detailed laws (20.22–23.33). On the basis of these commandments and laws there is celebrated a solemn ceremony of establishment of the covenant (24.3-8). Of course, this was meant to be the definitive inauguration of the covenant between God and Israel. The relation to God's covenant with Abraham is not mentioned, but whatever the history of the individual traditions might have been there is no tension between them. The Sinai covenant has two additional preconditions: Israel has become a nation, and the commandments are declared. So it would be necessary to re-establish the covenant.

After the covenant ceremony Moses has to go up the mountain in order to receive the tablets with the divine commandments and also the blueprints for the sanctuary that has to be built (24.12-18). He stayed there 40 days and 40 nights. That was too long for the people. Already before they had demonstrated that they had actually no idea why it was good to have left Egypt: just to die in the wilderness (16.3; 17.3)? The same happened now when they said: 'As for this Moses, the man who brought us up out of the land of Egypt, we do not know what has become of him' (32.1). In a sense this is a prefiguring of what is later reported again and again about the behaviour of the Israelites, be it in the books of Kings or in the prophets: they do not understand.

Under the half-hearted leadership of Aaron, the Israelites started an action that was strictly against the first of the Ten Commandments which had just formed the basis for the newly-confirmed covenant with God: they made *'elōhîm*, a deity (or deities?). Aaron tried to veil the fact that the 'Golden Calf' he produced was not in any way an image of the God who brought Israel up out of the land of Egypt (32.4). But actually the covenant was broken. That is what God felt when he saw all this. He was willing to let the flame of his wrath blaze against the people to destroy them (v. 10). He wanted only Moses to survive and to make a great nation of him.

Moses' situation is on the one hand comparable with that of Noah: he should be the only one to survive God's destructive judgment. On the other hand, according to God's conception he would become a new Abraham, the forefather of a great nation. But even this parallelism evokes Moses' protest. He beseeches God to remember again as he did previously when he remembered his covenant with the fathers (32.13, cf. 2.24). He asks him not to establish a new nation but to act according to the promise he had given to the fathers of the now-existing nation. Moses did not want to become a new Abraham but to continue to be a member of the people of Abraham's descendants that lived because of God's promise and covenant.

By his intervention Moses became in a certain sense something like a new Noah. God regretted what he had planned to do as he had done before in the time of Noah when he established a new beginning (Gen. 6.6-7; 8.21-22). The parallelism between Moses and Noah really exists in one central point: the establishing or re-establishing of the covenant.[7] God had established the covenant with Noah as a sign 'that never again shall all flesh be cut off by the waters of a flood, and never again shall there be a flood to destroy the earth' (Gen. 9.11, 15, cf. 8.21). God did this in spite of his insight that 'the inclination of the human heart is evil from youth' (8.21, cf. 6.5). The situation at Mt Sinai is quite parallel with that. God realized that Israel is still, and ever will be, a 'stiff-necked people' (Exod. 32.9; 34.9), but nevertheless he declared: 'I hereby make a covenant' (34.10). He is thereby re-establishing the covenant he had previously made with Israel (24.3-8), which Israel had broken. Just as humanity does not live in an uncorrupted creation but only because of God's grace, so also Israel no longer lives in its original, uncorrupted covenant with God, but in a covenant re-established by God in spite of Israel's continuing sinfulness.

V

The covenant at Sinai is the last and definitive covenant between God and Israel. It is indissolubly connected with the personality of Moses. There are still more peculiar aspects in the image of Moses, each of which makes him a unique figure. Moses received from God the Torah

7. Cf. R. Rendtorff, '"Covenant" as a Structuring Concept in Genesis and Exodus', *JBL* 108 (1989), pp. 385-93 (reprinted in Rendtorff, *Canon and Theology: Overtures to an Old Testament Theology* [OBT; Minneapolis: Fortress Press, 1993], pp. 125-34).

for Israel. Moses built the first sanctuary where Israel could worship the one and only God. Moses installed the cult which Israel has to follow in its service of God forever. Moses led Israel out of Egypt and up to the border of the promised land; his successor had only to take the last step.

In all of this, Moses is depicted as *the* leader of Israel. But he is a leader of a totally unique kind. This becomes particularly clear if one compares Moses with the kings of Israel and Judah. The kings have exclusively political sovereignty, while they are totally without any specific religious functions. The story of the beginning of kingship in Israel expresses this clearly by the fact that only a prophet like Samuel could install the first king (or kings: 1 Sam. 9-12; 16). In that respect Samuel is a successor of Moses, but he had to hand over the political power to the kings.[8]

From that point of view Moses was the ideal leader or even ruler of Israel, because Israel could only be ruled appropriately through a close connection of political and spiritual leadership. Therefore it is not suprising that Moses is called a prophet.[9] It would be interesting to look from here at the way prophecy is presently dealt with in Old Testament scholarship. For some scholars the prophets are in effect outsiders, well respected, of course, but just in 'total opposition'.[10] Moses indeed was also in 'opposition' to his people as far as they did not understand the way God was leading them and did not follow the instructions of the Torah. But this was not an opposition from the outside; on the contrary, Moses, as well as the prophets after him, were speaking out of an intimate relationship with God and a deep understanding of God's will and God's way with Israel. But to explore this would take another study.

8.   Cf. R. Rendtorff, 'Samuel the Prophet: A Link between Moses and the Kings', in C.A. Evans and S. Talmon (eds.), *The Quest for Context and Meaning: Studies in Biblical Intertextuality in Honor of James A. Sanders* (Leiden: E.J. Brill, 1997), pp. 27-36.

9.   See R. Rendtorff, 'Kontinuität und Diskontinuität in der alttestamentlichen Prophetie', *ZAW* 109 (1997), pp. 169-87.

10.   Cf., e.g., R. Albertz, *Religionsgeschichte Israels in alttestamentlicher Zeit* (2 vols.; Göttingen: Vandenhoeck & Ruprecht, 1992), I, pp. 255-80 (ET *A History of Israelite Religion in the Old Testament Period. I. From the Beginnings to the End of the Exile* [London: SCM Press, 1994], pp. 163-80).

THE THEOLOGY OF EXODUS

Graham Davies

The book of Exodus stands at the heart (though not the midpoint) of the Pentateuch or Torah. As such it encapsulates the problem of the theology of the Pentateuch as a whole. Two widespread ways of defining the theological character of the Pentateuch were compared by James Barr in an essay published in 1973.[1] There, as part of a wider investigation of salvation in the Old Testament, he finds fault with the idea that the Pentateuch presents a religion of salvation and prefers apparently to say that it presents a religion of law.[2] It is ironic that Barr should have reached this conclusion just at the time when liberation theology was elevating the Exodus paradigm into a central pillar of its thought and doing so on the basis of a serious engagement with recent Old Testament scholarship.[3] Barr's remarks are based largely on the absence of 'salvation' vocabulary from the Pentateuch (most of the examples that he does give of such vocabulary—and some that he discounts or does not mention—come, significantly, from Exodus) and on the fact that the 'saving' events of the Pentateuch do not involve any change in the relationship between those affected by them and God.

There is perhaps rather more to be said than Barr allows for seeing the theology of the Pentateuch as a theology of salvation. It is not altogether clear why the general notion of salvation should have to include a 'change in relationship' with God (such an idea looks like an import

---

1. 'An Aspect of Salvation in the Old Testament', in E.J. Sharpe and J.R. Hinnells (eds.), *Man and his Salvation: Studies in Memory of S.G.F. Brandon* (Manchester: Manchester University Press, 1973), pp. 39-52; see especially pp. 41-46.

2. Barr, 'An Aspect', pp. 45-46.

3. Cf. G. Gutiérrez, *A Theology of Liberation* (ET; Maryknoll, NY: Orbis Books, 1973), pp. 155-59; J.S. Croatto, *Exodus: A Hermeneutics of Freedom* (ET; Maryknoll, NY: Orbis Books, 1981). The first edition of Croatto's study was published in the early 1970s.

from Christian theologies of salvation) and it is questionable whether the Hebrew words that belong to the semantic field of 'salvation' regularly carry this implication. Moreover, in relation to Barr's first argument, it is surprising to find the author of *The Semantics of Biblical Language* attaching so much significance to lexical statistics in a discussion of biblical theology. The distribution of 'salvation' words in the Old Testament (with, as Barr notes, a heavy concentration in the Psalms and the Latter Prophets) is a separate question (and an interesting one) from the identification of the leading theological themes of different 'blocks' of Old Testament literature.

At all events, a good case can be made for both alternatives, a religion (or theology) of salvation or law, in relation to the book of Exodus in particular, depending on whether more emphasis is placed on the Exodus narrative itself in chs. 1–15 or on the Sinai narrative from ch. 19 (18?) onwards. It might seem that Christians have tended more towards the former alternative, perhaps because of the typological understanding of Passover and the crossing of the Red Sea, for example, as foreshadowings of aspects of salvation in Christian theology, whereas Jews have given greater weight to the legal texts, as seen in the amount of legal commentary on them. But, as often, such a simplified view would be misleading, on both sides: for within the Christian church and Western culture more generally the best known and most widely displayed passage of Exodus is surely the Decalogue in 20.1-17, while the annual celebration of Passover in the Jewish home brings to mind the story of the Exodus as one of past, present and future salvation. One long-favoured way of bringing the two approaches together, both in the Pentateuch as a whole and in the book of Exodus, is the notion of covenant, with its twin foci of election and law, and Exodus 24 and 34 do indeed contain accounts of the making (or remaking) of a covenant.[4]

Each of the approaches so far mentioned, however, is in danger of passing by a major theological theme of the book of Exodus, which has a strong claim to be its central theological theme, not least because it is an important component of each of the themes of salvation, covenant and law and so can serve to link them together. To discuss it here is unusually appropriate, since it is a topic which was treated in some of

4.   For a review see E.W. Nicholson, *God and his People: Covenant and Theology in the Old Testament* (Oxford: Clarendon Press, 1986).

Ronald Clements's earliest work[5] and, although it is not one which I have discussed in any detail before, it has been explored further in various ways by some of my own doctoral students,[6] like (till now) an inherited characteristic which 'jumps a generation'. It is a pleasure to be able to dedicate this essay to the honour of one who has over the nearly 30 years since he took me on as a research student been a stimulating and innovative teacher, and later a dear colleague and friend.

In what follows I shall in the first place be concerned with the book of Exodus 'as it stands'. I remain fully convinced of the importance and value of the various kinds of historical criticism,[7] but I also recognize the usefulness of attempting a more synthetic account of Old Testament books, particularly at the theological level, and there can be value in doing this before (or as if before) the historical questions are raised. The wide-angle lens is a useful part of the photographer's equipment as well as the telephoto. A good example of how such study can actually contribute to historical criticism is in E. Blum's attempt to isolate the main contours of the Exodus narrative, which leads him on to identify a major 'composition-layer' which is the subject of his subsequent analytical studies.[8] Similarly, some of those who have been involved in recent research on the unity of the book of Isaiah have left questions of dating and authorship on one side and looked for connecting links in the text as it stands, so as to be able to trace the dominant theological strands of the book as a whole and say something about the distinctive way(s) in which they are handled there. Their findings will be useful to those who tackle the historical questions in the future. There is a very practical

5. See *God and Temple: The Idea of the Divine Presence in Ancient Israel* (Oxford: Basil Blackwell, 1965) and, for its relevance to Exodus, *Exodus* (Cambridge Bible Commentary; Cambridge: Cambridge University Press, 1972), especially pp. 210-17, 239-43.

6. See the references in subsequent footnotes to the work of R.W.L. Moberly, P.P. Jenson and D.L. Adams.

7. See my essays 'The Wilderness Itineraries and the Composition of the Pentateuch', *VT* 33 (1983), pp. 1-13; 'The Composition of the Book of Exodus: Reflections on the Theses of E. Blum', in M. Fox (ed.), *Texts, Temples and Tradition: A Tribute to Menahem Haran* (Winona Lake: Eisenbrauns, 1996), pp. 71-85; 'KD in Exodus: An Assessment of E. Blum's Proposal', in M. Vervenne and J. Lust (eds.), *Deuteronomy and Deuteronomic Literature: C. Brekelmans Festschrift* (BETL, 133; Leuven: Peeters, 1997), pp. 407-20.

8. E. Blum, *Studien zur Komposition des Pentateuch* (BZAW, 189; Berlin: W. de Gruyter, 1990), pp. 9-17, 45-72.

reason for approaching Exodus in such a way at the present time. Until fairly recently, most scholars accepted the source-analysis of Exodus (and the rest of the Pentateuch) into the four independent documents identified in the second half of the nineteenth century as having originated in the order J, E, D and P.[9] Over the past 25 years a different view of the composition of the Pentateuch has been developing, according to which early accounts covering only a part of the story of Israel's origins were edited into a larger whole and reinterpreted by two or more authors or redactors, one closely related in outlook to Deuteronomy and one with a major interest in the origin of priesthood and sacrifice. The scholarly world is still divided over the validity of such ideas and I myself, while I believe that they are flawed at some points, do not feel able to discount them altogether at present. An approach which tries to focus on the overall shape of the book of Exodus and its theology therefore has a certain pragmatic attraction at the moment. And, as Blum's example shows, it may even be that such an approach will provide useful material for a future evaluation of the historical issues.

I propose, again for pragmatic reasons, to begin my investigation of the theology of Exodus at the end of the book, in ch. 40. Endings can be as enlightening as beginnings for discerning the meaning of a text, and in some sense at least Exodus 40 constitutes an ending, exhibits closure (cf. vv. 33-35), even though in other ways it looks forward to a continuing narrative (cf. vv. 36-38), an important point to which I shall need to return later. Most of this chapter is about the erection of 'the tabernacle of the tent of meeting' (v. 2) and the installation of its furnishings within and without. It brings to an end the long section of the book beginning in ch. 25 which first prescribes how the tabernacle is to be built and then, after the interruption of chs. 32–34 (of which more later), describes how it was built, in practically the same words. The tabernacle, and more precisely the altar of burnt offering outside it, was of course a place of sacrificial *worship*, the regulations for which fill much of the following book of Leviticus. But it was more than this, as several considerations indicate. First, the Hebrew word for 'tabernacle' is *miškān*, which properly means 'dwelling-place' (lest I be accused of 'etymologizing' I refer, for example, to the occurrences in Num. 16.24-27), and Exod. 25.8 makes it clear at the outset that it is to be a 'dwelling-place' for Yahweh himself: 'Have them make me a sanctuary,

9.	This analysis is taken for granted in Clements, *Exodus*, pp. 2-5.

so that I may dwell among them' (*wᵉšākantî bᵉtôkām*). This is language that is also used of Yahweh's 'dwelling' in the temple in Jerusalem (Isa. 8.18; Ps. 135.21). The *miškān* is also described repeatedly as the *'ōhel mô'ēd*, now generally and probably rightly rendered in English as 'the tent of meeting', that is, the place where Yahweh will 'meet' with his people Israel: compare 25.22, 'There I will meet with you' (*wᵉnô 'adtî lᵉkā šām*, the niphal of *yā'ad*), referring specifically to the ark in the 'most holy place'.[10] At the end of ch. 40, when all is complete, we are told that 'the glory of the Lord filled the tabernacle' (vv. 34-35): 'This represents God's very presence dwelling with Israel in accordance with the promise given in 25:22; 29:45-6'.[11] The 'glory', that is, was the *visible manifestation* of the divine presence, not a substitute for it.[12] So the tabernacle is a place of divine *presence* and divine *encounter*. No doubt precisely because of this it is also a *holy place*: this is clearly implied in the term 'sanctuary' (*miqdāš*) in 25.8, but it is repeatedly underlined by countless occurrences of the derivatives of the root *q-d-š* throughout chs. 25–40: over eighty in all, with the highest concentration being in chs. 28–30. P.P. Jenson entitled his work on the theology of the Priestly Document *Graded Holiness*, to give expression to the distinctions made in the text between different degrees of holiness in various dimensions of the ritual system.[13] One of these dimensions, perhaps the easiest to relate to the concept of grading, is

---

10. Also 29.42-43; 30.6, 36. The Septuagint (*tou marturiou*) and Vulgate (*testimonii*), however, saw the tablets of the law (Heb. *'ēdût*, e.g. in 25.16, which is derived by these translators [and many others, including BDB] from *'ûd* and not *yā'ad*) as the basis of the designation. Some passages later in the Pentateuch where *'ōhel* or *miškān* is qualified by *'ēdût* (e.g. Exod. 38.21; Num. 9.15) may have contributed to the confusion. Clements interestingly commented on the imprecise rendering of *'ōhel mô'ēd* by the NEB as 'the Tent of the Presence': 'The N.E.B. footnote follows earlier versions in reading "Tent of Meeting". The Hebrew "Tent of *mo'ed*" may simply mean "Festival Tent", since *mo'ed* is regularly used for "season" and the religious festivals which accompanied them (cf. Gen. 1.14)' (*Exodus*, p. 176).

11. Clements, *Exodus*, p. 242.

12. It is in line with this conception that the Septuagint renders *wᵉšākantî bᵉtôkām* in 25.8 by *kai ophthēsomai en humin*, a point brought to my attention by C.T.R. Hayward in a paper read to the Society for Old Testament Study in January 1998.

13. P.P. Jenson, *Graded Holiness: A Key to the Priestly Conception of the World* (JSOTSup, 106; Sheffield: JSOT Press, 1992).

the spatial dimension, that is, the degree of holiness of place increased as one moved (if permitted!) from the outside to the inside. Jenson points out that the plan of the tabernacle distinguished a series of zones, separated by clear physical boundaries and variations in the materials used in their construction. The camp of the Israelites (mentioned in the tabernacle chapters only in 29.14 and 36.6) is not holy at all, but 'clean'; the court surrounding the tabernacle has a certain degree of holiness, but it is the tent itself which is properly called 'the holy place' (*haqqōdeš*) and the innermost chamber behind the veil is the holiest place of all (*qōdeš haqqᵒdāšîm*).

That it is the related ideas of worship, divine presence, encounter with God and holiness which are central to the tabernacle chapters in Exodus can scarcely be doubted. Two further points emerge especially strongly from ch. 40. The first is that the tabernacle is built according to the precise command of God through Moses (v. 19 and repeatedly; summarized in v. 16); the second is that the tabernacle is designed to be a movable shrine, displaying God's presence visibly to the Israelites throughout their journeyings through the wilderness (vv. 36-38): so it looks to the future. In fact it is generally agreed that it does so in a much stronger sense, being a kind of prototype of the Temple in Jerusalem itself.

The points that I have made so far are mostly not new, and their importance lies rather in the fact that they tend to be ignored when the theology of the book of Exodus is being studied, perhaps partly because the tabernacle chapters belong to what is generally thought to be the latest of the Pentateuchal sources, but also because of the frequent tendency to sideline the theology of the cult in accounts of Old Testament theology. I want now to try to justify the claim that these linked themes of worship, divine presence, encounter with God and holiness (especially the holy place) are also central to the theology of most of the remainder of Exodus.[14] First, I propose to look at chs. 32–34, whose

14. A similar case, with an important distinction between the 'accompanying' and the 'abiding' presence of God, has recently been argued by D.L. Adams for Gen. 12–50 in his thesis '*Deus Praesens*: The Present God in the Patriarchal Narratives' (unpublished PhD dissertation, University of Cambridge, 1996). The arguments of those, such as S. Mowinckel, J. Pedersen and W. Beyerlin, who claimed that the traditions that lie behind narrative sections of Exodus originated or were transmitted in a cultic *Sitz im Leben* could in some cases serve to reinforce the position being argued for here, but such investigations into the earlier history of the

setting in the midst of the tabernacle chapters suggests that the redactor responsible may have been sensitive to some theological relationship between them and their context.[15] My attention was drawn to the key thematic role of worship in these chapters by R.W.L. Moberly's doctoral work which was subsequently published as a book.[16] Not that he himself makes very much of this theme: indeed the drift of his argument in one chapter (Chapter 3, 'Exodus 32–34 as a Cult Legend') is very much to distance this section of Exodus from a cultic *Sitz im Leben*. But it was he who drew my attention to these chapters and to the possibility of reading them as a coherent whole, and when one does that it seems to me that a *theological* concern with worship (whatever the *Sitz* [or *Sitze*] *im Leben* behind the text may have been) is high on the agenda of whoever compiled this variegated material together into its present form. After all, the narrative begins by identifying alien worship, the worship of the golden calf, as the sin which threatens to bring to an end Israel's relationship to Yahweh; and one way in which this sin is dealt with is by the action of the Levites, the priestly tribe, who are said, by this display of loyalty to Yahweh, to have 'ordained themselves for the service of the Lord' (32.29: a combination of two technical priestly formulae). But these are only the first of a succession of passages in Exod. 32–34 which have a relationship to worship and associated themes. Thus 33.7-11 speaks of another 'Tent of Meeting' (*'ōhel mô'ēd*) where Moses would meet with God and hear his voice, and 34.29-35 is a rather similar passage focussing on Moses' veil. It begins by referring to a specific encounter between Moses and God on Mt Sinai (v. 29), but it concludes with references to 'going in' and 'coming out' which imply something like a tent again, and the iterative imperfects and consecutive perfects in vv. 34-35 also recall 33.7-11. The theme of Yahweh's 'accompanying' presence is taken up in 33.12-23 (cf. also 32.34; 33.3, 5), but in terms of Yahweh's *pānîm*, variously translated as 'presence' (vv. 14-15) and 'face' (vv. 20, 23). The normal

---

traditions lie for the most part outside the scope of the present study. For a partial exception to this limitation, see the remarks on Exod. 15.1-21 below.

15. A specific point of contact is of course 33.7-11, which uses the very term *'ōhel mô'ēd*, though without any direct indication that anything as elaborate as the Tabernacle is in mind; and the explanation of its origin and its location in v. 7, among other things, clearly distinguish it from the Tabernacle.

16. R.W.L. Moberly, *At the Mountain of God: Story and Theology in Exodus 32–34* (JSOTSup, 22; Sheffield: JSOT Press, 1983).

way in Israelite thinking to find the *panîm* of Yahweh and even to 'see' it (something from which Moses is here debarred) was to visit a temple or shrine (e.g. Deut. 31.11; Pss. 24.6; 27.8; 42.3; Isa. 1.12).[17] The implication is that the real theme of the dialogue is the transfer of Yahweh's cultic presence from Sinai to the land to which Israel was going, that is, the land of Canaan (cf. 33.1-3, which are linked with vv. 12 and 15 by the verb *'ālāh*).[18] In ch. 34 the proclamation of Yahweh's attributes (vv. 6-7), which leads to Moses' response of worship (v. 8), has often been noticed to have close parallels in the psalms (e.g. Ps. 86.15). Finally, when the covenant is renewed in 34.10-28, it is with Israel specifically as a worshipping community: the conditions of the covenant are almost entirely of a cultic character, which led an earlier generation of scholars to see here a 'cultic decalogue' parallel to the 'ethical decalogue' (but see below) of ch. 20. In view of all this it seems justified to see Exodus 32–34 both as a warning against false (idolatrous) worship and as a charter for true worship in the land of Canaan, providing it with a priesthood (ch. 32), a validation (ch. 33), and a pattern (ch. 34).

One step further back in the narrative, in the main Sinai-narrative of chs. 19–24, it is again not difficult to find pointers to the importance of the worship theme. The holiness of Mt Sinai as the place of God's appearance is strongly emphasized and protected by the consecration of the people (19.10, 14, 22) and the mountain itself (19.23). The Decalogue in ch. 20 begins with commandments about worship and the Book of the Covenant both begins and ends likewise (20.23-26 on images and altars; 23.12-19 on festivals, closely parallel to 34.17 and 34.18-26 respectively, though the order in the latter passage is different). In ch. 24 a group of the leaders of Israel are invited to worship (*hištah̬"wāh*) on the mountain (v. 1) and vv. 9-11 briefly describe this as including 'seeing the God of Israel'. In between the covenant is sealed, not just by words but by sacrifices and blood rites (vv. 3-8).

---

17. In Deut. 31.11; Ps. 42.3; Isa. 1.12 the Masoretic Text has the niphal of *rā'āh* with *pānîm*, implying the translation 'appear before'. The use of the passive of *horaō* in the Septuagint at these points shows that this is an ancient reading tradition. But the passive interpretation is clearly contrary to the syntagmatic structures in these passages and today the verbs are generally thought to have been originally in the qal, for which a verbatim translation would be 'see the face'.

18. Moberly several times refers to the cultic background of the language of vv. 12-23: *At the Mountain*, pp. 68, 74, 81.

Even in the Exodus narrative itself (chs. 3–15) the worship theme is prominent. Moses' call by God in chs. 3–4 takes place at the mountain of God, which is 'holy ground' (3.5) and the sign promised by God to him is that 'you shall worship God on this mountain' (v. 12).[19] This is taken up in the stratagem (or is it more than that?) which is meant to induce Pharaoh to allow the Israelites to leave Egypt: 'Let us now go a three days' journey into the wilderness, so that we may *sacrifice* to the Lord our God' (3.18: and repeatedly in the ensuing narrative, 5.3, 8, 17; 8.4, 21-25; 10.25). As a result Pharaoh's refusal is presented as opposition to the worship of Yahweh, and when he finally relents he uses language which, while ambiguous, probably has its primary reference to the worship of Yahweh: *ûlᵉkû ʿibᵉdû et yhwh kᵉdabberᵉkem* (12.31). The triumph is not simply one of liberation from bondage, but freedom of worship. Further, as the very moment of departure from Egypt is reached, the narrative is delayed by a long series of instructions about the celebration of Passover and the feast of Unleavened Bread and the dedication of the firstborn to God. All these observances are linked to adjacent aspects of the Exodus narrative, and their declared purpose is to provide a means for the people of Yahweh to remember their great deliverance from Egypt: Exodus faith is to find its expression in ritual and worship. A little further on the same idea is expressed in another way, in the hymn (or rather, hymns) contained in ch. 15: the Song of Moses (vv. 1-18), and the Song of Miriam (v. 21) which corresponds closely to the first verse of the former. These hymns celebrate the specific episode of the deliverance at the (Red) Sea described in narrative form in ch. 14, but that represents the final decisive act of the liberation from Egypt: 'The Egyptians whom you see today you shall never see again' (14.13). The Song of Miriam is limited in its scope to this:

> Sing to the Lord, for he has triumphed gloriously;
> horse and rider he has thrown into the sea!

The Song of Moses is much more complex. After the introductory v. 1, which summarizes the first part of the poem as far as v. 12, there are two verses of general praise, then a poetic narrative of the defeat of the

---

19. The importance of the revelation of the divine name itself for Israel's worship should also not be overlooked, as it had a focal role in both praise and lament. The use of *zēker* in parallel to *šēm* in v. 15 may strengthen the likelihood that worship is specifically in mind, in view of the use of *hizkîr* in liturgical contexts, several times with *šēm* as its object (Isa. 26.13; 48.1; 62.6; Ps. 20.8).

Egyptians at the sea, which provides the expected specific reason for praise (vv. 4-10), and then an exclamation about the incomparability of Yahweh backed up by a further brief reference to the deliverance (vv. 11-12). Then the poetic narrative continues on to new ground: the main points are the following. First, 'You [i.e. Yahweh] guided them by your strength to your holy abode (*n^eweh qodšekā*)' (v. 13)—language of holiness and divine dwelling again. Then come three verses describing the fear of the inhabitants of Canaan and Transjordan at the arrival of the Israelites—most obviously a reference to the later part of the wilderness journey and the conquest/settlement of Canaan. The natural conclusion to draw from these verses (and even more from v. 17—see below) is that this hymn was not composed or sung by Moses just after the deliverance at the sea, but originated at a time after the Israelites had entered the land of Canaan, perhaps a considerable time afterwards. Some pre-critical commentators, finding such an idea unthinkable, translated some or all of vv. 13-17 in the future tense, presumably regarding them as a prophecy.[20] Linguistically this is not a serious possibility. But in a way those commentators were right, because we must assume that the redactor who placed the poem here did so with an awareness of its contents, and presumably he wished to anticipate at this point a later part of the whole story of Israel's beginnings which he believed to be important for the full understanding and celebration of the Exodus events. The settlement of Canaan is in view throughout the earlier part of the book of Exodus (and already of course in Gen. 12–50) as the ultimate destination of the people (3.8, 17; 6.4, 8; 12.25; 13.5, 11), and other references to it are to follow (16.35; 20.12; 23.10, 20, 23-33; 32.13, 34; 33.1-3; 34.11-16, 24). In the light of this a closer look at vv. 17-18 is needed. The narrative continues, first, to include the entry into the land of Canaan and the settlement, specifically on 'the mountain of your own [sc. Yahweh's] possession' (*b^ehar nah^alāt^ekā*),[21]

---

20. Not all, however, took this view throughout the passage: the Septuagint and Vulgate both use past tenses in vv. 13-15. It seems to have been Calvin and the Geneva Bible which were responsible for introducing the consistently future interpretation of these verses, which is followed, for the most part, by the AV: see my paper 'Some Points of Interest in 16th-century Translations of Exodus 15', in W. Horbury (ed.), *Hebrew Study from Ezra to Ben-Yehuda* (Proceedings of the British Association of Jewish Studies, 1996 [Edinburgh: T. & T. Clark, 1999], pp. 247-55).

21. The existence of a closely parallel Ugaritic phrase (*bǵr nḥlty*), referring to

and then speaks of 'the place, O Lord, that you made your abode, the sanctuary, O Lord, that your hands have established'. Given the context in the poem and the language used, this is most likely to refer to a temple in Canaan. For my present purpose, which is a purely theological one, it is not necessary to decide whether Jerusalem or some other place was originally meant: all that matters is that the first climax of this hymn is Israel's arrival at a 'dwelling-place' of Yahweh where we may assume that worship would be offered to him, no doubt (inter alia) precisely in the words of this hymn.[22] The final climax, of course, is the celebration of Yahweh's eternal kingship, a frequent theme of the cultic psalms (e.g. 29.10; 93.1-2, 5). But what about the reference to Yahweh's 'holy abode' in v. 13? One possibility is that it refers, like v. 17, to a sanctuary in Canaan: we have seen in the first part of the poem the use of the 'introductory summary' which goes straight to the main climactic point of a narrative. In the same way, v. 13 may summarize in advance what is to be said in vv. 14-17. Alternatively, if the order of events in vv. 13-17 is taken to represent a chronological succession, then the natural interpretation is to refer v. 13 to something that came between the deliverance at the Sea and the arrival in Canaan. In the familiar (and only firmly attested) version of the story this could only be Mt Sinai.[23] Some support for this interpretation might be sought in the Hebrew phrase *nᵉwēh qodšekā*, as *nāweh* seems basically to mean a place out in the open for a shepherd or sheep. However, metaphorical uses of this term (such as in 2 Sam. 15.25, referring to the tent-shrine in Jerusalem) show that it is not a decisive argument. The precise identification does not matter for my purpose here: the key point is that from their deliverance Yahweh is said to have led his people on to the holy

Baal's sacred mountain (*CTA* 3.3.27; 3.4.64), has often been noted.

22. There is a recent discussion of this issue in M.S. Smith, *The Pilgrimage Pattern in Exodus* (JSOTSup, 239; Sheffield: Sheffield Academic Press, 1997), pp. 223-26, which concludes from a comparison with Ps. 78 that Shiloh may have been the place originally referred to, even if the terminology was subsequently transferred to Jerusalem. The latter concession weakens the case (especially when Ps. 68 is brought into the argument), but the suggestion remains attractive. I shall consider later in this study whether Smith is correct in his contention that the intention of the (Priestly) redactor who inserted the hymn into the narrative was to identify the sanctuary with Mt Sinai.

23. A reference to Kadesh-barnea might be considered possible, in view of its importance in the wilderness narratives, but evidence is lacking that it was thought of in the way implied by the terms used here.

place (or places) where he would dwell and, we may understand, be worshipped by them. For those who worship him so, the God of the Exodus is still present in their midst and the God who is present in their midst is the God of the Exodus, no less.

From this review of the textual evidence it is clear that, to a much greater extent than might have been expected, the related themes of divine presence and encounter, holiness and worship, are quite central to the book of Exodus, often being the main theme in long sections of the book and also appearing at important transitional points. The need to give a more central place to such matters in the presentation of Old Testament theology has received greater recognition in the past twenty years, perhaps most strikingly in Samuel Terrien's *The Elusive Presence*.

> The reality of divine presence proved to be the constant element of distinctiveness throughout the centuries of biblical times... Israel maintained her historical existence as a people only in so far as she remembered and expected the manifestation of divine presence. It was the presence that created peoplehood.

> Because it refuses to accept a separation between cultus and faith and carries at the same time the seed of corporate continuity in history, the biblical theology of presence may provide a prolegomenon to a new biblical theology that in its turn may play a central part in the birth of an authentically ecumenical theology.[24]

Of course it cannot be denied that liberation and law, and also the fulfilment of Yahweh's oath to the patriarchs (6.8; 13.11; 32.13; 33.1) and his covenant with them (2.24; 6.4-5), are vitally important theological themes of the book of Exodus too. But they are inseparable from the focus on worship and divine presence.[25] This is an important cor-

---

24. S.L. Terrien, *The Elusive Presence: Toward a New Biblical Theology* (Religious Perspectives, 26; New York: Harper and Row, 1978), pp. 42, 43. See also R.E. Clements, *Old Testament Theology: A Fresh Approach* (London: Marshall, Morgan and Scott, 1978), pp. 40-46, 66-72.

25. The importance of these themes, especially the presence of God, for the theology of Exodus has been noted above all (in addition to Clements's works) by G. Henton Davies, *Exodus* (Torch Bible Commentary; London: SCM Press, 1967), and by J.I. Durham, *Exodus* (WBC; Waco, TX: Word Books, 1987), pp. xxi-xxiv and *passim*. Compare also Davies's wider-ranging earlier essay, 'The Presence of God in Israel', in E.A. Payne (ed.), *Studies in History and Religion: H. Wheeler Robinson Festschrift* (London: Lutterworth Press, 1942), pp. 11-29.

rective in two ways: to the tendency to give a purely political slant to the theology of Exodus, as in extreme versions of liberation theology; and to an undue focus on ethics alone, which might arise from an exclusive concentration on the Decalogue and the Book of the Covenant. At the risk of over-simplification, one could say that the theology of Exodus is a theology of liberation for worship as well as order in society and, specifically in chs. 32–34, a theology of restoration for worship as well as order in society. Or, to put it more dynamically, the book of Exodus tells the story of the people of God as they pass from persecution and slavery through liberation, revelation and rebellion to the establishment of a place for true worship in the presence of their God. And (although this is not the primary focus of this essay) it will not be difficult to see, for those who are familiar with the discussion of the composition of the Pentateuch, that this theology is not restricted to only one level of the text but goes back as far as we can discern the history of the tradition.

In a recent study M.S. Smith has suggested that the motif of 'pilgrimage' is determinative for the literary structure of Exodus as it stands.[26] If this were true, it would strengthen the case for a central focus of the theology of Exodus being of the kind suggested here. According to Smith the 'pilgrimage pattern' in Exodus appears twice in the form of the 'journey to Sinai', first in chs. 1–15 (strictly speaking concluding at 15.21) and then again from 15.22 to the end of the book. Traces of a pilgrimage motif have occasionally been found in the Pentateuch before. Thus M. Noth argued that many of the names in the itinerary in Numbers 33 come from a list of stopping-places on a pilgrim-route which he believed he could trace into north-west Arabia;[27] and the verb *ḥāgag* and the noun *ḥag*, which are commonly taken to be technical terms for pilgrimage-feasts, are used in Exod. 5.1 and 10.9. Smith's argument, however, has a much broader base than this and his book includes valuable discussions of approaches to Old Testament theology, pilgrimage in ancient Israel generally (especially to Jerusalem), recent research on the composition of Exodus and the literary structure of the present form of the text, with much of which I am in full agreement.

Nevertheless, I believe that there are a number of reasons for doubting whether it is correct to speak of a 'pilgrimage pattern' in Exodus.[28]

26. See Smith, *Pilgrimage Pattern*.
27. 'Der Wallfahrtsweg zum Sinai', *Palästinajahrbuch* 36 (1940), pp. 5-28.
28. I do not dispute the presence of a pilgrimage *motif* at certain points in both

An important consideration is whether it is legitimate to isolate Exodus as a 'work of literature' from the books which surround it in the Pentateuch. Smith's argument relies on Sinai being the goal of the journey(s) in Exodus. For several reasons this cannot be so. First, whether one is considering the present form of the text, the intentions of the final ('priestly') redactor or the older sources as various scholars have reconstructed them, the story of Exodus and Sinai is not complete in itself. The story goes on, to reach the land promised to the patriarchs. To attempt to interpret a part of that story as if the continuation did not exist is bound to distort the meaning that is seen in it. While Exodus 40 does exhibit an element of 'closure', as noted above, it is in no sense the end of the story. Secondly, there are numerous indications in the text of Exodus itself that the real goal of the story it tells is the land of Canaan (see the references given above). From the programmatic commissionings of Moses in chs. 3 and 6 onwards it is clear that this is constantly in view. Thirdly, there is no indication in the account of the journey itself that it is modelled on a pilgrimage. Such indications as there are suggest, rather, that it is thought of as a military campaign. The Israelites leave Egypt *'al ṣib'ōtām,* 'in their tribal divisions' (6.26; 12.51; cf. 7.4; 12.17, 41), a phrase with strong military overtones, and *ḥᵃmūšîm* (13.18), which probably means 'in battle array' (cf. Josh. 1.14; 4.12 [as explained in v. 13]; Judg. 7.11). On the formal level, the itinerary-chain (Exod. 12.37a, etc.) belongs, as I have argued elsewhere, to a genre which biblical, ancient Near Eastern and classical evidence shows to belong primarily in accounts of military campaigns.[29] Fourthly, the proposal that Sinai is viewed as the goal of a pilgrimage in Exodus weakens both the role of Sinai as a place of legislation and covenant-making and the indications in the text that its main concern is with a sanctuary in Canaan. The former point is too obvious to need elaboration; the latter is particularly evident in the role of the tabernacle as a prototypical temple, in the concern in ch. 33 for the transfer of Yahweh's cultic presence to the land of Canaan, and in the first climax of the hymn in Exod. 15.1-18. Smith seeks, in line with traditional Jewish exegesis, to relate Exod. 15.17 in its present context to an arrival at

the narrative and the laws, but that is not the same as a *pattern* in the book as a whole.

29. 'The Wilderness Itineraries: A Comparative Study', *TynBul* 25 (1974), pp. 46-81.

Sinai.[30] But, as already noted, the preceding verses do not support this at all and point rather to a sanctuary in the land of Canaan. Smith himself recognizes that this is probably what was intended by the original form of the hymn, and there is no good reason to suppose that it was applied in a different sense by the 'priestly redactor'. The more so (and this is very interesting in the light of Smith's argument [see n. 22 above] that the verse may originally have had Shiloh in mind) because in the book of Joshua the Tent of Meeting is set up on the soil of Canaan, at Shiloh, in passages with an undeniably Priestly style and ideology (Josh. 18.1; 19.51; cf. 22.19, 29).[31] Once this is seen, it undercuts Smith's claim that there is a first 'arrival at Sinai' in 15.17 and on the contrary encourages the reader once more to seek the goal of the journey not at Sinai but in the land of Canaan. In so far as elements of a pilgrimage to Sinai are present in Exodus (e.g. 3.12), they are a relatively minor motif, not the 'pattern' of the whole book.

These conclusions have importance for the lasting theological significance of the book of Exodus, a significance which can be real for Christians as well as for Jews, if they recall the Passover symbolism which is rooted in the very historical setting of the events of Christ's death and resurrection and, perhaps, recover the liturgical use of the Song of Moses in Exodus 15, which was once a central part of the Easter celebrations. Just as the Israelites made their journey to a holy place in the desert, so the people of God at all times have a point of encounter and orientation which lies 'outside' and 'beyond'. But this is not to be, according to the book of Exodus (and still more the larger narrative of which it forms a part), their final goal: it is rather a place from which they must move on and enter again the here and now. Nevertheless they do not, according to the 'pattern' in Exodus, leave the holy, the presence of God, behind them, but by his mercy take it with them as they go to the tasks which lie ahead of them. For, if the first part of Exodus places the emphasis on what God has done and how he has made

30. *Pilgrimage Pattern*, pp. 214-18.

31. The Priestly provenance of the references to Shiloh in Joshua has recently been defended and their interpretation expounded by D.G. Schley, *Shiloh: A Biblical City in Tradition and History* (JSOTSup, 63; Sheffield: JSOT Press, 1989), pp. 101-26; cf. J. Blenkinsopp, 'The Structure of P', *CBQ* 38 (1978), pp. 275-92, on whom Schley depends at several points. Schley's claim that the Priestly references go back to an early north Israelite, anti-Jerusalem, tradition is most improbable.

himself known to his people (Exod. 1–20), the second part (chs. 21–40) sets out what, in response to that action and revelation, they must seek to accomplish, both in the ordering of society according to justice and in the ordering of worship according to holiness.

ON 'SEEING' THE TREES WHILE MISSING THE FOREST: THE WISDOM OF CHARACTERS AND READERS IN 2 SAMUEL AND 1 KINGS*

Iain W. Provan

Introduction

It is one of the more remarkable features of human behaviour that we are often to be found believing things beyond all reason and in the face of impressive evidence to the contrary. We recognize the reality readily enough in the case of the 'end-times' specialist who continues to believe that the end is nigh, even though he has been wrong on all 47 previous occasions that he has prophesied it. We scoff, indeed, at the political enthusiast who maintains that his party's programme will usher in Utopia, in spite of the evidence of all previous periods in power. We even possess a sophisticated vocabulary with which to describe such a phenomenon, whereby belief is not readily swayed by counter-evidence, nor apt to be awed by mere facts. Psychologists refer to 'cognitive dissonance'. Sociologists, thinking more corporately, write of the 'sociology of knowledge'—the way in which we know what we know in community, reinforcing each other's point of view and understanding of the world more by what we *assume* than by what we *argue* to be true, and creating an atmosphere in which dissent seems unimaginable, where a difference of perspective is named 'mental ill-ness' or even 'sin'. Human beings knew all about this phenomenon, however, long before the rise of the social sciences, and communicated this knowledge through stories. They told, for example, of the emperor

* The substance of this essay represents my inaugural lecture as Marshall Sheppard Professor of Biblical Studies at Regent College, Vancouver, delivered on 22 February 1998. I am delighted to be able to contribute it in honour of my esteemed friend and colleague Ron Clements, with particular gratitude for his kindness and support during my first tenure of an academic post at King's College, London, during the years 1986–88. I should like also to thank my teaching assistant, Ian Scott, for his help in preparing this essay for publication.

and his new clothes: of the emperor, vain and gullible enough to think himself resplendent, when in fact he is parading through the streets of the city naked; of the crowd, their sense of self and security bound up with the king, unwilling to rock the royal boat by allowing their minds to register what their eyes are seeing; and of the child in his integrity and innocence, puzzled by the madness that he sees around him, and foolish enough to state the obvious. The emperor has no clothes! We are, as this story reminds us, resolutely tribal beings. We live in groups; we know things as part of a tradition; we are apt to get swept along in crowds. Without the still, small voice to alert us to our self-deception, we are prone to perish in groups as well, charging lemming-like over the cliffs of history, muttering, as we hit the water, 'but everyone else believed it too'.

As in life, so we find in biblical scholarship too that same 'mob momentum' that tends to sweep everyone along with it, making direction and purpose seem inevitable, a matter almost of destiny. It happens at both ends of the theological spectrum. It is a feature of the kind of conservative scholarship that tends to confuse its own traditional understanding of the truth with the truth itself, seeing no possibility of a distinction between these two things, and marginalizing all dissent. It is a feature, likewise, of the kind of non-conservative scholarship that, with a magician's sleight of hand, turns the tentative outcomes of intellectual inquiry into 'the assured results of scholarship', beyond doubt and question, and likewise marginalizes dissent. The latter case is particularly interesting, involving as it usually does an appeal to 'consensus' (a term generally preferred over 'crowd mentality'). The word implies agreement about objective fact among a variety of free-thinking individuals who have studied the matter in depth, without prejudice or preconception, and now pronounce themselves satisfied that the matter really is so. Yet the reality is that all learning is inevitably guided by conscious or subconscious expectations; that all knowledge is modification of previous knowledge; that everyone stands in a tradition while doing their supposedly 'free' thinking. In other words, in spite of that rhetoric of the Enlightenment which opposes reason to tradition, biblical scholars—like everyone else—are all still governed and led by tradition even as they reason. They know as part of a group, part of a crowd; they are inducted into that particular crowd's reading tradition; and it is from that basis that they may (or may not) go on then to think their own thoughts. Consensus may not in reality be the *result* of the exercise of free thought by individual scholars at all, so much as something that exists *before* freedom of thought is ever conceived of. It is the consensus of the crowd watching the naked emperor.

The history of non-conservative biblical scholarship over the past 150 years illustrates this reality. Relatively few scholars have dared to distance themselves entirely from such great originators of tradition as Wellhausen or Gunkel or the like, preferring to bow in their direction even if their feet are at the same time moving off on their own path. When individuals have made moves that tend to undermine the authority of these giants, the broader community of scholars has often managed, by acts of quite remarkable cognitive dissonance, to ignore the individual contribution, and to go on articulating the truth of the interpretative tradition in any case. They may adjust it a little here and there; they may absorb this or that detail into it; but they are most reluctant to believe that any modern thinker can actually *replace* the apostles and saints of the nineteenth and early twentieth centuries. It is one thing, after all, to allow sparrows and swallows in under the roof of the scholarly temple. It is another thing to allow moles in under the foundations. The consequence, at the extreme, is that theories are held in blatant contradiction of the facts or at least with little or no grounding in evidence—interpretative paradigms that survive on the faith of the community that believes in their veracity, and on little else.

To put this in another way: just as crowd mentality in general can disable people from seeing clearly the reality of the *world* that truly exists, so also crowd mentality in biblical scholarship in particular can disable readers from seeing clearly the reality of the *text* that truly exists. There may be a missing of the forest due to over-concentration on the trees. This general argument might be supported with any number of particular cases from the history of biblical interpretation, and could be directed against all varieties of readers. The example chosen for consideration here, however, is a particular twentieth-century reading tradition in regard to 2 Samuel and 1 Kings—that tradition which places at the centre of its concern a 'Succession Narrative' or 'Court Narrative' and a 'Deuteronomistic History'. Both hypotheses have had their share of criticism, some of it quite fundamental criticism, over the course of the years since they were first articulated; yet both they, and the reading tradition which rests upon them, survive. This endurance, I believe, has much more to do with the faith of the community of readers than with anything else; and indeed, the reading that this faith produces is in my view deeply flawed. The text itself is in fact not clearly seen at all; for attention is focused elsewhere, and in the wrong place.

Sources and Redaction in Samuel–Kings

To begin with the hypotheses themselves:[1] where does the imagined Succession Narrative end? Does it end in 1 Kings 1–2, and if it does, has the ending been adjusted by pro-Solomonic redactors in order to whitewash Solomon and perhaps David? This view has indeed been advocated. Alternatives have also been advanced, however. Is the entire work as it stands anti-Solomonic, and perhaps anti-Davidic as well? Where, in either case, does the document begin? Can it really begin with 2 Samuel 9, when David's request for survivors of the house of Saul in that chapter presupposes the death of Ishbosheth in the opening chapters of 2 Samuel? Then again, can it really begin even with 2 Samuel 2, when other aspects of the story in chs. 9–20 presuppose, not only the stories of Ishbosheth and Abner, but also the story of David as far back as 1 Samuel 18–20? Moreover, is it really a 'Succession Narrative' at all, whether in its shorter or longer form? The difficulties with this label are well known, even if they have not prevented many continuing to refer to the hypothetical work in this way. Not the least of the problems is that the legitimate successor around whom the story allegedly revolves (Solomon) is a shadowy figure at best in the book of Samuel, and emphatically the product of the adulterous relationship between David and Bathsheba; and that 1 Kings 1 (even if part of the document) provides no clear signal to the reader of his legitimacy. Are we dealing, then, with a 'Court History', beginning perhaps in 2 Samuel 13? The question then arises, of course, as to whether 2 Samuel 13–20 is any more viable as a self-contained document than the others suggested, particularly given these chapters' links with passages elsewhere in Samuel.

So the discussion goes on. It might have been supposed that by this

---

1.　I shall spare the reader long footnotes in respect of what follows—the listing of scholars who have taken this or that view of the hypothetical entities now under discussion. Those who do not know the field may consult either of the following recent books: S.L. McKenzie, *The Trouble with Kings: The Composition of the Book of Kings in the Deuteronomistic History* (VTSup, 42; Leiden: E.J. Brill, 1991); G. Keys, *The Wages of Sin: A Reappraisal of the 'Succession Narrative'* (JSOTSup, 221; Sheffield: Sheffield Academic Press, 1996).

stage there should be some general feeling of unease about a method of dealing with our texts which could produce such wildly disparate accounts of their origin and meaning, but this is apparently not the case. As Gillian Keys has recently observed, Rost's thesis has dominated scholarly thinking on 2 Samuel for some time now, and even though his ideas have been challenged and questioned, as she reminds us, 'they still form the pivotal point of every argument'. It was Rost who, as she puts it, '*authoritatively* established the view that 2 Samuel 9–20 and 1 Kings 1–2 was a single literary unit'.[2] That is to say, people may disagree about this or that aspect of Rost's thesis, and cumulatively this may add up to the questioning of the whole idea, but somehow the thesis survives as the base-line from which the discussion moves on, that presentation of the matter which sets the parameters. We cannot agree on where this hypothetical source document behind our text begins, or where it ends or even what it is really about. We do not know who wrote it, or anything about the circumstances of its production. But we all 'know' that it exists, that there is a 'literary unit' there somewhere, for we have been told authoritatively that it is so. It is part of the fundamental structure of our community discourse, and apparently beyond criticism. Thus it is that even when quite authoritative little boys or girls point at the emperor and cry 'Naked', their voices are apt to go unheard. As long ago as 1981, for example, Peter Ackroyd wondered aloud whether the Succession-Narrative hypothesis was in danger of becoming an article of faith for the crowd—a matter of 'critical orthodoxy'. His conclusion is worth quoting:

> If our reading and response are to be with fullest effect, we must not be hindered by restrictions imposed by artificial and hypothetical categorizing of the text; and one such may appear to have been the supposition that there is an identifiable unit to be described as the 'succession narrative,' when, in reality, such a unit is to be seen rather as the product of a too narrow reading and too great a desire to find uniformity where there is in reality diversity and richness. A less rigid reading may open up a wider perspective.[3]

In spite of this, and in spite of a broad sea-change in the academy in our approach to Hebrew narrative texts which might have been expected to allow the less rigid reading of which Ackroyd speaks, we

2. Keys, *Wages*, p. 14. The emphasis is my own.
3. P.R. Ackroyd, 'The Succession Narrative (so-called)', *Interpretation* 35 (1981), pp. 383-96, on p. 396.

have not in fact seen a general move away from such thinking about 'units of text' as he describes here. There has been no general move towards a more holistic approach, in which 2 Samuel 9–20 and 1 Kings 1–2, for example, are thought of simply as 'a part of the story of David and Solomon', and no further label is attached to them. There has been no general move away from the neat simplicities of redactional theory and towards the treatment of the text as a complex unity, the ambiguities in the text about David or Solomon taken as cues for interpretation of the text as we find it rather than for holy war among redaction critics.[4] The paradigm survives, more or less intact.[5] We still see the publication of dissertations such as that of Keys, for example, which take issue with Rost, only in the end to offer yet another modification of his theory.[6] I cite this example not in any sense to blame

---

4. It is indeed striking that even those readers who have moved in the direction of 'complex unity' have often found themselves unable quite to leave the past behind. Thus even D.M. Gunn, *The Story of King David: Genre and Interpretation* (JSOTSup, 6; Sheffield: JSOT Press, 1978), whose overall approach to the content of 2 Samuel is quite different from that of many preceding scholars, nevertheless offers his reflections within the Rost framework (note his apology for doing so, pp. 13-16), opining that the narrative begins with 2 Sam. 2. Likewise J.P. Fokkelman, *Narrative Art and Poetry in the Books of Samuel: A Full Interpretation based on Stylistic and Structural Analyses.* I. *King David (2 Sam. 9–20 and 1 Kings 1–2)* [Studia Semitica Neerlandica, 20; Assen: Van Gorcum, 1981]), thoroughly unconvinced of the Rost hypothesis in terms of the thematic question—claiming that Rost's spell has already been broken, and evidently not entirely comfortable with the traditional delimitation of the text as including only 2 Sam. 9–20, 1 Kgs 1–2— nevertheless accepts precisely this material as the subject matter upon which he is to work (pp. 1-20), and this despite some scathing commentary on the treatment of the text to which the Rost hypothesis has led (e.g. pp. 417-19). The intervening years have not seen much change, in this respect, to scholarly approaches to this section of text (see further below).

5. Thus R.A. Carlson, *David the Chosen King: A Traditio-Historical Approach to the Second Book of Samuel* (Uppsala: Almqvist and Wiksell, 1964) still stands out as an oddity in his thoroughgoing rejection of the Rost hypothesis. Subsequent scholarship has generally sought to marginalize Carlson more than it has sought to engage with his arguments—one notable exception being Ackroyd, 'Succession Narrative', who has himself largely been ignored to this point.

6. Keys's view (*Wages*) is that there is indeed a major textual unit to be found in 2 Samuel, but that it stretches only from ch. 10 to ch. 20, and is not particularly concerned with any succession. The idea of the 'textual unit' survives, even though the idea of succession does not; and yet Keys herself assembles in one volume most of the evidence which calls into question any Rost-like approach to the text, and

Keys: graduate students have to play by the rules of the game in which they find themselves. I cite it to illustrate rather that old rules still apply, and that orthodoxy is (as ever) resilient in the face of criticism. It does not need to face criticism, indeed, so long as it can keep on producing disciples who know the creed.

What of the Deuteronomistic History? Here, too, we are dealing with a work whose existence is characteristically simply presupposed, as if we all just 'knew' of its existence—as if it were currently sitting in a library somewhere and could be compared with the biblical texts that we actually possess. The novice simply would not guess from reading scholarly work in this area that we have to do here with an intellectual construct rather than a solid reality. Nor would she guess the extent to which the construct is so vulnerable to critical scrutiny. Yet there is no agreement in this case, either, as to the original extent of this hypothetical work. Was it perhaps originally a pre-exilic work, reaching only as far as Hezekiah or Josiah? Might it rather have been an exilic work, taking in the whole story from Deuteronomy to the fall of Jerusalem? Discussions about the coherence (or not) of its theology are interminable—discussions forced upon the perceptive reader by the evident fact that particular books of the so-called History tend to display much greater theological subtlety and complexity than any description of 'standard' Deuteronomistic theology ever captures. In the manner of pre-Copernican astronomy, wildly improbable solutions are then proposed for this problem, involving differing groups of Deuteronomists with differing perspectives reworking the text within a few years of each other, rather in the manner of pro- and anti-Solomonic redactors.

All this contributes to our difficulty in talking about 'Deuteronomists' even moderately coherently. Why should we assume that such people existed at all? The answer, seemingly, is that the biblical texts imply as much, since they have been shaped by a relatively uniform ideological perspective on the world which has some connection with Deuteronomy. But is there not evidence in the texts, in fact, that the ideological perspectives therein are not entirely uniform, and sometimes far from being so? Then, the reply comes, the textual evidence is to be disregarded, or at most it is to be understood as implying that the Deuteronomists had broad interests and worked over a long period of time. It is worth reflecting on just how seriously one ought to take such a

herself presents her position as a departure from the Rost paradigm (see in particular pp. 213-16, where she refers with approval to Ackroyd).

selective approach to what the texts 'imply'. It is also worth asking just
how broad 'Deuteronomistic interests' can be before the idea of 'Deuteronomists' begins to lose any coherent sense. It is certainly important
to note the extreme difficulty that scholars have had when they have
tried to put any flesh on these skeletal and shadowy figures who are said
to lie behind books like Kings and to be so crucial to their understanding. Some say Levites or priests; some, prophets; some, the wise
men of the Jerusalem court. 'Who do *you* say that they are?', seems the
next reasonable and biblical question. All of the above, perhaps? A
'Deuteronomistic School' to which people of varying traditions
belonged? At this point, however, the question sharpens as to whether
the Deuteronomistic Hypothesis is being kept alive more by the faith of
the scholarly community than by the quality of the arguments. It is,
after all, very difficult to know what to make of a 'school' which seems
to have no unified ideological perspective and no plausible social location. Is the hypothesis, then, the presupposition of scholarly inquiry or
its result? Is it *necessary* to posit 'Deuteronomists' with a 'Deuteronomistic theology' at all, when thinking about the Former Prophets?
And yet the paradigm continues unscathed. The enduring hold which
the Deuteronomistic theory retains on scholarship is well demonstrated
in the fact that even among scholars who are now more interested in
reading the Old Testament books in their final form (which is presumably, on any theory of composition, a *post-Deuteronomistic* form)
than in speculating about the history of their composition, terms like
'Deuteronomistic theology' and 'Deuteronomistic History' should still
be so widely used. It seems that the construct, once embedded in the
mind, is difficult to dislodge.

Both the 'Deuteronomistic History hypothesis' and the 'Succession
Narrative hypothesis' thus seem strangely immune from the many and
varied criticisms to which they have been subjected, apparently having
the capacity endlessly to change shape without in general giving rise to
the suspicion that they are not the same entities as they were when their
scholarly journeys began. Perhaps it is because of the respect in which
the founding fathers, Noth and Rost, are held—authority figures of
great stature, and the sort of people whose perspectives must be vali-
dated if we are not to feel generally insecure about our modern tradition
of reading. Whatever the reason, the community continues simply to
'know' that it makes sense to talk of a Succession Narrative or something like it, and to speak of a Deuteronomistic History. All the criti-

cism of the past decades has made little difference to this 'knowledge'. It is the wisdom that the reader brings to the text. Presupposed, unquestioned, it is simply 'there'. It survives even where those same readers know, in part or all of their minds, that it is unlikely to correspond to reality.

One's assessment of whether any of this matters will depend upon one's beliefs about texts and about truth. We are no longer living in times in which everyone believes that texts have meanings independent of their readers or that truth exists 'out there' to be grasped. It is possible in these times, confronted by the tale of the emperor, to object to the suggestion that the crowd had a problem. Perhaps some of them sincerely did think that the emperor was wearing clothes. If so, that is all that matters—that they had a perspective, and it was sincerely held as their own. Perhaps it is true that many of the crowd knew he was naked: but even then, we could not say that they were wrong to act as they did. Did the crowd not have the right to react to the king as they wished, forbidding reality to impinge on their community values or interfere with their fun? On this kind of view, there would be no sense to any critique of scholarship in terms of dogged persistence in a particular perspective in the absence of, or contrary to, evidence. If biblical scholarship is mainly about playing with texts and making a living and a reputation out of them where we can, then my observations thus far are beside the point. Assuming, however, that most readers of this paper still imagine that truth does matter and that there is more to reading than shaping the text in our own image, I can continue. My assertion is this: that the reading which the faith described above produces in respect of Samuel–Kings is deeply flawed. The commitment to and focus upon hypothetical entities behind the text, and the filtering of the textual data through that lens, have disabled readers from seeing what the actual text that exists is saying. The 'trees' of scholarly theory, which although only constructs are clearly 'seen' by the reader, in fact lead to a blindness with regard to the complex forest of the text as it exists. In the remainder of this paper, I should like to illustrate that this is so by referring to one overarching theme in 2 Samuel and 1 Kings that has clearly received insufficiently perceptive treatment among scholars— precisely because, I believe, theories about composition have so dominated in the readers' minds that they have been unable or unwilling to see the theme clearly. To return to Ackroyd, we have been 'hindered by restrictions imposed by artificial and hypothetical categorising of the text', and this has resulted in a 'too narrow reading [of the text]…too great a desire to find uniformity where there is in reality diversity and richness'. A less rigid reading, I suggest, 'opens up a wider perspective'.

Having alluded to the questionable wisdom that readers have brought *to* the text, then, I now turn to the wisdom of the characters *in* the text, wishing to suggest that in reality the question 'what is wisdom and who possesses it?' is one which dominates 2 Samuel 13–1 Kings 11.[7] I shall conclude by suggesting that the coherence which is thus found in 2 Samuel and 1 Kings, once a particular interpretative paradigm regarding the history of the text is set aside and the text is read in itself, in turn provides us with further reason to question whether that paradigm corresponds to the reality. In short, I shall be arguing that hypothesizing in terms of a 'Deuteronomistic History' or a 'Succession Narrative' is not only unhelpful in reading Samuel–Kings, but in fact that reading Samuel–Kings in the first instance without reference to these hypotheses itself renders them even less plausible than they were to begin with. The coherence of the picture which emerges is itself evidence against the idea of a self-contained 'Succession Narrative', and indeed against any narrow notion of what Deuteronomistic theology was.

The Wisdom Theme in 2 Samuel and 1 Kings

It is one of many extraordinary aspects of exegetical work on the book of Kings in the last 50 years that exegetes, on the whole, have shown themselves quite unwilling to read the first 11 chapters as if they followed each other consecutively. They have been unwilling in particular to do the obvious and read ch. 3 as if it followed ch. 2. The reason is clear enough: most scholars 'know' that these chapters do not belong together, because they 'know' about the compositional history of the text. 'Knowing' this, they tend to think of 1 Kings 1–2 as providing an ending and 1 Kings 3 as representing a fresh beginning.[8] This percep-

---

7. Intriguingly, Ackroyd himself ('Succession Narrative', p. 396) already refers, in the context of his plea that we should not read the text too narrowly, to the possibility that the wisdom aspects of the text might point, explicitly or implicitly, to the significance of the stories. It is this intuition, I believe, that is confirmed by the less rigid reading of 2 Samuel–1 Kings that he advocates.

8. Thus, e.g., G.H. Jones, *1 and 2 Kings* (NCB; 2 vols.; Grand Rapids: Eerdmans, 1984), straightforwardly accepts the existence of a Succession Narrative

tion lies at the root, then, of what we might call the dominant perception of Solomon's reign in Kings. It is a reign usually divided into two fairly self-contained parts: an earlier period, in which Solomon was obedient to God and was blessed by God; and a later period, in which he was disobedient to God and God's judgment fell upon him. A further step in the process is then to criticize this representation of Solomon as being artificial and schematic, and indeed simplistic theologically. We thus move by degrees from a theory about the genesis of the text to a particular reading of the text which leads on to critical judgments on the text. What are we to make of this line of argument?

I have argued elsewhere,[9] and I shall not repeat it at length here, that the popular reading of Solomon I have just described in fact represents an entirely shallow understanding of the Solomon story. The Solomon of many exegetes has little to do with the Solomon of the biblical text. The Solomon of the *text* is a king who, even at the zenith of blessing, invites divine cursing in various ways—a questionable character right from the beginning of his reign. Here we must note in particular the obvious textual fact that Kings does not present Solomon's reign as beginning in ch. 3, as modern scholarship characteristically does, but rather as beginning in 2.12. It is in ch. 2 that we read of the early days of the reign, during which Solomon enacts the advice of his father David and rids himself of his enemies; and here we come to our first consideration of the wisdom theme in Samuel–Kings. David urges Solomon to 'act according to his wisdom' in getting rid of Joab son of Zeruiah (v. 6), and he refers to this wisdom again in advocating the removal of Shimei son of Gera (v. 9). The emphasis is upon subtlety: Solomon must not act rashly, but use his brain, and find some justifica-

without raising any fundamental questions about it. Rost is said to have 'established' that 2 Sam. 9–20, 1 Kgs 1–2 originally formed an unbroken narrative, and a detailed discussion of this source is then provided (Jones, *1 and 2 Kings*, I, pp. 48-57). Later, at the beginning of his detailed discussion of 1 Kgs 1–2 (p. 88), Jones has this to say: 'For reasons noted in the Introduction...these first two chapters are to be separated from the account of Solomon's reign in 3.1–11.43'. The fact that we so obviously have a source in chs. 1–2 means that there is to be a 'separation' between chs. 1–2 and 3–11; and indeed, later in the commentary it is the latter chapters only, treated as a block and independently of 1–2, that are included under the heading 'The Reign of Solomon' (pp. 119-247).

9. I.W. Provan, *1 and 2 Kings* (Peabody, MA: Hendrickson; Carlisle: Paternoster Press, 1995), pp. 41-98. My reading of Solomon in this commentary builds upon and extends the insights of various other scholars noted therein.

tion for removing these people from the scene. The word used for wisdom is, however, *ḥokmâ*, exactly as in ch. 3 and elsewhere in the Solomon story. Its usage here, in a chapter which is highly ambiguous about the rights and wrongs of the executions and banishments described in it, and thus raises questions both about the quality of the wisdom that is being described and about the character of David and his successor, must surely influence our understanding of its usage later.

Read in this context, 1 Kings 3 clearly presents Solomon as a king aware of the deficiency of his previous wisdom, and addressing God about this fact. The emphasis of the whole section 3.4-15 falls upon wisdom as a supernatural gift from God, rather than as something that is innate (as it is implicitly in ch. 2) or acquired by patient hard work, utilizing careful observation and self-discipline (as it is explicitly in much of Proverbs and in 1 Kgs 4.29-34).[10] It is wisdom from above, not below. A 'wise and discerning heart' is granted by God, which will enable Solomon to govern his people and to distinguish between right and wrong (3.9)—a veiled allusion to the events of ch. 2 by a God who expresses pleasure that the king has not sought long life, wealth or the death of his enemies (3.10-11) and then grants him long life and wealth, but specifically not the death of enemies (3.13-14). The whole implication is that Solomon has recognized, and that God is confirming, that the 'wisdom' of ch. 2 was of a highly unenlightened, self-serving kind, which must now be replaced with a higher wisdom in order that the king may rule justly and well over his subjects (3.9, 11). The fear of the Lord is truly the beginning of wisdom (as elsewhere in the Old Testament; e.g. Job 28.28; Ps. 111.10; Prov. 15.33). The latter part of ch. 3 then illustrates the difference that the new wisdom makes, as Solomon uses his sword, not for arguably unjust executions, but to threaten execution in order to achieve justice. The glory of Solomon's wisdom is then further celebrated in 1 Kings 4, with questions asked about it in chs. 9–10, just before the collapse into apostasy in ch. 11. Ultimately, the Solomon story, from chs. 2–11, is exploring these questions: what is the source and the nature of true wisdom; and can wisdom truly be wisdom that does not issue in obedience to divine Torah? I believe that this is quite easily seen, once we are dealing with the text as we have it rather than with hypothetical entities of dubious extent and nature which may once have lain behind it. It is only such theorizing, and

10. For an excellent brief treatment of the biblical wisdom theme, see R.E. Clements, *Wisdom in Theology* (Grand Rapids: Eerdmans, 1992).

associated theorizing about the Deuteronomists and their theology, that has disabled us from seeing the reality. Our inherited expectations about the extent of the text and the theology of its authors have led us off the right track. Such theorizing has had, among others, this conse-quence: that it has produced a two-dimensional Solomon vastly less interesting and colourful than the Solomon who actually inhabits the text in all his complexity and ambiguity—the Solomon of the scholar rather than the Solomon of the artist.

As 1 Kings 3–11 has its immediate and proper background in 1 Kings 2, so the entire Solomon story of 1 Kings 2–11 has its own background in the David story that precedes it. Here, too, we find the wisdom theme explored, as part of a presentation of King David which likewise por-trays him as an ambiguous and complex character from whom the reader is invited to learn. And here too, theory *about* the text has dis-abled perceptive reading *of* the text.

We begin in 1 Kings 1. Here we find the king from whom Solomon takes his first example—a dying king, now out of touch with reality, now fully in control, with a curiously ambivalent attitude to oaths and a selective memory. The chapter opens with the story of David and Abishag—a beautiful woman whom we are told David does not 'know' sexually. The days in which David took possession of Bathsheba are now far behind; and Adonijah sees his chance, in the midst of the king's impotence, to gain power. David's lack of knowledge is not confined to the matter of sex, however. As the chapter progresses we discover that he is also lacking in knowledge about Adonijah's coup. Verse 18 has Bathsheba herself, whom David had clearly 'known' addressing him thus: 'Adonijah has become king, and you, my lord the king, do not *know* about it'. We ourselves need to know the preceding story to get the whole point here. This is the king, apparently, who had previously had the reputation of possessing 'wisdom like that of the angel of God [to know] everything that happens in the land/on the earth'—at least that is what the wise woman of 2 Samuel 14 has to say (v. 20). A declining king indeed, who now does not 'know' things or people, even though they live in his own house! We are thus directed still further back in our story, if we wish to discover the full extent of our wisdom theme—to the wisdom of David that provides the background for the description of the wisdom of his son. What manner of wisdom is this?

In exploring this question we are by no means lacking in already existing resources, upon which I shall now in turn build in outlining the

overall picture as I see it.[11] It has been noted before that one of the
themes which runs throughout 2 Samuel 9–20 and 1 Kings 1–2 is that
'the role of the king involves a keen discernment that helps him judge
between good and evil...almost a superhuman knowledge like that of
the angel of God'.[12] This is a theme that comes before the reader again
in 1 Kings 3, as Solomon's endowment with divine wisdom is put to the
test in the case of the two mothers who claim the one child. The David
who responds to the challenge to display such wisdom in 2 Samuel is a
complex character, like his son—a king for whose interpretation the
reader himself feels in need of divine wisdom, plumbing the depths of
David's actions and their motivations. How are we to explain his
actions and words when his first son by Bathsheba dies; or his inaction
in the case of the rape of Tamar? The narrative leaves such matters
unclear. What *is* clear, however, is that David after 2 Samuel 11–12 is a

---

11. I refer to literature which contributes directly to an understanding of the
wisdom theme in 2 Sam. 9–20, 1 Kgs 1–2, and/or which helps us to understand
more fully the overall narrative as an artistically-constructed piece of work and thus
to appreciate how its various wisdom elements function. Aside from the volumes by
Carlson, Gunn and Fokkelman already cited, I am thinking chiefly of: J. Blenkinsopp, 'Theme and Motif in the Succession History (2 Sam. XI 2ff.) and the Yahwist
Corpus', in G.W. Anderson *et al.* (eds.), *Volume du Congrès: Genève 1965*
(VTSup, 15; Leiden: E.J. Brill, 1966), pp. 44-57; L. Delekat, 'Tendenz und Theo-
logie der David-Salomo Erzählung', in F. Maass (ed.), *Das ferne und nahe Wort*
(L. Rost Festschrift; BZAW, 105; Berlin: A. Töpelmann, 1967), pp. 26-36;
W. Brueggemann, 'The Trusted Creature', *CBQ* 31 (1969), pp. 484-98; R.N. Why-
bray, *The Succession Narrative: A Study of II Sam. 9-20 and I Kings 1 and 2* (SBT;
London: SCM Press, 1968); J.L. Crenshaw, 'Method in Determining Wisdom Influ-
ence upon "Historical" Literature', *JBL* 88 (1969), pp. 129-42; H.-J. Hermisson,
'Weisheit und Geschichte', in H.W. Wolff (ed.), *Probleme biblischer Theologie:
Gerhard von Rad zum 70. Geburtstag* (Munich: Chr. Kaiser Verlag, 1971), pp. 136-
54; W. Brueggemann, 'On Trust and Freedom: A Study of Faith in the Succession
Narrative', *Interpretation* 26 (1972), pp. 3-19; J.S. Ackerman, 'Knowing Good and
Evil: A Literary Analysis of the Court History in 2 Samuel 9–20 and 1 Kings 1–2',
JBL 109 (1990), pp. 41-60; and R. Polzin, *David and the Deuteronomist: A Literary
Study of the Deuteronomic History* (Bloomington: Indiana University Press, 1993).
A considerable amount of insight into the way in which wisdom functions within
the story can be gained from this literature, even though the authors mentioned are
sometimes so interested in other questions (such as *Tendenz* or genre) that they
themselves do not develop the insights, and are sometimes so captivated (in my
view) by a romantic view of David that they do not develop the insights rightly.

12. Ackerman, 'Knowing', p. 42.

divided man with a divided family, who in the later years of his reign fosters division in his kingdom in pursuit of power, foreshadowing in his own person the divided kingdom of his grandson's day. What kind of wisdom is it, that produces the results which are the story of David in 2 Samuel 13–20? Is David truly a wise man? Or are the words of the wise woman of Tekoa which I just cited simple flattery, more evocative of Davidic ideology than of Davidic reality?

Several features of 2 Samuel 14 certainly give us further pause for thought. For one thing, it is the *woman* who is clearly in control of the situation, manipulating the king so that he moves by stages to the place in which she needs him to be. David, allegedly possessing the wisdom of a messenger of God, does not even get to first base when confronted by this wise messenger of Joab, who disarms him through disguise and deception, shocks him with direct speech, and finally praises him, in order to give him the chance to get over the painful surprise.[13] Even though David has previously suffered a similar manipulation through story at the hands of Nathan in 2 Samuel 12, he has not the first idea where the woman's story is leading, and he is caught in the same trap—slow learner more than swift-comprehending angel. His sole moment of insight in the story is the stunning deduction in v. 19 that perhaps Joab might be involved somewhere in the affair—a response which must raise a smile in the reader who has followed the speeches of the woman to this point, in all their depth and eloquence and artistry. 'Speak', says David in v. 12, and the wise woman weaves her spell. 'Speak', says the woman in v. 18; and David, befogged, and confessing that she knows much more than he, offers his dim perception of reality in the midst of illusion. It is for this amazing feat of discernment that David is then lauded by the woman for possessing divine wisdom. We are justified in asking whether we should take her words as ironic,[14] particularly in view of two other factors. First, the woman's double comparison of David to an angel recalls two other texts. Both the Philistine Achish (1 Sam. 29.9) and later the Saulide Mephibosheth (2 Sam. 19.27) make

---

13. Fokkelman, *Narrative Art*, pp. 126-47.

14. Fokkelman himself resists this reading (*Narrative Art*, pp. 142-44), arguing for the cleverness of David and the sincerity of the woman. He is only able to defend this position, however, by introducing the most extravagant of speculations about what is implicit in the text. Far more convincing is the reading of Whybray, *Succession Narrrative*, pp. 36-37, who writes of David's 'absurd ineptitude' when confronted with (among other things) the fictions of 2 Sam. 12 and 14.

similar statements to David. In both cases these statements by characters in the narrative are undermined by the narrative itself. David is not
as angel-white as Achish thinks, nor is angelic wisdom much in evidence in the king's erratic decisions about Saul's property. He fails to
discover whether it is Ziba or Mephibosheth who is lying, and contents
himself with dividing Saul's estates between them—effectively *dividing* between good and evil, rather than *divining* between good and evil,
as Solomon later manages to do (1 Kgs 3).[15] In the context, the words
of the Tekoan woman in 2 Samuel 14 thus indeed sound with 'unavoid-
ably ironic tones. All three situations underline in various ways how far
off the mark are such servile statements about David, who is either a
deceiver or a dupe at the point in the story when such comparisons are
made... David only *appears* to be wise "like...a messenger of God".'[16]

A second factor influencing our reading here is what has just happened in ch. 13. For the woman from Tekoa is not the only wise person
to appear in the story as a foil to David. In ch. 13 we have met Jonadab,
Amnon's friend: a wise man, anxious to help this son of the king who,
like his father, desires to possess a woman. He, too, contrives a story
for David. He knows only too well how to manipulate the allegedly all-
knowing king; and his plan to facilitate the rape of Tamar duly succeeds. At the end of the chapter, too, Jonadab reappears as someone
who again knows vastly more than David about what is going on in
David's own kingdom. David simply believes what he is told: Absalom
has killed all the king's sons. Jonadab knows differently: only Amnon
is dead. How he knows is never made clear: perhaps his wisdom resides
partly in knowing when to stick with his friends, and when to keep
quiet about plots to have them murdered. The main point, however, is
this: that David knows nowhere near as much in these stories as the
other wise people around him. His ignorance here foreshadows his
ignorance in 1 Kings 1, when he is unaware of what is happening at the
feast of another of his sons. By the same token, Jonadab's manipulation
of the king foreshadows the manipulation in 1 Kings 1 by Nathan and
Bathsheba, both of whom 'know' of a Davidic oath from the past that
the biblical narrator does not otherwise mention, and manage to convince David to remember it too.[17]

15. Ackerman, 'Knowing', p. 52.
16. Polzin, *David*, p. 141.
17. The way in which David adheres to the letter of the oath regarding Absalom
in 2 Sam. 14.21-24, while failing to adhere to its spirit, also foreshadows his advice

Fokkelman has summed up quite excellently the movement of the narrative in 2 Samuel 13–14. A combination of illusion and reality holds together the texts in this section of the book:

> The illusion: David thinks that he is visiting an ailing Amnon, that he is sending his sons to a feast, and that he is hearing a widow pleading for her son. The reality: Amnon, full of energy, is on the way to gratifying his sexual appetite, Absalom kills his brother, and Joab tries to arrange a reconciliation.[18]

As he goes on to suggest, David, blinded by his ego, repudiates the unity of life and people, dividing Bathsheba from Uriah, divorcing himself from God, dividing his family against itself. From that point onwards the world that is presented to him becomes steadily less reliable, more fragmented and difficult to put together. As David has abused people around him mercilessly, now he is abused. His sons manipulate him, using him for their own crimes.[19] Yet David knows little throughout of what is really happening.

The play on the nature of wisdom and who possesses it does not stop with 2 Samuel 14. The theme of 'the overturning of the king's counsel' is central to chs. 15–17, the story of the decline of Ahithophel forming a meditation on the divine destruction of human plans.[20] In both the stories in 2 Samuel–1 Kings, in fact, in which the king's counsellors are central figures during crucial turns in the monarchy, the particular counsel chosen by the king leads to disaster for that king—Absalom here in Samuel, and Rehoboam in 1 Kings 12.[21] What is striking about 2 Samuel 16–17 in particular is first of all the remarkable statement in 16.23 that both David and Absalom (but not the narrator) regarded the counsel of Ahithophel as equivalent to a word from God. The narrator himself at first appears to lend some weight to the equivalence of the word of Ahithophel and a prophetic oracle, since Ahithophel's advice to Absalom in 16.21 leads on to the fulfilment of Nathan's prediction of

---

to his son about Shimei, and Solomon's subsequent behaviour in respect of the latter, in 1 Kgs 2. See further Provan, *1 and 2 Kings*, pp. 31-42; *idem*, 'Why Barzillai of Gilead (1 Kings 2.7)?: Narrative Art and the Hermeneutics of Suspicion in 1 Kings 1-2', *TynBul* 46 (1994), pp. 103-16.

18. Fokkelman, *Narrative Art*, pp. 156-57.

19. Fokkelman, *Narrative Art*, pp. 158-61.

20. Polzin, *David*, p. 169.

21. The theme continues in passages like 1 Kgs 22, where it is demonstrated that false prophets are as hopeless from this point of view as counsellors.

12.11 about David's wives. It becomes clear in 17.14, however, that
Absalom and David are guilty of a misperception; for God is perfectly
well prepared to frustrate even the good counsel of Ahithophel in order
to carry out his plans. Indeed the very point appears to be this: 'whether
good or bad, wise or foolish, merely human advice lacks the providential status and epistemological guarantees that result from seeking
out or inquiring of the LORD'.[22] The way the story is told makes it
clear that it is indeed to be the word of God, and not the counsel of
men, that carries out God's curse upon the house of David. Human wisdom, of itself, is not up to the task.

We follow our theme, finally, into 2 Samuel 18–20. We have already
met Ziba and Mephibosheth, but here we also meet Barzillai—someone
who refuses David's offer of patronage because of his great age, and
the fact (among others) that he is unable to tell the difference between
good and evil (19.35). It may be that this is at one level simply a statement about his inability to enjoy life at the royal court. It is difficult in
the context of the story as we have read it, however, not also to see in
Barzillai's words the implication that service in the royal court, as an
extension of the crown, involves the keen discernment claimed for
David earlier in the story,[23] and that old age does not necessarily bring
improvement to this ability to discern which kings and their courtiers
require. It is that sad reality which 1 Kings 1 goes on to illustrate with
its picture of the aged David, never very *good* at discerning things, and
now utterly *unable* to do so. We are thus faced with the irony that Barzillai, in questioning his own ability to discern and in refusing a place at
court, shows considerably more wisdom than the aged David, still on
the throne yet unable to know anything of what is around him. It is
perhaps no surprise in this context that it is not even his own wisdom
that David eventually deploys on his death bed, when advising Solomon to deal decisively with his enemies. David had never proved himself so decisive. This is very much wisdom learned from someone
else—the last wise person mentioned in 2 Samuel, and the last foil to
the wise king David. I refer to the wise woman from Abel beth-maacah
in 2 Samuel 20 who saves her city by having the rebel Sheba executed.
The political wisdom which David requires of his son is the wisdom of
this resourceful woman, much more than it is the wisdom of the angel
of God. It is the wisdom also of the doomed counsellor Ahithophel in

22. Polzin, *David*, p. 168.
23. Ackerman, 'Knowing', pp. 42, 51.

2 Samuel 17—the wisdom which seeks blessing through the death of the enemy—rather than the wisdom of 1 Kings 3, which looks for better ways of governing the people.

Conclusion

What manner of wisdom is this wisdom of David, then, that provides the background for the description of the wisdom of Solomon? It is a highly questionable sort of wisdom, I believe. It is not just the waning David of 1 Kings 1–2 who does not know good and evil, and who hands on a dubious view of wisdom to his son. The David of the entire preceding Samuel narrative is a king whose mind is darkened as he lives his life under divine judgment, 'under the curse'.[24] Under these circumstances his wisdom is of no avail as he faces his troubles. He is no match for Jonadab or the Tekoan woman; he comes off badly in comparison to Barzillai, and he fails to convince us of his wisdom in regard to Saul's family. On the one occasion in the story that the failure of another's wisdom redounds to David's advantage, the narrator pointedly tells us that it was not David who truly engineered it, but God.[25] It is not that we are to think, of course, that the wisdom of the other characters in the story is necessarily beyond question either. The wisdom that in 2 Samuel 13 facilitates rape, or that in ch. 14 eases Absalom's return and rebellion, or that in chs. 16–17 advocates the humiliation or execution of David—this is not intended to be wisdom of which the reader should think well. It is not just Davidic wisdom that is under a cloud in 2 Samuel, therefore, but the very notion of human wisdom *at all*, as it seeks to function in independence of the divine will.

The whole David story from 2 Samuel 12 onwards therefore helps to prepare us for Solomon's vision at Gibeon in 1 Kings 3 and what comes afterwards. If one way of looking at the David story of the latter part of 2 Samuel is to see it as the tale of a king divided against himself because he is divided from God, and therefore fostering division in his

24. The phrase is Carlson's, *David*, who places the entire second part of 2 Samuel (chs. 9–24) under this heading. This precise division of the book at ch. 9 owes more to Rost's theory that Carlson disavows, of course, than to his own analysis of the content (since David does not, in fact, come under the curse until chs. 11–12)—a further indication of the tenacity of critical tradition.

25. On this point, see further W. Brueggemann, *First and Second Samuel* (Int; Louisville: John Knox Press, 1990), pp. 312-13.

family and his land, then one way of looking at the beginning of the
Solomon story is to see it as the tale of a king putting his father's later
example behind him, learning once again what it is to be a man after
God's own heart, and being able therefore to govern a united kingdom
once again with justice. If the theme of 2 Samuel 9–1 Kings 2 is 'that
which has been divided cannot be reunited, unless one has the wisdom
of the angel of YHWH',[26] then Solomon's early and later reigns *both*
illustrate that truth. The early Solomon illustrates it positively and the
later Solomon negatively; for it is as the later Solomon himself forgets
that the fear of the Lord is the beginning of wisdom—that wisdom can
only truly be wise when it springs from worship and obedience—that
the kingdom is once more divided. Solomon, like his father, begins
under divine blessing and ends under divine curse. I would therefore
want to affirm these words of Ackerman, near the end of his article: 'the
Court History is a critique of the wisdom of the wise'.[27] It is important,
however, to make this qualification: that in the light of the Kings sequel
to Samuel we can see that it is in fact a critique of a *particular* sort of
wisdom only—wisdom that is not rooted in God and the divine Torah.
We find the same two wisdoms, of course, in the New Testament, and a
similar critique of one and praise of the other. There is the wisdom from
below which is vain philosophy; and the wisdom from above, which we
must embrace if we are to think and act in accordance with the divine
will.

It is to my mind fairly evident that our biblical text of 2 Samuel–
1 Kings as a whole text addresses the theme of wisdom in much the
way I have described it. It is only inherited assumptions brought to the
text without much reflection from outside it that are capable of dulling
our wits sufficiently to miss the point. It is because these assumptions
have been so widely held, indeed, that the kind of holistic reading of the
wisdom theme in both Samuel and Kings that I have attempted here has
not generally been pursued, even though various scholars over the years
have touched in different ways on the theme in Samuel in offering revi-
sions of Rost's position. The Rost paradigm had already set boundaries
in their minds as to what their task should be. It is also quite clear, in
my view, that the sort of cross-referencing and allusion that we find
throughout this section of text, as the authors invite us through the way
in which they tell the story to ponder a particular section in the light of

26. Ackerman, 'Knowing', p. 60.
27. Ackerman, 'Knowing', p. 56.

the whole, is in fact a feature of the entire David and Solomon story, and beyond that of the whole narrative of the Former Prophets. If this is so, and the level of interwovenness of our narrative texts is thus vastly greater than was ever suspected by traditional source or redaction critics, then it can readily be seen how the very constructs which have rendered readers just as blind as David to the reality around them will increasingly come under pressure. If it was difficult enough under the old rules of the game to talk convincingly about a Succession Narrative or a Court History, partly because Rost's claims (and indeed other claims after him) about the self-containedness of his literary unit could not be sustained, how much more difficult will it continue to be under the new. That is not to say that the attempt will not be made; for the power of the constructs themselves, and the will of the crowd to believe in them, or at least to use words which imply that they do, should not be underestimated.[28] It would be comforting to think that the time must surely come when exegetes begin to question whether it is worth holding on to words and concepts which have long since lost their meaning—and which indeed run the risk of distorting their reading of the text—just because they happen to be words and concepts found in the official dictionary of critical orthodoxy. If I really thought this, however, I would surely be guilty of the naivety of the boy who thought he saw the emperor clearly, when he was merely under-educated in the sociology of knowledge.

---

28. I note, for example, that Ackerman ('Knowing', pp. 56-57), almost a decade after Ackroyd and for all his perceptiveness about the ways in which the books of Samuel constitute a unified work, cannot quite bring himself to believe in one author for the work, but posits instead a Court History which deliberately continues themes and elements from the History of David's Rise. I note further that Polzin (*David*) whose wonderful treatment of the David story provides countless examples of the art and ambiguity, the theological complexity of the book, cannot prevent himself speaking about a Deuteronomist, even though his description of the story bursts through the boundaries which exist in most people's minds regarding what this term means.

'FROM ONE DEGREE OF GLORY TO ANOTHER':
THEMES AND THEOLOGY IN ISAIAH

H.G.M. Williamson

It is now some 30 years since I wrote my first series of undergraduate essays on the Old Testament prophets under the supervision of Ronald Clements. The titles, so far as I can recall, were all fairly standard: 'The marriage of Hosea', 'The early prophecies of Jeremiah in their historical setting', and so on. In this series, the book of Isaiah was, of course, treated in its separate sections, 'The Immanuel prophecy' and 'Isaiah and Hezekiah' covered the first part of the book, while a more synthetic treatment of 'The major themes of Deutero-Isaiah' introduced the second. For many of these assignments I was happy to find that there was an essay by Rowley to guide me.[1] Here common sense was applied to the evaluation of a wide range of scholarly opinion to enable the tyro to arrive at what seemed to be solid historical ground for understanding the life and authentic spoken ministry of each individual prophet. There was a sense of confidence about the results, even if it sometimes drove rather a wedge between the scholar and other members of the community who wished to make constructive use of the Bible for their theology and praxis.

If the scene looks different today, then that is due in no small measure to the many probing and innovative writings of Clements himself, from whom we have all continued to learn, sometimes in agreement and sometimes in dialogue. With regard to the book of Isaiah in particular, he is rightly credited with being one of the first to open up the study of the unity of the book as a legitimate field of inquiry. Indeed, so common has this approach now become that it is difficult for us to recapture the atmosphere of those days when another pioneer in the field, Clements's predecessor in the chair at King's College, London, could broach

1.   See especially H.H. Rowley, *Men of God: Studies in Old Testament History and Prophecy* (London: Thomas Nelson, 1963).

the subject in public only after carefully guarding himself against the charge of a return to fundamentalism[2]—and that was scarcely 20 years ago!

Briefly to trace the course of these changes through Clements's writings, we may note that a characteristic of his earlier work on the first half of the book was to adopt and develop international trends in the redaction-critical approach to these chapters, an approach which had long typified his work in general.[3] In particular, he moved beyond Barth's well-known theory of a Josianic, anti-Assyrian redaction[4] to argue in addition for a less extensive redaction which reflected on the fall of Judah and Jerusalem to the Babylonians in 587 BCE.[5] This conclusion, which indicated that work on an early form of Isaiah continued into the exilic period and aligned it to a certain extent with the other two major prophetic books of Jeremiah and Ezekiel, seems to have

2. P.R. Ackroyd, 'Isaiah i-xii: Presentation of a Prophet', in *Congress Volume, Göttingen 1977* (VTSup, 29; Leiden: E.J. Brill, 1978), pp. 16-48, reprinted in Ackroyd, *Studies in the Religious Tradition of the Old Testament* (London: SCM Press, 1987), pp. 79-104. This latter collection includes some other of Ackroyd's influential essays on this topic.

3. See especially *Isaiah and the Deliverance of Jerusalem: A Study of the Interpretation of Prophecy in the Old Testament* (JSOTSup, 13; Sheffield: JSOT Press, 1980), and *Isaiah 1-39* (NCB; Grand Rapids: Eerdmans; London: Marshall, Morgan and Scott, 1980). A number of essays both at that time and since continue in this vein, e.g., ' "A Remnant Chosen by Grace" (Romans 11:5): The Old Testament Background and Origin of the Remnant Concept', in D.A. Hagner and M.J. Harris (eds.), *Pauline Studies: Essays Presented to Professor F.F. Bruce on his 70th Birthday* (Exeter: Paternoster Press, 1980), pp. 106-21; 'Isaiah 14, 22-27: A Central Passage Reconsidered', in J. Vermeylen (ed.), *The Book of Isaiah* (BETL, 81; Leuven: Leuven University Press/Peeters, 1989), pp. 253-62; and 'The Immanuel Prophecy of Isa. 7:10-17 and its Messianic Interpretation', in E. Blum, C. Macholz and E.W. Stegemann (eds.), *Die hebräische Bibel und ihre zweifache Nachgeschichte: Festschrift für Rolf Rendtorff zum 65. Geburtstag* (Neukirchen–Vluyn: Neukirchener Verlag, 1990), pp. 225-40, reprinted in Clements, *Old Testament Prophecy: From Oracles to Canon* (Louisville: Westminster/John Knox Press, 1996), pp. 65-77.

4. H. Barth, *Die Jesaja-Worte in der Josiazeit: Israel und Assur als Thema einer produktiven Neuinterpretation der Jesajaüberlieferung* (WMANT, 48; Neukirchen–Vluyn: Neukirchener Verlag, 1977); see too J. Vermeylen, *Du prophète Isaïe à l'apocalyptique: Isaïe, I-XXXV, miroir d'un demi-millénaire d'expérience religieuse en Israël*, I (Etudes bibliques; Paris: Gabalda, 1977).

5. 'The Prophecies of Isaiah and the Fall of Jerusalem in 587 B.C.', *VT* 30 (1980), pp. 421-36.

played a significant role in the development of his thought about the connection between the main parts of the book. In his first publication directly to address this issue, the problem is approached very much as an extended exercise in redaction criticism, for

> once the connection between the prophecies of Isaiah and the destruction of Jerusalem is recognized as a factor in the way the book of Isaiah came to be developed, we have the single most essential clue towards understanding why the prophecies of chapters 40 and following came to be incorporated into the book.[6]

It is a characteristic of all the major prophetic collections that divine threats 'are followed and counterbalanced by divine promises'. Along with this point, there are also observations on other redactional adumbrations of the later parts of the book now included in chs. 1–39 as well as the fact that parts of chs. 56–66 have links back to the earlier chapters in such a way that they cannot ever have been meant to be understood in isolation from them.

Specific themes which cut across the traditional boundaries of Isaiah receive only brief mention, but they became the subject of a later, separate study[7] to which frequent reference has subsequently been made by others, and indeed Clements has himself continued since to add further examples of such overarching themes.[8] Initially he restricted himself to

---

6. 'The Unity of the Book of Isaiah', *Interpretation* 36 (1982), pp. 117-29 (127), reprinted in Clements, *Old Testament Prophecy*, pp. 93-104 (102).

7. 'Beyond Tradition-History: Deutero-Isaianic Development of First Isaiah's Themes', *JSOT* 31 (1985), pp. 95-113, reprinted in *Old Testament Prophecy*, pp. 78-92. This essay has also appeared in P.R. Davies (ed.), *The Prophets: A Sheffield Reader* (The Biblical Seminar, 42; Sheffield: Sheffield Academic Press, 1996), pp. 128-46.

8. For instance, 'Patterns in the Prophetic Canon: Healing the Blind and the Lame', in G.M. Tucker, D.L. Petersen and R.R. Wilson (eds.), *Canon, Theology, and Old Testament Interpretation: Essays in Honor of Brevard S. Childs* (Philadelphia: Fortress Press, 1988), pp. 189-200; 'A Light to the Nations: A Central Theme in the Book of Isaiah', in J.W. Watts and P.R. House (eds.), *Forming Prophetic Literature: Essays on Isaiah and the Twelve in Honor of John D.W. Watts* (JSOTSup, 235; Sheffield: Sheffield Academic Press, 1996), pp. 57-69; 'Zion as Symbol and Political Reality: A Central Isaianic Quest', in J. van Ruiten and M. Vervenne (eds.), *Studies in the Book of Isaiah* (W.A.M. Beuken Festschrift; BETL, 132; Leuven: Leuven University Press/Peeters, 1997), pp. 3-17; '"Arise, shine; for your light has come": A Basic Theme of the Isaianic Tradition', in C.C. Broyles and C.A. Evans (eds.), *Writing and Reading the Scroll of Isaiah: Studies of an Interpretive Tradition*

material in Deutero-Isaiah, where a case could be made out for the view that the later prophet was aware of, and specifically alluded to, the work of his predecessor. More recently, this has been extended to examples of two-way influence, that is to say, from the earlier part of the book on to the later, and then back again to still later redactional material now included within the first part of the book. The effect of the accumulation of such examples is to stress the unity of the book in two ways: first, to indicate that it is not just a case of the late stitching together of works which were originally written separately, but that the later writers always had the work of the earlier ones in view and so wrote consciously in continuation of their work; and, secondly, to suggest that the whole book has in turn been the subject of what may be called overall editorial work.

In all this activity, Clements has been far from a lone voice, and the number even of survey articles of works which follow similar paths has grown considerably. Some, of course, would urge that we should go one step further by dropping all pretence that we can arrive at a satisfactory reading of the book—theological or otherwise—through attention to the stages of its growth. The questions of literary analysis and dating are so uncertain of resolution that to base an interpretation upon them is to build our hermeneutical house on sand; it would be better to acknowledge the fact and locate meaning firmly in the reader.[9] For most, however (and I believe this would include Clements himself), the unity of Isaiah, such as it is, is too complex for this to be satisfying. It is precisely because as modern readers we are aware of the many tensions and different points of view in the text, of the facts that the book is by no means seamless and that it manifests abundant testimony to historical depth and development, that we crave a reading which will do justice to our sense of hard-won critical gain. To be postcritical implies that we have first been critical; in the scholarly world, there is no short-cut to modernity.

To pursue this line does not, of course, make the task of interpretation any easier, and in the present essay it will not be possible to do more than indicate guidelines for further work. I propose, therefore, to take two examples, each of which follows a separate (though related)

    9.   See, for instance, the discussion of these issues in R.F. Melugin and M.A. Sweeney (eds.), *New Visions of Isaiah* (JSOTSup, 214; Sheffield: Sheffield Academic Press, 1996). The volume is dedicated to Ronald Clements.

path of the kind which Clements has outlined, to discuss them in their own right, and to reflect briefly upon them as illustrations of reading strategies to which, if I understand them aright, the texts themselves would seem to point.

The first, and easier, example concerns a passage from the last section of the book. It has become a commonplace nowadays to observe that much of the material in Isaiah 56–66 picks up, reflects on and develops material from the earlier parts of the book. This suggests that those responsible for these chapters had a sense of seeking to draw the diverse lines of thought together in order to bring a sense of closure to the whole. Indeed, writing on Isaiah 60 Clements has most recently found so many allusions to earlier material as to label the chapter 'midrashic', explaining that it is designed 'to give a new coherence and credibility to themes and mythical motifs which had a very long history', and observing that it was 'intended to provide a kind of summarising and framing role within a much larger collection'.[10] If such a view can be sustained, then it will suggest that the interpreter of the finished book would do well to read the earlier passages through the synthesizing lens of these closing chapters.

What Clements has proposed for ch. 60 has equally been suggested for other passages. In development of this approach, I should like to propose that the same applies to the figure who presents himself in the first person at the start of ch. 61. This appears not to have been considered before because commentators generally try to conform him to one particular 'type', such as that of the servant or a prophet. I shall argue that this fails to do justice to the many lines of thought from earlier in the book of Isaiah which lead into this description, so making of him a far more composite character than has previously been recognized.

The figure states first that 'The spirit of the Lord God is upon me'. This is generally recognized as an allusion to the endowment of the servant in 42.1, and behind that verse there is probably a further specific reference to the royal figure of 11.1. In both these earlier occurrences endowment with the spirit was to prepare the figure in question to exercise a judicial role, appropriate to his royal status.[11] Although that is not

10. '"Arise, shine"', pp. 450 and 449 respectively.
11. For the royal characteristics of the servant in Isa. 42, see, e.g., O. Kaiser, *Der königliche Knecht: Eine traditionsgeschichtlich-exegetische Studie über die Ebed-Jahwe-Lieder bei Deuterojesaja* (FRLANT, 70; Göttingen: Vandenhoeck & Ruprecht, 1959), pp. 14-31, and A. Laato, *The Servant of YHWH and Cyrus: A*

so obviously the case in ch. 61, it would be possible to see in the continuation of the passage a description of part of the royal task of defending the cause of the poor and disadvantaged.

Influenced, no doubt, by what is to follow, most commentators prefer to see in this phrase a reference to a prophetic role,[12] not least because that may be thought the most obvious interpretation for a first-person reference in a prophetic book. In a passage where references to previous written texts are so prominent, however, it seems to me preferable to say that the speaker is marking himself out as in the succession not just of the old established offices of king or prophet, but rather of the newer role of servant, a role which in itself, of course, combined elements of both the earlier ones.[13]

The figure tells us, secondly, that 'the Lord has anointed me'. Reading within the context of the book of Isaiah, this can allude only to the role of Cyrus as conqueror of Babylon and liberator of Israel (cf. Isa. 45.1). In view of the tasks entrusted to our present figure in the following lines, it is surprising that, so far as I am aware, the possibility has been ignored that he is here claiming to take over those parts of Cyrus's role which still remain to be fulfilled.[14] That seems to be the obvious implication.

The reason for this neglect is again that the commentators have been too quick to try to accommodate all that is said in this passage to one specific office. However, because outside the book of Isaiah anointing is mostly associated with the king, a role not thought suitable for the present figure, it is frequently stated that the reference here must be understood metaphorically.[15] It would seem more plausible, however, to

Reinterpretation of the Exilic Messianic Programme in Isaiah 40-55 (ConBOT, 35; Stockholm: Almqvist and Wiksell, 1992), pp. 74-87. In the light of Isa. 55.3, this does not, of course, rule out an identification of the servant in this passage with (a possibly idealized) Israel.

12. See, for instance, C. Westermann, *Das Buch Jesaja, Kapitel 40-66* (ATD, 19; Göttingen: Vandenhoeck & Ruprecht, 4th edn, 1981), p. 291 (ET *Isaiah 40–66: A Commentary* [OTL; London: SCM Press, 1969], p. 365), and R.N. Whybray, *Isaiah 40–66* (NCB; London: Oliphants, 1975), p. 240.

13. Cf. W. Lau, *Schriftgelehrte Prophetie in Jes 56–66: Eine Untersuchung zu den literarischen Bezügen in den letzten elf Kapiteln des Jesajabuches* (BZAW, 225; Berlin: W. de Gruyter, 1994), pp. 66-79.

14. Though see briefly O.H. Steck, *Studien zu Tritojesaja* (BZAW, 203; Berlin: W. de Gruyter, 1991), p. 132 n. 60.

15. E.g.: 'The second line uses the word "to anoint" in a non-literal and trans-

speak here rather of a literary allusion to the role of Cyrus. This would help explain the obviously royal overtones of the combining of spirit and anointing, at which most commentators have baulked. It does not, of course, make the speaker a king, but he fulfils some of the same functions. Nor need we conclude that he necessarily identified the servant as Cyrus, as some have done at least with regard to 42.1-4. Rather, a picture begins to emerge of this figure taking over a combination of some of the major actors in Deutero-Isaiah's salvation drama.

The next thing that our figure says of himself is that the Lord 'has sent me'. Here, there is general agreement, which there is no need to question, that this is particularly characteristic of the call to the prophetic office.[16] It certainly cannot be derived from the royal tradition, and indeed it stands in some tension with it, since 'anointing' is generally to a permanent office, whereas 'sending' implies a specific task. The uneasy juxtaposition of the two verbs here, therefore, is a further indication that we should hesitate before trying to press all the characteristics of this speaker into a single institutional mould.

It is likely that the prominence of the theme of sending in the commissioning of Isaiah himself in 6.8 has been particularly influential here,[17] especially in view of the links between that chapter and Isaiah 40 (itself recalled more than once in the present passage, as we shall

---

ferred sense, something like "to give full authorization"' (Westermann); 'this is obviously to be taken metaphorically' (Whybray); 'just as the anointing of Cyrus in 45.1 is metaphorical, so too is the servant's anointing metaphorical and not literal' (P.A. Smith, *Rhetoric and Redaction in Trito-Isaiah: The Structure, Growth and Authorship of Isaiah 56-66* [VTSup, 62; Leiden: E.J. Brill, 1995], p. 25). The alternative attempt to associate the anointing with that of the high priest seems less likely; cf. W. Caspari, 'Der Geist des Herrn ist über mir', *Neue kirchliche Zeitschrift* 40 (1929), pp. 729-47; H. Cazelles, *Le messie de la Bible: Christologie de l'Ancien Testament* (Paris: Desclée, 1978), p. 156; P. Grelot, 'Sur Isaïe LXI: la première consécration d'un grand prêtre', *RB* 97 (1990), pp. 414-31.

16. For references, see W.A.M. Beuken, 'Servant and Herald of Good Tidings: Isaiah 61 as an Interpretation of Isaiah 40–55', in Vermeylen (ed.), *Book of Isaiah*, pp. 411-42, especially p. 415, and Smith, *Rhetoric*, p. 24. K. Koenen, *Ethik und Eschatologie im Tritojesajabuch: Eine literarkritische und redaktionsgeschichtliche Studie* (WMANT, 62; Neukirchen–Vluyn: Neukirchener Verlag, 1990), p. 104, emphasizes in particular the importance of the construction with dependent infinitives following in this connection, while Beuken, 'Servant and Herald', pp. 416-17, observes that strings of infinitives also characterize the servant's task in chs. 42, 49 and 50.

17. Cf. P. B. Wodecki, 'šlḥ dans le livre d'Isaïe', *VT* 34 (1984), pp. 482-88.

see) which suggest that Deutero-Isaiah's commissioning was under-stood as in some sense an extension of that of his eighth-century prede-cessor.[18] In addition to what has already been noted, therefore, the char-acter depicted in Isaiah 61 also claims prophetic status for himself, and in particular that he stands in continuity with the prophet(s) of the ear-lier parts of the book.

We come next to what the speaker is commissioned to do. Basing ourselves on the usual line in two halves of Hebrew poetry, this may be summed up by the string of four infinitives: 'to bring good news...to proclaim...to proclaim...to comfort'. Each of these is given a degree of emphasis by different means, the first by the unusual word order in the Hebrew text, the second and third by virtue of repetition, and the last by the fact that it is amplified by an additional complete line.[19]

'To bring good news ($l^e ba\acute{s}\acute{s}\bar{e}r$)' is a prominent verb in Deutero-Isaiah. In 41.27 God says that he is going to 'give to Jerusalem a herald of good tidings ($m^e ba\acute{s}\acute{s}\bar{e}r$)'. This is the climax of one of the trial speeches directed against the idols in which particular reference is made to the exploits of Cyrus. The good news in question, therefore, is the very heart of this prophet's message, and it is directed to Jerusalem, which here stands in parallel with Zion. At 52.7 we find the verb used twice at the start of a passage which is rightly recognized by many as marking the climax of Deutero-Isaiah's work. Again, as at 41.27, the good news is relayed by some unidentified messenger to Zion. And finally, it is difficult to overlook the close connection in both language and thought between this verse and 40.9 in the prologue to the work. Here, a slight distinction is to be noted, in that Zion/Jerusalem probably

18. Cf. C.R. Seitz, 'The Divine Council: Temporal Transition and New Proph-ecy in the Book of Isaiah', *JBL* 109 (1990), pp. 229-47, and 'How is the Prophet Isaiah Present in the Latter Half of the Book? The Logic of Chapters 40–66 within the Book of Isaiah', *JBL* 115 (1996), pp. 219-40; R. Albertz, 'Das Deuterojesaja-Buch als Fortschreibung der Jesaja-Prophetie', in Blum *et al.* (eds.), *Die Hebrä-ische Bibel*, pp. 241-56; K. Holter, 'Zur Funktion der *Städte* Judas in Jesaja xl 9', *VT* 46 (1996), pp. 119-21.

19. Something seems to have gone wrong with the text at the start of v. 3, which slightly obscures the otherwise balanced structure. A plausible solution is the pro-posal that the words translated 'to provide for those who mourn in Zion' should be bracketed as an exegetical gloss on the preceding 'all who mourn' (i.e. 'to be applied to those who mourn in Zion'), with the result that the poetic balance of the remainder is neatly restored; cf. K. Koenen, 'Textkritische Anmerkungen zu schwierigen Stellen in Tritojesajabuch', *Bib* 69 (1988), pp. 564-73 (567-68).

becomes herself the herald rather than the recipient of good tidings. It is striking, however, that there is an ancient and widespread alternative tradition of interpretation, going back at least as far as the Septuagint, which would make Zion/Jerusalem the recipient of the good news: 'O thou that tellest good tidings to Zion'.[20] It would not be at all surprising if Trito-Isaiah already understood the word in this sense, in view of its later use in Deutero-Isaiah. Either way, it seems that he saw here an additional role being portrayed in the work of his predecessor and that, like the others already examined, he absorbed it into his own new persona.

The verb 'to proclaim' (*qārā'*) is, of course, extremely common, so that we should be cautious about building too much upon its repeated occurrence here. Nevertheless, in view of the links that are already beginning to be established between this passage and the opening of Deutero-Isaiah's work (and there is more to follow), it is tempting to suppose that another specific reference is intended here, for the same verb comes no less than four times in Isa. 40.2-6. It is now generally agreed that the imperative plural in v. 2 points to a scene in the heavenly court, where, as in other portrayals of such a setting, such as Isaiah 6 itself, there is a dialogue between, and commands issued to, God's attendant ministers. The voice of one crying out in 40.3-5 and the dialogue about what to cry in vv. 6-8 should then no doubt be seen in the same context. Of course, we cannot be sure that this will still have been understood by the time of Trito-Isaiah; in due course, the plural came to be understood as an address to the priests (so the Septuagint) or to the prophets (so the Targum). The most that we can suggest, therefore, is that whoever he thought was entrusted with this message, he understood it as now being taken over by the character depicted in 61.1-3.

'To comfort' (*naḥēm*) is the last in this series of emphasized infinitives, and in view of what we have already seen the suggestion is obvious that it should be related to the very first words of Isaiah 40: 'Comfort, O comfort my people'. This indication of its importance to Deutero-Isaiah is reinforced by the fact that the verb recurs a number of times in his work (49.13; 51.3, 12, 19; 52.9; 54.11), and it is further of interest to note that in all these cases there is reference in the immediate context to Zion/Jerusalem, as was the case with 'bringing good news'.

20. Cf. R.W. Fisher, 'The Herald of Good News in Second Isaiah', in J.J. Jackson and M. Kessler (eds.), *Rhetorical Criticism: Essays in Honor of James Muilenburg* (Pittsbugh: The Pickwick Press, 1974), pp. 117-32.

To sum up on these three verbs, we have seen that they all appear in the prologue to Deutero-Isaiah, that in at least two cases they are also of thematic importance in the rest of Isaiah 40–55 and that in these same two cases they are closely associated with comfort/good news for Zion/Jerusalem. Interestingly, none of them is used to describe the work of the servant in the servant passages as usually designated, even though, as we saw, there are significant allusions to this material at the start of the passage, and some more evidence to the same effect will be presented shortly. The impression therefore continues to build up of a character who somehow gathers to himself every available role in Deutero-Isaiah which is related to the work of announcing and inaugurating God's salvation.

The remaining phraseology in Isa. 61.1-3 mainly describes those to whom this figure ministers. Since we have seen that our author was working particularly with Deutero-Isaiah in mind, it is possible that even casual references may potentially be of significance. On the other hand, individual words which lack the kind of wider contextual support which we have presented up till now cannot carry the same weight of argument. It therefore seems best simply to lay out the evidence without claiming that anything in our overall case stands or falls on it.

The noun '*ānāw*, 'oppressed', does not occur elsewhere in Isaiah 40–66, but its related adjective '*ānî* is used in Deutero-Isaiah in the plural as a description of exiled Israel (41.17; 49.13) and in the singular as a description of the present afflicted state of Zion/Jerusalem (51.21; 54.11). Words from the same root as *š^{e}bûyîm*, 'captives', are also used generally for the people in their Babylonian captivity (49.24, 25) as well as specifically for daughter Zion (52.2). The term '*^{a}sûrîm*, 'prisoners', is the same as the word used at 42.7 and 49.9 for those whom the servant is to release from prison, presumably an image for the Babylonian exile. The form of *p^{e}qah-qôah*, 'release', has occasioned much debate; however it is to be explained, it is clearly derived from the verb *pqh*, 'to open', and as such it is reminiscent of 42.7, 20. In 'the year of the Lord's favour' there seems to be, as many commentators recognize, an allusion to 49.8, 'in a time of favour I have answered you'. Finally, at the end of the passage the author uses an extremely rare word to describe the condition of those whom he is addressing, *kēhâ*, 'faint (of spirit)'. This may therefore be a conscious echo of the use of the same word to describe those to whom the servant ministers in 42.3.[21]

This list does not, of course, include all the terms found in 61.1-3, and the way some of those which are included is applied is somewhat different. This, however, is only to be expected, for the audience is now back in the land, not in exile in Babylon. The significant point is that the author seems consciously to address them in terms familiar from Deutero-Isaiah. They are the same community as that to which the promise was originally delivered, and he reapplies that same promise to them even in their changed circumstances. Within this, parts of the message coincide with the role of the servant, even though the servant passages by no means cover all the points of possible comparison. It seems reasonable to conclude that he expects to complete the as yet unfinished work of the servant, just as we have already seen that he expects to complete parts of the work of Cyrus and of the other figures alluded to in Deutero-Isaiah.

While these few remarks are very far from constituting a full exegesis of Isa. 61.1-3, enough has been said to draw some conclusions for the topic of interpretation of a decidedly unfashionable nature. In pre-critical days, the various 'messianic' passages in Isaiah, such as the royal oracles in 1–39 and the servant passages in 40–55, were regularly read in the light of each other in order to produce a composite portrait of 'the messiah', and the whole was related to a future figure. With the rise of a more historically-oriented approach to interpretation, this has dropped completely out of favour. Interpreters have been more concerned to draw distinctions, and to allow each passage to speak with its own voice to the times at which it is supposed it was originally written. While I should certainly not wish to argue that we either can or should return to pre-critical readings, it is equally clear that a passage such as 61.1-3 issues a challenge to modern readers not to stop with their historically-bound atomistic approach. Already within the text itself we have found a witness from a relatively late stage in the formation of the book of an attempt to draw together the various heralds and agents of God's salvation into a single figure and to throw off into the future those aspects of their work which remained as yet unfulfilled. This would seem to offer textual warrant, if not demand, for interpretation not to stop at a historically contextualized reading, as though that was all that

21. Cf. K. Pauritsch, *Die neue Gemeinde: Gott sammelt Ausgestossene und Arme (Jesaia 56–66)* (AnBib, 47; Rome: Biblical Institute Press, 1971), p. 110; Koenen, *Ethik*, p. 106.

there was to say. Beyond that, the text's witness to God's announcement of comfort and salvation remains open, and interpretation should ultimately involve moving beyond the historical conditions which first called forth the individual texts towards a synthesis of those underlying principles which unite their disparate expression in separate passages. In its own way, as with several other parts of Isaiah 56–66, 61.1-3 is a challenge to move beyond exegetical fragmentation towards a broader theological synthesis, while at the same time realizing that that synthesis is itself conditioned by the circumstances of the interpreter, so that the task must needs be repeated by each successive generation. Ours will not be identical with that of the author of 61.1-3, but we shall learn to recognize him as a kindred spirit.

The second example that I wish to consider is of a completely different nature, but is equally one that follows to some extent along a path which Clements has blazed for us. It concerns a theme on which various authors and redactors of the book of Isaiah appear to have reflected creatively, their attention to it therefore being scattered throughout the length of the book. The challenge which this will pose to the modern reader concerns the effect of this on the interpretation of the whole.

Clements's essay on the theme of the blind and the lame seems to me to be of particular importance in this regard.[22] Here he takes further his earlier consideration of this theme by pointing out how (partly under the influence of reflection on 2 Sam. 5.6 and 8) this metaphor in Isa. 6.9-10 was transformed into an expectation of literal healing as a mark of the arrival of the kingdom of God. This was already adumbrated in Deutero-Isaiah (where both metaphorical and literal applications of the theme appear side by side), but it reached its fullest expression in one or two late passages now included within the first half of the book (notably at 33.23 and 35.5-6), passages which in turn are raised to particular prominence by the New Testament accounts of the ministry of Jesus and the early church. Thus material which tends to be marginalized in an exclusively historical reading of the text is shown to become centrally important for the later reception of the book.

The situation seems to be not entirely dissimilar with regard to the theme of 'glory ($k\bar{a}b\hat{o}d$)'. While my main interest is in the latest stages of the redaction of Isaiah 1–39, it is necessary first to give brief attention to the background to this theme in earlier parts of the book.[23]

---

22. Clements, 'Patterns'.
23. See too the brief remarks in R. Rendtorff, 'Zur Komposition des Buches

First, when Isaiah hears the seraphim cry that $m^e l\bar{o}'$ kol-$h\bar{a}'\bar{a}re\d{s}$ $k^e b\hat{o}d\hat{o}$ (6.3), it seems probable that reference is made to God's majesty, and even his power. The word $k\bar{a}b\hat{o}d$ occurs in connection with human potentates with this sense at, for instance, 8.7, where 'the king of Assyria and all his glory' clearly includes prominently the thought of the Assyrian army as an impressive display of power; see, too, 16.14; 21.16; and 22.18, in each of which a reference to military might is present in the context. (For probably metaphorical extensions, see, for instance, 5.13; 10.3, 16, 18; 17.4.) Thus, when 6.3 declares of the thrice-holy 'Lord of Hosts' that 'the fulness of the earth is his $k\bar{a}b\hat{o}d$', we are pointed firmly in the direction of the natural world as a reflection of his royal majesty and military might.[24] As is to be expected from the setting in ch. 6, this is a theme which finds many resonances in the Psalms of the Jerusalem cult tradition,[25] and it is likely that its roots lie further back in Canaanite religion.[26] We may note too that, just as the vocabulary for God's exaltation in 6.1 becomes the basis for condemnation of anything else which seeks to usurp that position, so too with his $k\bar{a}b\hat{o}d$; see 3.8.

Deutero-Isaiah both takes up and develops this notion. First, in the eschatological hymn of praise (appropriately) at 42.12, various features of the natural world and their inhabitants are called upon to 'give glory to the Lord' (parallel with 'declare his praise'). Secondly, God continues jealously to guard his glory: 42.8; 48.11. Thus far, we are moving in the same realm of ideas as the earlier writer.

Jesaja', *VT* 34 (1984), pp. 295-320 (ET 'The Composition of the Book of Isaiah', in R. Rendtorff, *Canon and Theology: Overtures to an Old Testament Theology* [OBT; Minneapolis: Fortress Press, 1993; Edinburgh: T. & T. Clark, 1994], pp. 146- 69).

24. Alternatively, though I think less plausibly, T.N.D. Mettinger suggests that 'the entire beauty of Creation makes up the garments of God's majesty... This is appropriate dress for the heavenly King' (*The Dethronement of Sabaoth: Studies in the Shem and Kabod Theologies* [ConBOT, 18; Lund: C.W.K. Gleerup, 1982], p. 119).

25. See H. Wildberger, *Jesaja. I. Jesaja 1–12* (BKAT, 10/1; Neukirchen–Vluyn: Neukirchener Verlag, 2nd edn, 1980), p. 249-50 (ET *Isaiah 1–12: A Commentary* [Minneapolis: Fortress Press, 1991], pp. 266-67), for references.

26. So W.H. Schmidt, *Alttestamentliche Glaube und seine Umwelt: Zur Geschichte des alttestamentlichen Gottesverständnis* (Neukirchen–Vluyn: Neukirchener Verlag, 1968), p. 138 (ET *The Faith of the Old Testament: A History* [Oxford: Basil Blackwell, 1983], p. 154).

Thirdly, however, there seems to be a marked development of the theme at 40.5, and this is likely to be of particular significance in view of the many connections between Isa. 40.1-9 and ch. 6: 'Then the glory of the Lord shall be revealed, and all people ['flesh'] shall see it together'. We notice at once three things. First, the scene is again in the heavenly court. In this setting in ch. 6 God's holiness and glory were recognized and celebrated by the seraphim and, being overheard by the prophet, there is an indication that the same was true within the Jerusalem cult. But for 'this people' at large, it is clear that there was to be no seeing in the sense of understanding (v. 9). Now, however, secondly, this glory is to be seen openly, 'revealed'. That seems to involve not just a shift in human perception (though the emphasis on 'seeing' here suggests, by contrast with 6.9, that this too is included), but in the nature of divine glory itself; whereas previously it was identified with 'the fulness of the earth', now it transcends nature and is seen rather in God's mighty act of preparing the ground for a great and unmistakable epiphany.[27] Although there is still room for considerably further development of this notion, a decisive step has been taken towards God's 'glory' becoming a visible token of his presence. There can be little doubt that specifically Israelite notions which we commonly associate with the Priestly tradition (and behind it, those of Ezekiel) are beginning to make themselves felt here, and they will subsequently be taken up powerfully by later contributors to this book. Finally, however, we cannot fail to note that this epiphany will be witnessed by 'all flesh', a phrase with self-evidently universal overtones. While Zion/Jerusalem remains as the focus of the prophet's attention (vv. 9-11), the implications of what happens there go far beyond any narrowly nationalistic concerns.

In the final major section of the book (chs. 56–66), we again find that older uses of this theme are accompanied by further developments. To list the former briefly in the first place, 59.19 exemplifies the continuation of the notion of God's glory (again parallel with his name) as his exclusive prerogative, while 60.13 ('the glory of Lebanon'; cf. 35.2) and 61.6 indicate that the word can still be used in a theologically neutral sense. More adventurously, 58.8 develops the theme of 40.5 by combining it with the imagery of 52.12 to make clear that 'the glory of the Lord' will serve as a visible equivalent of the pillar of cloud and fire

---

27. The importance of this transformation is stressed in relation to other passages by Mettinger, *Dethronement*, p. 107.

which had guided and guarded the Israelites on their journey through the wilderness (cf. Exod. 13.21-22; 14.19-20). Indeed, it is of interest that 'the glory of the Lord' here stands in the place of God of Israel himself in 52.12 (as in the previous line 'your righteousness' [NRSV, 'your vindicator'] replaces 'the Lord' of 52.12). However, if that much could be gathered from the J narrative in Exodus,[28] we move further in Trito-Isaiah into decidedly more priestly territory as well, with the introduction of the notion for the first time in our survey of the glory of God also resting on Jerusalem, just as it had on the tabernacle in Exod. 29.43; 40.34-35; Lev. 9.6, 23; Num. 14.10; 16.19; 17.7 [ET 16.42], and 20.6, and as Ezekiel asserted had been, and would again be, the case with regard to the Jerusalem sanctuary (cf. Ezek. 9.3; 10.4, 18; 11.23; 43.2, 4).[29] In Trito-Isaiah, however, this is associated less with the sanctuary alone, and more with Jerusalem as a whole; see 60.1-2 and 62.2.

Now it might be suggested that all these varied uses have reached the point where it has become a mistake to speak of a 'theme' here at all; not all word studies in a book can be said to amount to a theme. However, it is striking that the word *kābôd* occurs no less than five times in the closing section of the book, sometimes with evident allusions back to earlier texts, in such a way as to suggest that one ancient author, at least, did see some serious connection between the uses we have been tracing. And this will be all the more significant if indeed, as seems probable, those authors are correct who find in this passage a conscious attempt to provide a suitable conclusion for the book of Isaiah as a whole.[30] Thus in 66.11 there is a reference to the glory of Jerusalem,

28. Cf. B.S. Childs, *Exodus: A Commentary* (OTL; London: SCM Press, 1974), pp. 218-21.
29. See the careful study of S. Tengström, 'Les visions prophétiques du trône de Dieu et leur arrière-plan dans l'Ancien Testament', in M. Philonenko (ed.), *Le trône de Dieu* (WUNT, 1.69; Tübingen: J.C.B. Mohr [P. Siebeck], 1996), pp. 28-99, especially pp. 49-58, who sees clearly the distinction between the representation of God's glory in Isa. 6.3 and in these later texts; see, too, Mettinger, *Dethronement*.
30. See most recently M.A. Sweeney, 'Prophetic Exegesis in Isaiah 65-66', in Broyles and Evans (eds.), *Writing and Reading*, pp. 455-74, with references to earlier studies. Sweeney argues that not only do these chapters function 'as the conclusion of the book of Isaiah' (p. 457), but further that '66.5-24 also makes extensive reference to earlier Isaianic texts, but it does so in a manner different from Isa 65.1–66.4 in that it tends to develop motifs at length rather than simply to cite or allude to an earlier textual tradition. Furthermore, in citing earlier texts and motifs, it builds on statements from Isa 65.1–66.4' (p. 468). It thus serves as a conclusion

and in 66.12 a use of 'glory' more in the sense of wealth which will be transferred to her from the nations. In 66.18 we are told that all nations and tongues 'shall come and shall see my glory', an obvious reflection on 40.5[31] which further makes clear that God's glory is localized in Jerusalem.[32] Then in 66.19 we hear of distant nations 'who have not heard of my fame or seen my glory', and that an unspecified 'they' 'shall declare my glory among the nations'. It seems, therefore, that the 'hardening' saying of 6.9 is to be reversed, not just for Israel but, in the spirit of Deutero-Isaiah, for the nations as well. In short, it is clear that this concluding author of the book was aware of several of the earlier passages to which we have referred and that he deduced synthetically from them that God's exclusive glory was to be seen in Jerusalem and that this would act as a magnet to the nations who would surrender their 'glory' to her in acknowledgment. Thus the glory of God as presented initially in 6.3 has been transformed both by its closer identification with the visible revelation of God himself and by the fact that this is to be seen universally from Jerusalem, not just perceived within the narrow confines of the national cult.

In the light of this cursory outline, we turn finally to three verses now included within the first part of the book: 4.5-6; 11.10; and 24.23. So far as I am aware, they have not previously been considered together, but they are united by some distinctive features. The most striking of these is that they each include a reference to *kābôd* without further qualification, whether definite article, pronominal suffix or construct relationship. This certainly makes an initially disturbing impression when reading, and it is not surprising that commentators have often sought to improve on the text in each case taken separately. The likelihood of the same kind of error occurring three times independently seems remote, however; the three verses are mutually reinforcing. It is also widely agreed that they all come in late—possibly very late—pas-

---

to the conclusion. It is perhaps surprising in this regard that Sweeney makes no mention in his careful study of those points which concern us here.

31. It is noteworthy that the 'all flesh' of that verse recurs in 66.16, 23 and 24, though not specifically in relation to the glory of the Lord. This repetition reinforces the fact that 40.5 was in our author's mind.

32. Isa. 35.2 is another obviously related text ('they shall see the glory of the Lord'), though in this case it is less clear who 'they' are (ransomed Israel or the desert); for introductory discussion, with references, see Rendtorff, 'Komposition', p. 300 n. 19 (ET p. 151 n. 25).

sages. Thus 4.2-6 as a whole is certainly postexilic, and many consider that the closing section, which includes our reference, is a still later addition. As we shall see, 11.10 is an obvious redactional link between the adjacent passages; one, 11.11-16, is exilic, in my opinion,[33] and the concluding verses of the other (11.6-9) probably postexilic. So 11.10 must be even later. And 24.23 comes at the end of the first major unit in the so-called 'Isaiah Apocalypse' (Isa. 24–27), whose date and unity are much debated. The current consensus, with which I agree, is that the section as a whole must be postexilic,[34] and some further consider 24.21-23 to be an even later addition to that.[35] Finally, as we shall see, the use of *kābôd* in each passage shows some similarities. Whether this is sufficient for us to speak of a *kābôd-Schicht* need not, perhaps, be discussed here, though it is tempting!

Isaiah 4.5-6 looks forward to the time following the purification of a remnant left in Jerusalem, and says first that 'the Lord will create over the whole site of Mount Zion and over its places of assembly a cloud by day and smoke and the shining of a flaming fire by night'. Among several remarkable, if not unique, features in this passage, we need note here only that the accounts of the wilderness wanderings, to which we referred earlier, have obviously been drawn upon here again,[36] but that a peculiar development has been introduced, namely that whereas previously the cloud and pillar were to guide and guard Israel on her journey, here they have come to rest, as it were, as a permanent feature of Mt Zion. Priestly notions of the sanctuary have clearly been fused with other expressions for the visible presence of God, and this is both clarified and amplified in the following: 'for over everything *kābôd* will

33. Cf. my *The Book Called Isaiah: Deutero-Isaiah's Role in Composition and Redaction* (Oxford: Clarendon Press, 1994), pp. 125-43; many other commentators would maintain an even later date.

34. See Williamson, *Book*, pp. 175-83, with further references. The most decisive argument, in my opinion, is the wealth of citations in these chapters both from elsewhere in the book of Isaiah as a whole and from a number of other Old Testament books.

35. See recently, for instance, H. Wildberger, *Jesaja. II. Jesaja 13–27* (BKAT, 10/2; Neukirchen–Vluyn: Neukirchener Verlag, 1978), pp. 898-99 (ET *Isaiah 13–27: A Continental Commentary* [Minneapolis: Fortress Press, 1997], p. 453), followed in this instance by Clements, *Isaiah 1–39*, p. 205; Vermeylen, *Du prophète Isaïe*, pp. 360-61, who cites some earlier commentators to the same effect.

36. Cf. J. Vollmer, *Geschichtliche Rückblicke und Motive in der Prophetie des Amos, Hosea und Jesaja* (BZAW, 119; Berlin: W. de Gruyter, 1971), pp. 176-77.

be a canopy and a pavilion; it will serve as a shade by day from the heat, and as a refuge and a shelter from the storm and rain'.[37] These latter images are stereotypical of divine protection, not least elsewhere in Isaiah, and literary dependence is not unlikely. Whereas in 32.2 the reference is to human rulers, in 25.4-5 it is ascribed to God. In the present passage, it is likely that the reference was originally to the cloud and pillar, but, possibly under the influence of 25.4-5, the addition of the intervening *kî 'al-kōl kabod ḥuppâ wᵉsukkâ* turns this even more in the direction of God's personal overshadowing of Mt Zion. Since in this addition *kābôd* is separated from the cloud and pillar as a yet further level of protection, it seems that it serves virtually as a 'buffer' for God himself. The lines of development which we traced above through the earlier parts of Isaiah are here brought to their ultimate conclusion, 'glory' being taken in the most concrete or literal manner possible. The path traced is not unlike that which Clements found in the increasingly literal interpretation of the blind, the deaf and the lame.

A similar outlook may be found, too, in the different context of 11.10. As already noted, the first line of this verse is clearly intended to join the two main halves of this chapter, identifying 'the root of Jesse' from v. 1 with the 'signal to the nations' of v. 12.[38] He or it, we are then told, will be sought by the nations. The different ways in which the 'root of Jesse' and the 'signal to the nations' are used in this verse by comparison with their use in 11.1 and 12 is a further indication that we

37. The text here is uncertain, and commentators are not agreed about the best solution. Since the Masoretic Text's apparent assertion that there will be a canopy over all the glory seems to me to be most unlikely, and since further we have been led to expect, not that God's glory will be veiled, but rather highly visible, I follow those who take *kol* as an absolute, *kōl* (cf. K. Marti, *Das Buch Jesaja* [Kurzer Hand-Commentar zum Alten Testament, 10; Tübingen: J.C.B. Mohr, 1900], p. 51), rejoin the phrase now divided by the Masoretic verse division, and follow the Septuagint in reading *wᵉhāyâ* in place of *tihyeh*, the latter being a reading which will have arisen as a result of the mistaken verse division; cf. G.B. Gray, *A Critical and Exegetical Commentary on the Book of Isaiah I–XXVII* (The International Critical Commentary; Edinburgh: T. & T. Clark, 1912), p. 81. It is also possible that *yômām*, 'by day' (v. 6) should be deleted as a mistaken repetition from v. 5 (cf. Septuagint).

38. For a discussion of the use of metaphor here, together with a survey of the disputed issue whether the reference is to a messianic figure or to the postexilic community as a whole, see K. Nielsen, *There is Hope for a Tree: The Tree as Metaphor in Isaiah* (JSOTSup, 65; Sheffield: JSOT Press, 1989), pp. 140-43.

are dealing here with the work of a later redactor. It is the nations them-selves that are now attracted to this figure rather than their being the place from which the dispersed Israelites will be drawn.

The verse then concludes with what Wildberger rightly describes as 'a strange-sounding clause':[39] $w^e h\bar{a}y^e t\hat{a}\ m^e n\bar{u}\d{h}\bar{a}t\hat{o}\ k\bar{a}b\hat{o}d$, 'and its (or his) resting place will be glory (?)'. The 'resting place' can, of course, be used neutrally of 'home' (as in Ruth 1.9), rest (Isa. 28.2), or a rest-ing-place on a journey (Num. 10.33). More commonly in the Hebrew Bible, however, it refers to the promised land as a place where the Israelites finally came to settle and where they hoped to find security (as, e.g., in Deut. 12.9 [and contrast 28.65]; 1 Kgs 8.56; Isa. 32.18; Ps. 95.11), while sometimes the further step is taken of identifying Zion as the resting place for the ark and so for God himself (Ps. 132.8, 14; 1 Chron. 28.2; in polemical contrast, Isa. 66.1)[40] In so theologically charged a context as Isa. 11.10, it is difficult not to believe that these more specific senses are implied. Although the reference is to 'his' rest-ing place, it is likely that there is also included the overtone that this is the place where the nations' quest will find fulfilment, namely in Zion, the dwelling place of God, a theme anticipated in 2.2-4, and picked up frequently in the second half of the book, some occurrences of which we have noted above in particular association with the idea of Zion's glory. Once again, notions originally associated specifically with the sanctuary are expanded to encompass the city as a whole.

The use of an unqualified $k\bar{a}b\hat{o}d$ at the end of the phrase has not attracted as much comment as might have been expected. Most seem to translate it adjectivally without further elaboration; at the most, it is sometimes suggested that the nations will bring their wealth to Zion, so making it glorious,[41] again a notion which we have already met else-where. In the light of what we have already seen, however, Wildberger is surely right in finding this ultimately unsatisfying and in pressing the sense one step further:

> He is certainly not thinking simply of pomp and circumstance, as would
> be a normal part of life in a royal residence, but might mean that the resi-
> dence of the king would be the place from which the divine, heavenly

39. Wildberger, *Jesaja*, I, p. 459 (ET p. 482).

40. See H. D. Preuß, 'נוח', *ThWAT* V, cols. 297-307.

41. E.g., O. Kaiser, *Das Buch des Propheten Jesaja: Kapitel 1–12* (ATD, 17; Göttingen: Vandenhoeck & Ruprecht, 5th edn, 1981), p. 249 (ET *Isaiah 1–12: A Commentary* [OTL; London: SCM Press, 2nd edn, 1983], p. 263).

glory would break out at the time of salvation. From there, however, it would stream forth across peoples throughout the entire inhabited world.[42]

It seems, therefore, that this verse adds to the culmination of the theme of glory which we found with regard to Israel alone in 4.5-6 that universal dimension which we also expect on the basis of its development in chs. 40–66.

I turn finally to Isa. 24.23. Once again, the focus is explicitly on Mt Zion and Jerusalem, where, we are told, the Lord of hosts 'will reign' (*mālak*). This is set in a truly universal context, for the affirmation of the Lord's rule follows a statement about the punishment of both 'the host of heaven in heaven' and 'the kings of the earth on earth' (v. 21). In view of the fact that references to the Lord as king are extremely rare in the first part of the book (they become more common in the second), it is difficult not to see a reflection on, and extension of, the scene in Isaiah 6, the previous occasion on which the Lord of hosts was celebrated as king. In line with the general outlook of Isaiah 24–27, however, this is now stated to have universal, and even cosmic, implications.

The verse then concludes with another terse expression of the type with which we have by now become familiar: *w^{e}neged z^{e}qēnāw kābôd*, which the NRSV paraphrases as 'and before his elders he will manifest his glory', but which Millar (with a different line division), renders more strikingly as 'And opposite His elders, in Jerusalem, the *kabod*'.[43] The precise identification of 'his elders' is uncertain. Willis has argued forcefully against most other commentators that members of the divine council are intended,[44] but even if he is right it is impossible not to see that there has been influence in the choice of word from Exod. 24.9-11, where in an unprecedented scene various leaders of the people, including the 70 elders, 'saw the God of Israel', and where the following verses further specify that 'the glory of the Lord settled on Mount Sinai, and the cloud covered it' (v. 16) and that 'the appearance of the glory of

---

42. Wildberger, *Jesaja*, I, p. 459 (ET p. 483). Note, too, how Calvin concludes that 'Here, therefore, we have a remarkable proof that God is pleased to dwell continually in his Church' (J. Calvin, *Calvin's Commentaries*. III. *Isaiah* [Grand Rapids: Associated Publishers and Authors, no date], p. 179).

43. W.R. Millar, *Isaiah 24–27 and the Origin of Apocalyptic* (Harvard Semitic Monographs, 11; Missoula: Scholars Press, 1976), p. 36.

44. T.M. Willis, 'Yahweh's Elders (Isa 24, 23): Senior Officials of the Divine Court', *ZAW* 103 (1991), pp. 375-85.

the Lord was like a devouring fire on the top of the mountain in the sight of the people of Israel' (v. 17). Rather like in Isa. 4.5-6, our verse seems therefore to indicate that the manifestation of God's presence in connection with the time of Moses is now transferred to Zion and is referred to without further qualification as *kābôd*.

These three passages, then, gather up a number of the developments of this theme which we have seen elsewhere in the book: the focus on Zion as a whole as the place where God is revealed and seen, the relationship with him there of the nations and their leaders, whether for punishment or salvation, and the drawing together of various depictions of God's presence with his people from the Exodus narratives by a conflation of Sinai, the desert sanctuary and the pillar and cloud. Most striking of all, 'glory' has become virtually a 'buffer' term for God himself, adumbrating the later use of *Shekinah* in the Targums.

Now this is, of course, only one small example of a much wider phenomenon whereby the diachronic development of important theological themes in the book of Isaiah has left its mark even on late additions to the early chapters. From a purely historical perspective we do not have too much difficulty in sorting out the different levels and rearranging them in order of progression. However, as Darr has recently reminded us,[45] this is not the way in which we normally read books. Either, as moderns, we generally start at the beginning and work our way through, so that reading is affected by the order in which the various elements are met in literary succession, or, if it is true that ancient readers worked more atomistically, then they will have been influenced in their interpretation of any one particular passage by their recollection of other passages, regardless of their particular (and least of all their historical) context. Either way, we are confronted with another version of what we saw earlier with regard to Isa. 61.1-3, namely that the drive towards synthesis is far stronger than we have been inclined to allow in scholarly study, and interpretation should in turn take fuller account of this.

Indeed, the theme which I have outlined gives us a particularly striking example of just this. When discussing Isa. 6.3, the point was made strongly that for Isaiah himself the reference to God's glory was very far from what it became later in the book. But in the book as it has reached us, 6.3 cannot be read in this narrow sense alone: it follows

45. K.P. Darr, *Isaiah's Vision and the Family of God* (Louisville: Westminster/John Knox Press, 1994).

4.5-6 in particular, and equally cannot be divorced from the other passages which serve to give it a wider literary context for interpretation. And in this connection we should not fail to notice that the Septuagint translated our phrase in that light: 'the whole earth is full of his glory'. Some commentators inveigh against such a 'misunderstanding' of the Hebrew text,[46] while others propose emending the Masoretic text to make it conform (*māle⁾â* for *me lō'*).[47] Neither are right; the translator was working responsibly to interpret his text in the light of its wider context.[48] It is a theme which was to have a profound influence on many later writers, not least of the New Testament and those who later shaped the heart of the Church's liturgy. We do well not to historicize it away.

46. E.g. R. Wagner, *Textexegese als Strukturanalyse: Sprachwissenschaftliche Methode zur Erschließung althebräischer Texte am Beispiel des Visionberichtes Jes 6, 1-11* (Arbeiten zu Text und Sprache im Alten Testament, 32; St Ottilien: EOS Verlag, 1989), p. 182.

47. Cf. E. Nestle, 'Miscellen 13. Zum Trisagion', *ZAW* 25 (1905), pp. 218-20; Gray, *Isaiah I–XXVII*, p. 108.

48. See L.H. Brockington, 'The Greek Translator of Isaiah and his Interest in ΔΟΞΑ', *VT* 1 (1951), pp. 23-32, who concludes that as *doxa* gained 'more and more emphasis on external appearance, it was an appropriate portmanteau word to use in relation to the appearance of God in theophany. The Hebrew text of Isaiah, notably in the later chapters of the book, had already paved the way for the concentration of interest on the brilliant shining of God's presence and this would be carried by the word δόξα in every [*sic*] reference that had theophanic implications' (pp. 31-32). Specifically on ch. 6, he observes that 'in transmitting the story in Greek the translator substituted "glory" for "train" in the first verse and then evidently intended his readers to take the reference to "glory" in verse 3 in the same way. The whole earth would be full of God's brilliance as was the temple at the moment of Isaiah's vision' (p. 28).

'BECAUSE OF YOU!': AN ESSAY ABOUT THE CENTRE OF THE BOOK OF THE TWELVE

Knud Jeppesen

More than 10 years ago the present writer published a two-volume work on the book of Micah in Danish.[1] For various reasons, which are irrelevant here, the book was never, as planned, translated into English, and consequently, it is not much known outside Scandinavia.

The main thesis of the study was that the formation of a prophetic book like the book of Micah is an example of inner biblical interpretation. The purpose of the book was by means of old or supposedly old prophetic oracles to explain a disaster which the Israelites had experienced, and to inspire a hope through which they could overcome the results of the disaster.

The disaster in question was, I suggested, the destruction of Jerusalem's temple and the exile, but I did not find evidence for a historical fulfilment of the hope in the book of Micah; the return to Jerusalem and the rebuilding of the temple was yet to come. Consequently, I dated the redaction of the book to the period in which 'Evil-Merodach, king of Babylon...lifted up the head of Jehoiachin, king of Judah' (2 Kgs 25.27) near the end of the Babylonian exile. On the other hand, I did not find it impossible to date most of the original oracles, both the prophecies of doom *and* the prophecies of salvation, to the eighth century BCE—but it was not the original date which was the focus of my investigation.

---

1. K. Jeppesen, *Græder ikke saa saare: Studier i Mikabogens sigte* (2 vols.; Aarhus: Århus University Press, 1987). The planned English title was *Weep ye not at all: Studies in the Purpose of the Book of Micah*. The title is a quotation of Mic. 1.10 from old translations, and the point is that the book of Micah in its final form is a comforting text.

Today, where the idea of a history of Israel, including the exile, and the possibility of reconstructing the original prophetic preaching are very much questioned,[2] I do not think we have enough evidence to date an Old Testament text as exactly as I did then, and that is the case when we ask for both the original and the redactional settings. The final form of the book of Micah is later than 587 BCE, no doubt about that, but how much later is impossible to say, and exactly how many of the oracles used in the book come from the eighth century BCE, it is impossible to tell.

But I still think my principal approach to the text of Micah was correct; I agreed and still agree with R.E. Clements, to whom the present volume is dedicated: the interest of the redactional work as part of the canonical process 'lies in the message, not in witness to the prophetic personalities as such'.[3] It is a great honour and pleasure for me to have this opportunity to express gratitude for Professor Clements's inspiration, not only through his printed works, but also and probably even more through the oral discussions we have had over the years, beginning in 1974–75, when I a spent a whole academic year in Cambridge.

2.   The catchwords 'a history of Israel' and 'the original prophetic preaching' bring us into the centre of two large areas of discussion in modern Old Testament research. A very great deal has been written in recent years about the history of Israel narrated in the Old Testament as a tendentious construction rather than historiography; of the voluminous literature I restrict myself to referring to the ongoing discussion in the *European Seminar in Historical Methodology*, of which two volumes have been published; see L.L. Grabbe (ed.), *Can a 'History of Israel' be Written?* (JSOTSup, 245, Sheffield: Sheffield Academic Press, 1997) and *Leading Captivity Captive: 'The Exile' as History and Ideology* (JSOTSup, 278; Sheffield: Sheffield Academic Press, 1998). The problem whether the prophetic books contain biographical material has also provoked many contributions. On this problem, too, I shall restrict myself and mention only one of the books which for me, when I worked on the book of Micah, was an eye opener: R.P. Carroll, *From Chaos to Covenant: Uses of Prophecy in the Book of Jeremiah* (London: SCM Press, 1981).

3.   R.E. Clements, 'Patterns in the Prophetic Canon' in *idem*, *Old Testament Prophecy: From Oracles to Canon* (Louisville: Westminster John Knox Press, 1996), p. 196 (first published in G.W. Coats and B.O. Long [eds.], *Canon and Authority: Essays in Old Testament Religion and Theology* [Philadelphia: Fortress Press, 1977]). The quotation continues, 'even though [the prophetic personalities] cannot remain altogether hidden', a point with which I do not now agree as much as I once did.

In my redactio- and traditio-historical research I compared the book
of Micah with the book of Isaiah, and my approach was then very much
inspired by R.E. Clements. In particular, his book *Isaiah and the Deliverance of Jerusalem* and the articles 'The Prophecies of Isaiah and the
Fall of Jerusalem in 587 B.C.', 'The Unity of the Book of Isaiah', and
not least 'Beyond Tradition-History: Deutero-Isaianic Development of
First Isaiah's Themes' were very much used in my research in those
days.[4] In the following essay I will take up some themes that I worked
upon 10 years ago; I will take my point of departure in a verse from the
book named after Micah, a prophet from the eighth century BCE, and
yet a verse which is mythically as well as historically related to the fall
of Jerusalem in 587 BCE; and then I will discuss the context of this
verse.

1. *The Centre of the Book of Twelve: Micah 3.12*

According to the Masoretes' notes in the Hebrew Bible the reader is
half way through the Book of the Twelve Prophets, when coming to the
words *lākēn biglalᵉkem ṣiyyôn śādeh* in Mic. 3.12. This verse is number
526 out of 1050 verses in the whole Book of the Twelve. The words
'therefore, because of you' connect the claim of some Israelite officials:
'Is not Yahweh in our midst? No evil can come upon us!' with the
threat of God: 'Zion shall be ploughed as a field'. Thus the verses in the
centre of this biblical book deal with topics which are in the centre of
both the theology of the Hebrew Bible and the history of the Israelite
people, and this is probably not without importance

The idea that God is dwelling in the midst (*bᵉqereb*) of Israel is one
of the expressions for God's presence (see, e.g., Exod. 17.7; Num.
11.20), a variant of the formula *Immanuel*, 'God is with us' (cf., e.g.,
Isa. 7.14). And God's presence in Zion is of special ideological and
theological importance.[5] When Yahweh is in the midst of Zion or the
temple, the future is secure and no harm will fall upon the people; his
presence indicates his *ḥesed*, his steadfast love (Ps. 46.6; 48.10).

---

4. *A Study of the Interpretation of Prophecy in the Old Testament* (JSOTSup,
13; Sheffield: JSOT Press, 1980); *VT* 30 (1980), pp. 421-36; *Interpretation* 36
(1982), pp. 117-29; *JSOT* 31 (1985), pp. 95-113.
5. Cf. the subtitle of R.E. Clements, *God and Temple* (Oxford: Basil Blackwell, 1965): *The Idea of the Divine Presence in Ancient Israel*.

The claim, God is 'in our midst', would normally in a Zion context be heard as a manifestation of faith in God, and of piety. But the people who in Micah 3 express their confidence in Yahweh's presence, are leaders, priests and prophets, who have taken advantage of their office and earned money for their own advantage; and as often pointed out, according to the prophets a declaration of piety must not be isolated from the way of life of those who make the declaration. If their ways are wrong, it is in vain that they refer to God's authority.

It is, therefore, no surprise that after the phrase 'because of you' we find a text which speaks of events that express the very opposite of Yahweh's protective presence in Zion. Zion will become field and forest, and the abode of God will become ruins. This probably means that God, at least for the time being, will not reside on Mt Zion.

Just as it is part of biblical ideology or theology that God is present with his blessing and his love, it is also part of that ideology that God can leave a person or a place,[6] and thus take his blessing and love away. Most dramatically this feeling of forsakenness has found an expression in the words of the poet in Ps. 22.2: 'My God, my God, why have you forsaken me?', and indirectly the same feeling is found in prayers for salvation (e.g. Ps. 38.22-23).

Sometimes Yahweh, according to the myth, left the country if not the earth (*hā'āreṣ*), with disastrous consequences for humankind. In the book of Ezekiel we read that 'the elders of Israel' misused this myth and said, 'Yahweh does not see us; Yahweh has left the country' (Ezek. 8.12; cf. 9.9). They behaved like the leaders in Micah 3 and did not acknowledge that their abominations were of consequence for themselves and their people. But in the following chapters Yahweh's glory (*kābôd*) left the temple area (10.18) and the city to go to the mountain east of the city (11.22-23); thus Jerusalem and Zion were laid open to

6. It was already recognized long ago that the idea that Yahweh *left* somebody has its background in Canaanite cultic tradition. F.F. Hvidberg found some traces of the idea, e.g., in Hos. 5.15 in his book, *Graad og Latter i Det gamle Testamente: En Studie i kanaanæisk-israelitisk Religion* (Copenhagen: Bianco Luno, 1938). The posthumous English translation is called *Weeping and Laughter in the Old Testament* (Leiden: E.J. Brill, 1962); see especially Chapter 4, 'Traces of Cultic Weeping in Israelite Life and Literature' (pp. 98-137); in the above-mentioned example, we read: 'When Yahweh leaves his people, they will, in the affliction with which they are visited, seek his face ([Hos. 5] Verse 15)'.

disaster, because Ezekiel's contemporaries did not accept the ethical consequences of Yahweh's presence in the temple.

There is no doubt that the myth about Yahweh's protection of Zion and his presence has been used to interpret events in the history; this has been shown for instance in Clements's above-mentioned book, *Isaiah and the Deliverance of Jerusalem*. The myth about Yahweh leaving the country and not least the temple was used to explain what happened in 587 BCE. This is what is described in an artistic way in Ezekiel 10–11; what the prophet saw in his vision was applied to what happened in history in his days. Another prophet expressed the idea in a poem, Jer. 12.7-13: 'I have left my house, I have given up my heritage, I have given the life of my beloved in the hands of her foe'. The consequence is that the people were given to the wild animals, and the vineyard, the country, became a wilderness.[7]

When scholars in the commentaries discuss the authorship of the prophetic oracles in the book of Micah, most of Micah 3 is normally considered to be Micah's *ipsissima verba*. As already noted, modern research into the prophetic literature has put a question mark against the possibility of proving this. But if, as a working hypothesis, we keep the idea that the words in Mic. 3.11-12 were first spoken in the eighth century BCE, we have to explain what kept this oracle alive among people in Judah and Jerusalem in Micah's time and the years following.

To leave an impression and to be remembered, it is necessary for an oracle to evoke a response in the audience, but there was not, as far as we know the history of the period in question, any event in Micah's day which could be seen as the fulfilment of the disaster described in 3.12— on the contrary, the biblical as well as the extra-biblical sources agree that Sennacherib's siege of Jerusalem was given up without much harm done to the temple and the town. A destruction of Jerusalem, which could be interpreted by means of the words 'Zion shall be ploughed as a field, Jerusalem become ruins, and the mount of the temple hills[8] with

---

7. In Lamentations the same sentiment is found expressed in different types of imagery.

8. It might be of some significance for the understanding of the book of Micah that Jerusalem is twice connected with *bāmôt*, which is a word for pagan sanctuaries. In 1.5 it is used about contemporary Jerusalem, but often considered by commentators to be en error (see n. f to Mic. 1.5 in *BHS*); here in 3.12 it is part of the description of Jerusalem after the disaster. It is a matter of taste, whether to stress a point and a word-play like this in a translation.

forest' and the ideology behind it, did not happen until the Babylonian conquest, more than a century later.

Consequently, if the oracle comes from the eighth century BCE, it seems that the application of the myth concerning a town, which will become ruins if its God leaves it, made sense at least to some of the contemporary audience. The impact of the words cannot have been absurd for all of them, and the possibility that the temple might perish cannot have been totally unknown to them.

On the other hand, the oracle was not outside history, in spite of the fact that the words, as far as we know, were not related to an event in history. The oracle was related to people, contemporary with the text— 'because of *you*', the oracle said; and this is understandable, even when we do not know the exact period. Probably not all officials, who according to v. 11 were accused of superficial worship of God, would accept a connection between what they did and the possibility of a coming disaster—but some people saw the connection, and therefore the saying was remembered without an event to connect it to.

Through the book of Jeremiah, this possibly eighth-century oracle is brought closer to the historical destruction of Jerusalem. In Jer. 26.18 the oracle of doom from Mic. 3.12 is quoted; and it is said indirectly in the following verse that the meaning of 'because of you' had been understood already when Micah prophesied in the days of King Hezekiah. The king and the people of Judah showed their fear of God and pacified him, so the disaster of the prophecy based upon the myth did not happen at that point in history. But, and this is the point of Jeremiah 26, the disaster was still a possibility, and the phrase 'because of you' was therefore reinterpreted in relation to Jeremiah's contemporaries: 'we are inflicting great disaster (*rā'â gᵉdôlâ*) upon ourselves' (v. 19).

It is beyond doubt that the great disaster in the book of Jeremiah is the Babylonian conquest of Jerusalem and the destruction of the temple.[9] This means that in the greater biblical context, Mic. 3.12 is read as a text about the destruction in 587 BCE. This point is also stressed by the fact that the Zion texts in Micah 4 follow immediately after Mic. 3.12 in the present book. In most of this chapter the reader is placed between the fact that the disaster had happened and the hope that the results of the disaster can be cancelled.

9. See, e.g., the context of the same expression in Jer. 32.42.

2. *The Centre of the Book of Micah: Micah 4.12*

The Masoretes did not mark the centre of the single book among the twelve; they considered the *Dodekapropheton* to be one book. There is doubtless much to be learnt from a holistic or a canonical reading of the Book of Twelve—and that is what happens in the modern discussion.[10] But just as it is and has always been legitimate to take units out of the prophetic books and discuss them separately as single entities,[11] so it is still legitimate to deal with, for example, the text between the introductory lines 'The word of Yahweh that came to Micah...' (Mic. 1.1) and 'An oracle (*maśśā'*) about Nineveh' (Nah 1.1) as one unit and look for its centre.

Micah 4.12 is verse number 53 out of the 105 verses in the book of Micah; thus the centre of the book says, 'But they do not know the plans of Yahweh'. This means that a shift of emphasis has taken place in comparison with 3.12. There a *you* (plural), a group of people, is spoken to, while here in 4.12 a *they*, a group of people, is spoken *about*. It is not the same group of people in the two verses; *you* in 3.12 are the Israelites, because of whom Jerusalem was going to be destroyed, and the *they* in 4.12 are the foreigners, who were involved in the act of the destruction and humiliation of Zion.

The contents of Micah 3 are accusations, which with variations lead to the conclusion that the catastrophe had to come; God has hidden his

---

10. It is characteristic that R. Alter and F. Kermode (eds.), *The Literary Guide to the Bible* (London: Collins, 1987) has one article about the Book of the Twelve with the same naturalness as it has one article about the book of Isaiah. It is also suggestive that among the titles in the JSOT Supplement series is found a book called *The Unity of the Twelve* by Paul R. House (JSOTSup, 97; Sheffield: Almond Press, 1990). In the article from 1977 mentioned above (n. 3), reprinted in his *Old Testament Prophecy* (1996), Clements's argumentation takes the direction that the canonical prophets became canonical, because their prophecies of doom fitted into a pattern of threats, and because they in the end became *Heilspropheten*, since their messages contained trends, which could be used to strengthen the prophecy of hope after 587 BCE. The book of Micah fits well into that pattern.

11. For example, the units in the book of Isaiah, which are marked with the Hebrew word *maśśā'* in the introductory line (13.1; 15.1; 17.1; 19.1, and others). See my discussion of the text between *maśśā' bābel* and *maśśā' mô'āb* in Isa. 13-14: K. Jeppesen, 'The maśśa Babel in Isaiah 13-14', *Proceedings of the Irish Biblical Association* 9 (1985), pp. 63-80.

face from the leaders (v. 4) and gives no answers to the prophets (v. 7). The only hope in this chapter is the fact that a true prophet, *I* Micah, was inspired to reveal the sins of the people (v. 8). From the interpretation in Jeremiah of the conclusion in Mic. 3.12, it seems as if Micah succeeded in this prophetic office; his contemporaries drew the only sensible deduction from the prophet's accusations and changed their attitude towards God.

According to the book of Micah itself, however, his preaching about the transgressions of Jacob and the sins of Israel does not seem to have been a success; there are no traces of the leaders' conversion. On the contrary, the centre of the book, the context of 4.12, deals in four *tempi* (4.6-8; 4.9-10; 4.11-13; 4.14-5.5) with a disaster which had come upon Zion. The sad situation is described in different ways: the lame, probably a metaphor for the population or part of it, have been driven far away (4.6-7); Zion's daughter has pain like a woman in labour (v. 9); Zion is or will be defiled (v. 11) and is under siege (v. 14). This is, with variations, the situation foreseen in 3.12; the accusations had obviously not worked, and the 'great disaster' had come.

But where the variations of the preaching of doom in ch. 3 lead to the arrival of the disaster, the various descriptions of the situation in ch. 4 lead to the overcoming of the disaster, to a prophecy of hope. After the humiliation the former kingdom returns to Zion (4.8), Zion shall be delivered in Babylon (v. 10) and become as strong as a threshing heifer (v. 13), and a new ruler will go out from Bethlehem in Judah (5.1-5).

This will happen because the destruction of Zion and the scattering of the people is not Yahweh's final plan. This is part of the point of the central verse in Mic. 4.12. The people who take part in the humiliation of Zion have gone too far, and therefore they will be gathered as sheaves on the floor to be threshed by the inhabitants of Zion.

The leaders of Jacob-Israel in Micah 3 did not realize what the will of Yahweh behind his threat was, and consequently in the end it was necessary that the disaster came. On the other hand, the foreign people did not realize either that the disaster was not the final will (*maḥš^{e}bôt* and *'ēṣâ*) of Yahweh; in short, the destruction was not what God really wanted.

The commissioning of the prophet (3.8) and the destruction of Jerusalem (3.12) were in a way different attempts to reach the same goal, the preserving of the people. History showed that the sending of a prophet was not enough; 'because of you'—because of the sins of the people and their officials—a stronger medicine was needed. This is reflected in the outline of the canonical book of Micah.

But a strong medicine can, wrongly used, become poisonous for the patients. The people who experienced historically the fall of Jerusalem and the deportation far away were almost dead. In Babylon the house of Israel said: 'Our bones are dried up, and our hope is lost' (Ezek. 37.11); but it was still the will and plan of God to cause them to get out of their graves and to return them to the land of Israel (v. 12); the myth about death and resurrection was activated to prove the possibility of salvation in a specific historical situation.

A parallel mythical idea, but developed less dramatically, is found in the first variation on the overcoming of Zion's misfortune, the gathering of the suffering people in Mic. 4.6-7. The lame and the dispersed are interpreted as those upon whom Yahweh had brought disaster (*r'* hiphil). As a good shepherd Yahweh will bring back his suffering people, reign as their king on Mt Zion forever (4.7), and, as already mentioned, restore the former kingdom.

Another mythical way of expressing the ending of a period of misfortune which is comparable with death, is the birth of a child. This imagery is found in the second variation, in 4.9-10. Here the disaster is described in terms of the daughter of Zion's being a woman screaming in pain, because she is in labour. The deliverance is in this case that the woman gives birth in another place than where she normally lives.

The salvation is not that she gives birth to a special child. In an attempt to find the reason for her birth pains the question is raised whether there is no king or advisor left. Because of the question about the missing king, one expects that the important point in the salvation part of vv. 9-10 would be the outcome of the birth, probably a boy. But this is not developed until the fourth variation on the theme, future salvation from the present disaster. The catchword *yôlēdâ* from 4.10 is taken up in 5.2. But at least in later tradition history (cf. Mt. 2.1-12) the woman giving birth in ch. 5 is different to the one in ch. 4; she is the mother of the coming ruler, and not the daughter of Zion. The ruler in his turn will receive universal power and become the guarantee of peace.

One of the trends in Deutero-Isaiah is that Zion is the mother of the people,[12] but in the present situation she finds herself bereaved, sterile,

---

12. Cf. K. Jeppesen, 'Mother Zion, Father Servant: A Reading of Isaiah 49–55', in H.A. McKay and D.J.A. Clines (eds.), *Of Prophets' Visions and the Wisdom of*

exiled and gone away (Isa. 49.21), and consequently without an off-spring that would guarantee her a happy future. And then suddenly some children[13] of hers are hastily on their way from somewhere (v. 17), which could be Babylon; but if they are the same as those mentioned in v. 12, they come from far away, from north and west, and from the land of Sinim. But the miracle is that these children are the fruit of Zion's bereavement (v. 20).

Somewhere in the tradition history of the text, Mic. 4.9-10, the emphasis seems to have been moved from the outcome of the birth to the place of the birth. The next thing, the salvation, will happen in a special place, and the birth metaphors recede into the background. The daughter of Zion who gives birth is told to leave the town, which prob-ably means something like a flight of the population of Jerusalem. The flight will take place in two *tempi*; the daughter is told to go out and dwell in the field. If the original idea was that the salvation would hap-pen in the field, where she was alone, the imagery was then not far from that of the punishment and subsequent salvation of the unfaithful wife in Hos. 2.16-17.

In the last clause of v. 10, however, the daughter of Zion is told to go to another place, where she will be saved (*nṣl*, niphal). The place is Babylonia, 'from where Yahweh will redeem you (fem. singular) from the hands of your enemies'. It has long been recognized that 'Baby-lonia' is not a very likely place name in an oracle of an eighth-century prophet, and therefore most commentaries consider the line with 'Babel' an addition,[14] if, indeed, the whole pericope is not thought to be later.

Sages (R.N. Whybray Festschrift; JSOTSup, 162; Sheffield: Sheffield Academic Press, 1993), pp. 109-25.

13. According to the Masoretic punctuation; other texts read 'your builders', which also makes sense in the context; cf. n. a to Isa. 49.17 in *BHS*.

14. See the commentaries from J. Wellhausen, *Die kleinen Propheten übersetzt und erklärt* (Berlin: W. de Gruyter, 4th edn, 1963), p. 144 ; and cf. n. b-b to Mic. 4.10 in *BHS*. Scholars who argue in favour of the authenticity of the Babel oracle in the book of Micah often point to the fact that the book of Isaiah also has a Babel text, namely Isa. 39; but 'the date of the composition of the present narrative is after 598' (R.E. Clements, *Isaiah 1–39* [NCB; London: Marshall, Morgan and Scott, 1980], p. 293). An exilic date has also been supported by the observation that *gā'al* with Yahweh as the subject is typical of Isa. 40–55.

Modern research on prophecy does not find it as important as earlier study did to decide whether a prophetic saying is original or not; furthermore, the research using traditio-historical methods has realized that the given object we have to investigate is the text in the present form; earlier layers can be found as the result of research carried out on the basis of working hypotheses, which are always questionable. So here the important thing is that in the final text of the book of Micah we find the place name *bābel* in the midst of a text, dealing with Zion and Jerusalem.

In other words, we have here two geographical points, Jerusalem and Babylon, which have their respective places at each end of a line in biblical historical thinking. Zion, which in our text is destroyed, means in this context the beginning of the exile; and Babylon, which is the place of the release, means the end of the exile. In the traditional *history of Israel* the beginning is related to the Babylonian conquest of Jerusalem in 587 and the end to the Persian conquest of Babylon in 539 BCE.

Scholars have long since recognized that the events in 587 BCE did not imply that all inhabitants of Jerusalem and Judah went to Babylon.[15] It is also obvious from the sources that not all descendants of the people who were moved to Babylon went back in the years after 539 BCE. In other words, the country was never emptied and the exile never ended.

But the idea that there had been an exile with a beginning and an end became part of the Israelite myth.[16] The events in 587 and 539 and the period between were interpreted by means of the myth about death and resurrection, as we find it, for instance, in Ezekiel 37, as mentioned above. The history of the exile became *the* example which proved that no crisis was so devastating that it could not be overcome—with the help of God.

In my opinion there is no reason to doubt that the myth about the exile takes its point of departure in events that happened in history; the beginning and the end of the exile are instances where history and myth meet. The problem is that for the mythical interpretation of the historical events it was necessary to built upon a narration where both the

15. See, e.g., the discussion in H.M. Barstad, *The Myth of the Empty Land* (Symbolae Osloenses Fasc. Suppl., 28; Oslo: Scandinavian University Press, 1996).

16. It is no coincidence that Barstad, *Myth*, writes about a *myth* of the Empty Land. See also my essay, 'Exile a Period—Exile a Myth', in Grabbe (ed.), *Leading Captivity Captive*, pp. 139-44.

deportation and return was absolute. Therefore, while most of the biblical references are related more closely to the myth than to the events as such, we have gained the impression that all inhabitants were forced to leave Judah and Jerusalem in 587 and that all of their descendants went happily home in the years immediately after 539 BCE. That is why scholars have had problems with hints in the texts which suggest that something else happened in reality.

As shown above, the oracle about the destruction of Zion and Jerusalem in 3.12 draws on the myth rather than the history, if it is of eighth-century origin. But formulations about the disaster in the four pericopes in 4.6–5.5 also draw upon mythical language. True enough, it is said that the mountain of the temple is totally destroyed, and that the destruction happened during a foreign siege and conquest. But the enemy is anonymous, as in the Psalms. Furthermore, we hear that the population is scattered far away, and the place from where Yahweh will collect them and bring them back to Zion is not mentioned by name, either. What is said is not far removed from history, but the language has the touch of myth.

Only once is the information very precise; this is where it is said to the daughter of Zion that she will be redeemed in Babylon—but the rest of the language of the verse is still mythical. It is very difficult to judge whether the mentioning of Babel as the place for the daughter of Zion's release is an expression of hope, which came up in the middle of the events, or whether it is a later prophetic interpretation of what happened. And perhaps it is not so important; even if the words 'in Babylon…Yahweh will redeem you from the hands of your enemies' were first uttered before 539 BCE, at the point the words were placed in the present form of Micah 3–4, they came to fulfil a new purpose.

Of course, their purpose was to prove that it was part of Yahweh's plan to rescue his exiled people in Babylon; but beyond this proof the idea was to create further hope, when a new crisis threatened the future of the biblical people; next time a historical enemy tried to humiliate Zion and its inhabitants, they would be able to use the myth they now know in its full scope, from disaster to release. It would be a comfort for them to remember that the enemy does not know the thoughts of Yahweh or understand his counsel, as is said in the centre of the book of Micah.

3. Micah 3–4: A Prophecy of Hope

In the traditional *Literarkritik* in this century chs. 3 and 4 in the book of Micah have normally been separated from each other. In an article in the first volume of *ZAW*, B. Stade interpreted Micah 4–5 in the light of Zechariah 12–14, and thus he saw the former as an eschatological text much later than the prophecies of doom in Micah 3;[17] and this suggestion had a great impact on the criticism of the book.

But from the 1950s onwards several scholars have realized that even if the two texts were not from the same time, they now belong inseparably together. The outline of the book as a whole seems, according to some investigators, to show that chs. 3–5 form one coherent group of pericopes, and other researchers have suggested that there is a special pattern, which binds not least the end of ch. 3 and the beginning of ch. 4 together.[18]

One of the details, which makes it difficult to believe that Mic. 3.12 and 4.1-4 are by the same author is of course that Mic. 4.1-3 is so close to Isa. 2.2-4 that there is no doubt that we have here two editions of the same text.[19] The pericope is connected very well with the context in the

17. B. Stade, 'Bemerkungen über das Buch Micha', *ZAW* 1 (1881), pp. 161-72; see K. Jeppesen, 'How the Book of Micah Lost its Integrity: Outline of the History of the Criticism of the Book of Micah with Emphasis on the 19th Century', *ST* 33 (1979), pp. 101-31.

18. See, e.g., E. Nielsen, *Oral Tradition* (SBT; London: SCM Press, 1954), pp. 79-93; R. Renaud, *Structure et attaches littéraires de Michée IV–V* (Cahiers de la Revue Biblique, 2; Paris: Gabalda, 1964); and J.T. Willis, 'The Structure of Micah 3–5 and the Function of Micah 5,9-14 in the Book', *ZAW* 81 (1969), pp. 353-68. More recently, C.S. Shaw has, in his monograph *The Speeches of Micah: A Rhetorical-Historical Analysis* (JSOTSup, 145; Sheffield: Sheffield Academic Press, 1993), pp. 97-127, treated Mic. 3.1–4.8 as one authentic speech.

19. Again I abstain from offering a list of the many contributors to this topic. The biggest difference between the two editions is that where the text in Isaiah has *gôyîm*, Micah has *'ammîm* and vice versa. This is perhaps only a coincidence, but a possible explanation might be found in the redactional activity on the book of Micah; in this case it could be the result of an effort to stress the connection between 4.1-5 and 4.6-8. According to v. 7 Yahweh will make the invalid and scattered people into a remnant and a *gôy 'āṣûm*, a strong nation. Later in Mic. 4–5 one of the themes is that the saved Israel will play a role among the nations (see, e.g., 5.6-7); this is already hinted at here, because *a strong nation* now stands out as a reflection of *the strong nations* (*gôyîm 'ᵃṣumîm*) in v. 3. In Isa. 2.4 we find at the correspond-

book of Micah, but the ideology of the text fits better into the book of Isaiah.[20]

Even if one takes a long pause for breath between Mic. 3.12 and 4.1, the change in outlook for the future is surprising; it is like moving suddenly from night to day—and that is, of course, one of the reasons why scholars declined to read the two texts together. You cannot go directly from one statement that the mountain of the temple will become hills with forest, to another which claims that the mountain of Yahweh's temple will be placed on top of the other mountains as, so to speak, the centre of the world; so scholars thought.

It seems as if the two prophecies are alternative suggestions about what is going to happen in the future. Micah 3.12 could be the result if the people did not listen to the prophet, and 4.1-4 could be the result if they listened and repented. But, as we have seen above, the point in the present book of Micah is that the people did not listen; in the long run the people of Judah did not show their fear of God and did not pacify him (cf. Jer. 26.19). In the Micah context, therefore, 4.1-4 cannot be the consequence of the Israelites' attitude towards God; it can only be the result of a merciful act of God.

We have spoken earlier about what followed the sins of Israel: a stronger medicine than the commissioning of a prophet was needed, namely, what was foretold in 3.12. As in Ezekiel 8–9, alluded to above, the leaders in Micah 3 thought they could act as if God did not see them; but in both cases the disaster came. But the disaster was not, as the foreign nations thought, the final plan of God; to cure the world, Yahweh had also a strong medicine after the destruction of Jerusalem.

In the last days Zion and Jerusalem were to become the centre of the world, and all people would then from this centre gain a knowledge and an insight, which they did not gain by acting in a way that brought the disaster and humiliation to Jerusalem (4.12). The section 4.1-5 belongs

ing point *'ammîm rabbîm*, many peoples; in Mic. 4.3 this phrase is used in the parallel clause (where Isa. 2.4 has *gôyîm*)—and it is the phrase which is taken up in Mic. 5.6-7.

20. Concerning the relations to the context, see, e.g., Nielsen, *Oral Tradition*; and to the Isaianic ideology, see, e.g., H. Wildberger, 'Die Völkerwallfahrt zum Zion: Jes ii 1-5', *VT* 7 (1957), pp. 62-81. If Zion-hymns like Pss. 46 and 48 are pre-587 BCE, Isa. 2.2-4 and Mic. 4.1-4 could also be pre-exilic, but many scholars agree with R.E. Clements, who has stated: 'Quite certainly...we must ascribe the prophecy to a time after the destruction of Jerusalem in 587' (*Isaiah 1–39*, p. 40).

where the path from Jerusalem (3.12) to Babylon (4.10) and back again has been followed; what happened between Jerusalem and Babylon is now relegated to the background;[21] it is described in Mic. 4.6–5.5 and reminds future people about what happened *because of you*. But in another perspective the distance from Mic. 3.12 to 4.1 was not of very much importance any more.

The purpose of the redactional activity which connected 4.1-5 to ch. 3, which is the centre of the Book of Twelve, was to bring the people to the point, where they could appreciate what was said elsewhere, in an oracle from Yahweh in the book of Isaiah:

> For a short moment I left you;
> but with great mercy I take you back (Isa. 54.7).

---

21. Compare again Jer 32.42 (see n. 9).

'WHEN THE TOWERS FALL':
INTERPRETING NAHUM AS CHRISTIAN SCRIPTURE

Edward Ball

> It is the Text that saves us; the interlineary glosses, and the marginal notes, and the *variae lectiones*, controversies and perplexities, undo us.
>
> John Donne

> ...like it or not, interpretation is the only game in town.
>
> Stanley Fish

> For me, at any rate, the question of the true nature of interpretation is the supreme question.
>
> Karl Barth[1]

Though it may surprise at least some modern readers of his work (perhaps not a huge company), Nahum figures among the select 14 prophetic witnesses to Christ who flank the rising tree and the succession of kings portrayed in the breathtakingly beautiful Jesse Window in the west front of Chartres Cathedral.[2] Jonah is not there, nor Jeremiah, but Nahum has his place in the grand array. This is no real surprise, of course, since he, like all the other prophets, was seen in the Middle Ages, in line with earlier Christian understanding, as announcing in advance the coming Messiah. Nahum may have little in the way of messianic prophecy according to the 'literal sense', but as its three

---

1. The epigraphs come, respectively, from: G.R. Potter and E.M. Simpson (eds.), *The Sermons of John Donne*, III (Berkeley: University of California Press, 1957), p. 208 [16 February 1620]; S. Fish, *Is There a Text in This Class? The Authority of Interpretive Communities* (Cambridge, MA: Harvard University Press, 1980), p. 355; K. Barth, *The Epistle to the Romans* (ET of 6th German edn; London: Oxford University Press, 1933), p. 9.

2. In the north rose window (c. 1230), Nahum and his 11 companions among the minor prophets immediately surround the central Virgin and Child. See also, for instance, the west (c. 1220) and north (c. 1270) rose windows of Notre Dame de Paris for the same prophetic and incarnational emphasis.

major medieval commentators will show, the book could speak amply, according to the other senses, of the work of Christ and the life of his Church. Indeed, after the influential exposition of Jerome,[3] who worked with related 'literal' and 'spiritual' senses, a basic fourfold interpretative pattern is already found in summary fashion in an exposition formerly attributed to the seventh-century Julian of Toledo.[4]

> Nahum propheta in regnum Assyriorum invenitur: *historialiter* de Nineve, quae metropolis ejus fuit, destructione loquitur; *allegorice*, de desolatione mundi; *mystice*, de reparatione per Christum generis humani; *moraliter*, de restitutione in pristina dignitate, vel majore gloria peccatoris in sceleribus lapsi.

> The prophet Nahum is set in the kingdom of the Assyrians. According to the historical sense, he speaks of the destruction of Nineveh, its capital; in the allegorical sense, of the world's being laid waste; in the mystical sense, of the restoration of the human race through Christ; in the moral sense, of the restoring to his first dignified state, or to yet greater glory, of the sinner fallen into wickedness.

This points us also to another important dimension of the medieval exegetical tradition, which finds its best iconographic representation in the prophets on the west facade of Amiens Cathedral (c. 1220). Here the 16 statues are accompanied by medallion reliefs of scenes from the respective books. The significance (and, in some cases, the identification) of these scenes has been a matter for debate: are the prophets here to be seen as two correlated groups, one focused on penitence and promise, the other on the announcement of the final judgment and downfall of evil; or are they *all* to be viewed as heralds of the last judgment?[5]

3.   *S. Hieronymi Presbyteri Opera, Pars I: Opera exegetica 6: Commentarii in Prophetas Minores* (Corpus Christianorum Series Latina, 76A; Turnhout: Brepols, 1970); for Nahum, pp. 525-78. The senses are, respectively, *iuxta litteram* and *secundum αναγωγην* (among other terms).

4.   (Pseudo-)Julian of Toledo, *Commentarius in Nahum Prophetam*, PL 96, col. 705 (my italics). The extant work (cols. 705-58) covers only 1.1-4. For the (now usual) denial of it to Julian, see J.N. Hillgarth, 'St. Julian of Toledo in the Middle Ages', *Journal of the Warburg and Courtauld Institutes* 21 (1958), pp. 7-26 (p. 10 n. 22).

5.   For the former view (and illustrations), see A. Katzenellenbogen, 'The Prophets on the West Façade of the Cathedral at Amiens', *Gazette des Beaux-Arts* 40 (1952), pp. 241-60; for the latter, W. Sauerländer, *Gothic Sculpture in France 1140-1270* (ET; London: Thames and Hudson, 1972), pp. 465-66. Both argue for an interpretation in line with Jerome's commentary on the relevant passages.

Nahum is in any case indisputably among the latter in this particular display; among the scenes represented are the 'no one turns back' of 2.8 (Vulg.) and the 'falling figs' of 3.12, which even without literary correlations would point in this direction.

Both of these emphases—the prefiguring of salvation in Christ and the Church, and the proclamation of eschatological judgment—appear strongly and clearly in the medieval commentaries. First, from the west in the ninth century comes the *Enarratio in duodecim prophetas minores* by the influential Haimo of Auxerre.[6] 'His commentaries', says Beryl Smalley, '...are important because they were widely read from the tenth to the twelfth century, and because they give substance to the Carolingian revival'.[7] The literal/historical exegesis (*iuxta litteram*) is primary and foundational; alongside it stands the 'mystical' (*mysticus sensus*). So Nahum, whose very name means 'consolator', 'consolatur captivitatem decem tribuum, quas jam transtulerant Assyrii in Niniven, regnante in Judaea Ezechia rege' ('He comforts the captives of the ten tribes which the Assyrians had just then carried off to Nineveh, at the time when Hezekiah reigned in Judah') (col. 167), thus bringing comfort in fact not only to those already in captivity, but also to those besieged in Jerusalem, by the news that their Assyrian enemies were to be defeated by the Chaldeans; while, for instance, the summons to Judah to rejoice in 1.15 'mystice praecipitur Ecclesiae, quam diabolus

6.   *PL* 117, cols. 9-294; on Nahum, cols. 167-80. B. Smalley, *The Study of the Bible in the Middle Ages* (Oxford: Basil Blackwell, 3rd edn, 1983), p. 39 n. 3, follows E. Riggenbach, against the common earlier attribution to Haimo of Halberstadt (c. 778–853); so also B. Heurtebize, *DTC* 6.2 (1947), cols. 2068-69; J.J. Contreni, 'Haimo of Auxerre, Abbot of Sasceium (Cessy-le-Bois) and a New Sermon of I John V, 4-10', *Revue Bénédictine* 85 (1975), pp. 303-20 (303 and n. 2).

7.   Smalley, *Study*, p. 39; see her further general comments on Haimo on pp. 39-40. There is comment on Haimo's exegetical principles scattered through H. de Lubac, *Exégèse médiévale* (Aubier: Montaigne), e.g., 1.2 (1959), pp. 500-501: 'Pour Aimon d'Auxerre, "omnis Scriptura veteris Testamenti ad mysteria Christi et Ecclesiae contuenda nos invitat", et encore: "Vetus Testamentum, ubi mysteria Christi Ecclesiaeque sunt praedicta".' See further the essays by D. Iogna-Prat, 'L'œuvre d'Haymon d'Auxerre: Etat de la question' and J.J. Contreni, 'Haimo of Auxerre's Commentary on Ezekiel' in D. Iogna-Prat, C. Jeudy, G. Lobrichon (eds.), *L'école carolingienne d'Auxerre de Murethaci à Remi 830–908* (Paris: Beauchesne, 1991), pp. 157-79, 229-42. For the wider intellectual context, see J.J. Contreni, 'Carolingian Biblical Studies', in U.-R. Blumenthal (ed.), *Carolingian Essays: Andrew W. Mellon Lectures in Early Christian Studies* (Washington, DC: Catholic University of America Press, 1983), pp. 71-98.

gravissimo jugo idolatriae premebat, ut liberata per Domini passionem, celebret festivitates...' ('in the mystical sense is predicated of the Church, which the devil was oppressing with the crushing yoke of idolatry, that when set free by the Lord's passion it should celebrate its festivals') (col. 172). Conversely, 'mystice Ninive mundum diximus figurari' ('in the mystical sense Nineveh, as we said, symbolizes the world') (col. 174), so that of the disaster that befalls the city in ch. 2 Haimo can say 'haec omnia quae ad Niniven dicuntur, in judicio super diabolum et ejus complices ventura sunt' ('everything said to Nineveh is going to happen in the judgment on the devil and his associates') (col. 175).

The Chartres Jesse Window was constructed around 1150. Less than a century earlier, in the east, there was the Greek commentary of Theophylact, archbishop of Bulgaria,[8] while the window is predated by less than 30 years in the west by the *Commentariorum in duodecim prophetas minores* by Rupert of Deutz.[9] For Rupert the literal/historical sense is the necessary basis for the knowledge of the God made known through his works; but the spiritual sense, too, for him 'nearly always referred as well to *events*, acts of God in the history of salvation',[10] principally the saving works of God in the incarnation, passion, resur-

---

8. *Expositio in Naum Prophetam* (*PG* 126, cols. 969-1048). Again the 'literal sense' is foundational to the spiritual. So, e.g., Theophylact expounds 1.15 of the messenger announcing Cyrus's (!) capture of Nineveh, which would mean peace for Israel; but he also finds the 'feet' to be those of the apostles, sent to teach the Gentiles, and through whom the Lord announced peace (col. 997). Little has been done on Theophylact's exegetical work, but see K. Krumbacher, *Geschichte der byzantinischen Litteratur von Justinian bis zum Ende des oströmischen Reiches (527–1453)* (Munich: Beck, 2nd edn, 1897), pp. 133-35; R. Janin, 'Théophylacte', *DTC* 15.1 (1946), cols. 536-38.

9. *PL* 168, cols. 9-836; on Nahum, cols. 527-88. Rupert (c. 1075–1129), 'the most prolific of all twelfth-century authors' (J.H. Van Engen, *Rupert of Deutz* [Berkeley: University of California Press, 1983], p. 3), became abbot of Deutz around 1120; his work on the Minor Prophets, written in the period 1121–24, was well known. For Rupert's exegesis, see again scattered references and comments in de Lubac, *Exégèse médiévale*, and especially 2.11 (1961), pp. 219-38; also P. Séjourné, 'Rupert de Deutz', *DTC* 14.1 (1939), cols. 169-205 (esp. 174-84 on his exegetical work); and Van Engen, *Rupert of Deutz*, pp. 70-72, and especially pp. 237-42 on the Minor Prophets commentary.

10. See Van Engen, *Rupert of Deutz*, p. 70, who observes also that 'Rupert most often simply distinguished broadly between the historical and spiritual senses' (p. 71).

rection and ascension of Christ. This can again be illustrated from the comments on 1.15–2.2, which are interpreted in Christian terms of the Church's rejoicing in the work of Christ, as well as in relation to the deliverance from Sennacherib (cols. 549-52). The senses are carefully interwoven, and not simply juxtaposed: the things affirmed historically of Judah 'veraciter implentur in Evangelio Christi' ('are truly fulfilled in the Gospel of Christ') (col. 550), since Judah 'est confessor prophetikae et evangelicae fidei' ('is those who confess the prophetic and evangelical faith') (col. 551). Nineveh is both the historical city and, throughout, 'this world' (*mundus hic*)—as he comments on 2.8, 'mundum damnatum et extremo judicio damnandum' ('the world already condemned and still to be condemned in the final judgment').[11]

We might imagine that the visual images at Chartres and Amiens simply depend on and express the long literary tradition of Christian exegesis of the prophets, with the pictorial text so to speak parasitic on the verbal, the art work belonging to a wider 'history of influence' (*Wirkungsgeschichte*) whose real core and substance is 'history of interpretation' expressed in written texts. It is natural enough for those whose business is (verbal) texts to think in this way, but it gives a misleading impression of the dynamics of medieval interpretative experience. This is true not only in the general sense that for most of Christian history interpretation of Scripture has involved much more than written commentary; it is true also, more specifically, in respect of the interaction of text (not least biblical commentary) and visual image in medieval, perhaps especially twelfth-century, Europe.[12] John Milbank notes

> the fact that the Bible as one continuous, primarily *written*, and initially naked, uncommented-upon text was invented by printing, humanism, and the Reformation. Previously, the Bible was often apprehended in discrete manuscript rolls adorned with surrounding glosses (like Jewish Bibles to this day), and illuminated pictures. Moreover, liturgically performed scripture and graphically depicted scripture (for example, on church walls) were regarded as equally 'original' with the written text in a culture with continuing 'oral' characteristics.[13]

11. So the 'falling figs' image in 3.12 refers to the final judgment, when 'magno terrae motu cadent munitiones totius orbis' and those who have resisted the truth 'cadent in os devorantis inferni, glutientis abyssi, gehennalis incendii' (col. 577).

12. See, e.g, M. Curschmann, 'Imagined Exegesis: Text and Picture in the Exegetical Works of Rupert of Deutz, Honorius Augustodunensis, and Gerhoch of Reichersberg', *Traditio* 44 (1988), pp. 145-69.

13. J. Milbank, Review of M.S. Burrows and P. Rorem (eds.), *Biblical Her-*

Something depends, clearly, on the concept of 'interpretation' we are working with, and it is appropriate to remind ourselves that this is a highly-contested concept (are there *any* elements which belong unequivocally, self-evidently, 'objectively' to—whose?—interpretative practice?).[14] Does, then, the setting of those images of the prophet in the Jesse Window or the Amiens facade 'count' as *interpretation* of the book of Nahum? One good reason for attending to past engagement with the Bible, in its difference and strangeness, is precisely to help alert ourselves to the theoretical foundations of our own practice.[15] Such attention does not imply that we should not be *critical* of older interpretation,[16] but it does make us sensitive in turn to the precise nature and basis of our criticism.

Now we might suppose that the raison d'être of the Chartres window was in some sense to mediate spiritual experience to its viewers, and, indeed, the illustrious Abbé Suger of Saint-Denis spoke of the way such glass was to lead them from the material realm to the immaterial.[17] In Christian faith, the role of Scripture itself has been seen in similar ways. Yet attention has also been drawn to the *political* nature of the Jesse Tree, both in the general sense that it may be taken to express the Christian imperialism of a unified culture which leaves no space for contrary voices, and in the more specific sense that its iconography (especially the presence of the lily) relates the divinely-chosen kingship of Israel and the messianic reign of Christ to that of the rulers of twelfth-century France: heavenly and earthly kingship were unified, and 'it was believed that through the person of the king the union of Christ and His Church

meneutics in Historical Perspective (Grand Rapids: Eerdmans, 1991), in *JTS* NS 46 (1995), p. 667. 'The Reformation,' he adds, 'did not, therefore, make more widely available something which had previously existed; it disseminated something new'.

14. Note Richard Coggins's comment: 'Almost every feature of every commentary will be value-laden' ('A Future for the Commentary?', in F. Watson [ed.], *The Open Text: New Directions for Biblical Studies* [London: SCM Press, 1993], pp. 163-75 [166])—surely an understatement?

15. See, e.g., B.S. Childs, *Biblical Theology in Crisis* (Philadelphia: Westminster Press, 1970), pp. 139-47.

16. See D.J.A. Clines, *Interested Parties: The Ideology of Writers and Readers of the Hebrew Bible* (JSOTSup, 205; Gender, Culture, Theory, 1; Sheffield: Sheffield Academic Press, 1996), pp. 107-108 and n. 27.

17. For Latin text and translation, see E. Panofsky, *Abbot Suger on the Abbey Church of St.-Denis and its Art Treasures* (Princeton: Princeton University Press, 1946), pp. 72-77.

was accomplished'.[18] So here, we could say, in the context of a unitary vision of the world, Nahum and his companions are enlisted in the service of the kings of France, and biblical interpretation is put to what we would distinguish as political work. That is not very obvious, perhaps, to the casual modern observer for whom the aesthetic beauty of the window which mediated its ideological concern now helps to mask it.[19] Refusal to acknowledge that socio-political function might be regarded as a wilful disregard of the historical context and ideological structuring of the image, an unwillingness for whatever reason to recognize its use as an instrument of control. But the modern 'reader' of the glass, while alert to that function, may say: it doesn't *have* to be 'read' like that—rather than seeing an undergirding of earthly kingship by heavenly, why not find in it a limiting, a relativizing, a critique, of (all) human rule by that of Christ? Who would such a reader be, and why would she or he want to read it in that way? What is there to prevent such a reading? What, or who, could constrain it—or 'validate' it? To read thus would certainly be to find another ideology inscribed in the image/text; and it would be open to discussion whether this is any less oppressive and destructive—or any more creative and sustaining— of human flourishing than the former. (This in turn would raise the prior and crucial question of the terms in which human well-being is best understood.) If both readings are *ideological*, both are *theological*, too. Is one of those adjectives reducible, straightforwardly or otherwise, to the other? From what standing-ground, or astride what metanarrative, may such a question be decided? Can it in fact be decided at all without a commitment, overt or covert, to *some* metanarrative?

Here, of course, I am implying many recent questions about the nature of interpretation, which then cast back their light on what is often referred to as 'pre-critical' interpretation—as expressed, say, in the windows or the facade and the written texts they interact with. Are such texts, visual or verbal, worth the modern interpreter's attention? That will depend in part on what one thinks the nature and goal of the modern interpreter's work is—and it is surely time not only to recognize, but also to accept the legitimacy of, a plurality of responses to

18. See especially J.R. Johnson, 'The Tree of Jesse Window of Chartres: *Laudes Regiae*', *Speculum* 36 (1961), pp. 1-22 (8).

19. On the modern dissociation of 'aesthetic' from social life which is relevant here, see, e.g., T. Eagleton, *Literary Theory: An Introduction* (Oxford: Basil Blackwell, 2nd edn, 1996), pp. 18-19.

those questions (and, yes, with attention also to the socio-political con-
figuring of those responses: what is generated by and acceptable to
whom, and why?). Then, as Stephen Fowl puts it,

> to the extent that individual biblical scholars have recognized method-
> ological pluralism, they have been relatively slow to recognize that the
> theoretical arguments which underwrite interpretative pluralism also
> undermine the arguments against attending seriously to pre-modern bib-
> lical interepretation. One cannot treat pre-modern biblical interpretation
> as a failed attempt to uncover the single meaning of a biblical text if one
> has already abandoned the modern quest for a single, eternally-stable
> meaning.[20]

Fowl is evidently alluding here to some questioning of the role normally claimed for itself by that cluster of methods[21] somewhat loosely
referred to as 'historical criticism', which has, of course, made its own
attempts to interpret the book of Nahum. Let us rehearse briefly of
some of its salient features.

It has generally been supposed by their practitioners that historical-
critical approaches, by relating texts as closely as possible to the time,
culture and circumstances of their origin, furnish the fundamental and
indispensable—perhaps, indeed, the only *true*—means for eliciting the
(stable and determinate) meaning intentionally expressed in those texts
by their authors. Much attention has been given to tracing possible
stages in the literary growth of such texts as appear to offer evidence of
their composite character, often with the assumption (for one reason or
another) that most interest—and value (by whatever precise criteria that
is defined)—lies in the earliest stages in the total history of composition. The work of subsequent editors, once identified, may then be variously judged, again according to varying criteria within the broad
scheme. Such approaches have usually wanted to claim that they are
empirical, unbiased, objective; more, that they offer the *only really*
'objective' way of handling the texts (even when some ideal of 'pure,
scientific objectivity' is reckoned less than fully attainable): other approaches are deemed liable to subjectivity and arbitrariness. There are
other interesting, and interconnected, features of historical-critical consciousness and rhetoric, too: the sense projected that such criticism is

---

20. 'Introduction', in S.E. Fowl (ed.), *The Theological Interpretation of Scripture: Classic and Contemporary Readings* (Oxford: Basil Blackwell, 1997), p. xvii.

21. See F. Watson, 'A Response to Professor Rowland', *SJT* 48 (1995), pp. 518-
19.

engendered purely by its object, and discloses the meaning of the latter in a natural, common-sense way; the related moral claim that it involves empathetic, compassionate listening to the other—that is, the careful, demanding attempt to hear as precisely as possible what is being said, to read the text 'itself' 'on its own terms', while battling strenuously against the refracting prisms of the critic's own consciousness; sometimes—perhaps more attenuated now than a century ago, but still present?—the romantic self-projection of the scholar as the lonely seeker heroically pursuing truth in the face of opposition from dogma and tradition (the picture, perhaps, for some of us, of the scholar standing between church and academy, and suspected or mistrusted by both); and the expectation that historical criticism could supply the basis for a common discourse in its humane and tolerant stance grounded in a common approach to the biblical texts, which by its very objectivity could not only make possible a rapprochement between different confessions,[22] but also function in some measure apologetically towards those outside them. There is, therefore, in Francis Watson's words, 'an acute sensitivity to the danger of theologically motivated encroachments which are said to compromise the secularity and thus the credibility of the discipline. Theological reflection is optional and extra-curricular, and should begin only after a firm historical-critical foundation has been laid.'[23]

Now I know all this is over-simplified, perhaps even caricaturish, certainly itself rhetorically interested.[24] Here, though, is part of a review of a commentary on Nahum (and others) which appeared some years ago in the *SOTS Booklist*.[25]

---

22. See, e.g., the striking remark to this effect by J. Gray, *I & II Kings: A Commentary* (OTL; London: SCM Press, 1st edn, 1964), p. 10. (The forerunner of such a position is, perhaps, Hugo Grotius.)

23. F. Watson, 'Literary Approaches to the Gospels: A Theological Assessment', *Theology* 99 (1996), pp. 125-33 (131).

24. John Barton has tried to probe and evaluate the ways in which its recent critics have characterized 'historical criticism'; see, for instance, his 'Historical-critical approaches', in *idem* (ed.), *The Cambridge Companion to Biblical Interpretation* (Cambridge: Cambridge University Press, 1998), pp. 9-20.

25. R.A. Mason, Review of E.A. Achtemeier, *Nahum–Malachi* (Int; Atlanta: John Knox Press, 1986), in *Society for Old Testament Study: Booklist 1988*, pp. 53-54. But see also R.A. Mason, *Micah-Nahum-Obadiah* (OTG; Sheffield: JSOT Press, 1991), pp. 56-84.

> The editors state that the series...takes seriously 'the hermeneutical responsibility for the contemporary meaning and significance of the biblical text'. If this need not put the critical faculties on red alert, it is enough to set the amber hazard lights flashing. For, paradoxically, it is the zealous and scholarly exploration of the text in its historical context (including the whole history of its emergence into its final form) which most surely releases its contemporary relevance. Attempts to short-circuit this process in the name of 'devotion' or 'relevance' tend to usher in the subjective. The biblical text is called on to support the tradition of the expositor rather than standing over against that tradition in judgement.

The reviewer acquits the commentator of such grievous faults, and indeed reckons that she 'does the best anyone can with Nahum'. For, he asks, 'will any of us ever have the courage to admit in a popular commentary that the book really is rather a disgrace to the two religious communities of whose canonical Scriptures it forms so unwelcome a part?'

Now, leaving aside the questions raised by the earlier comments there, that last sentence looks remarkably like a value judgment, involving some hermeneutical standpoint or other and using some evaluative criterion or other. Is that, also, 'subjective'? Or is it a judgment which arises in some 'natural', unreflective, universally-obvious way from the text? On the one hand, the reviewer recommends an historical-critical method which in theory brackets out evaluation, and aims to look with zealous dispassion at 'what is there', according to the meaning determined in and by its 'historical context' of origin. On the other hand, he seems to have responded in advance to David Clines's summons to be properly critical, to take up a stance outside the ideology of the text, to judge it according to one's own standards of reference—and thus to practise a truly ethical criticism.[26] Whatever be the case in this instance, it would be better to acknowledge (wouldn't it?) that historical criticism is not 'objective', that it is not simply a 'natural' response to 'the text'—and that it has no uniquely authoritative status as defining the 'true nature' of biblical interpretation.[27]

How does Nahum fare, if one is willing to entertain at the very least a

26. Clines, *Interested Parties*, pp. 18-21, 107-10, 268-69, and elsewhere.

27. 'In endowing the observer with an ability to step outside his historical situation that it must necessarily deny to the object he scrutinizes, objectivist methodology is self-condemned to an irresolvable self-contradiction' (L. Patterson, *Negotiating the Past: The Historical Understanding of Medieval Literature* [Madison, WI: University of Wisconsin Press, 1987], p. 42).

relativizing of the status of historical criticism?

To begin with, there can be no denying the role which such criticism has played in the modern study of Nahum. It seems to have exemplified excellently the model of the determinate text in a determinate historical setting with a determinate meaning. From at least the Christian patristic commentators onwards, in fact,[28] Nahum was believed to have been written in a quite definite historical setting by a definite prophet from a definite locality (however much they might have disagreed on the location of Elkosh!): until the later nineteenth-century discovery that Thebes (the No-Amon of Nah. 3.8) had fallen to the Assyrians in 663 BCE, the great majority of scholars, both 'conservative' and 'critical', dated his work to the reign of Hezekiah,[29] putting it either during or shortly after Sennacherib's siege of Jerusalem, to which very clear reference was found in the language of ch. 1 (and for some v. 14 gave a *terminus ad quem*, as announcing Sennacherib's still future death[30]). Nahum thus presented a prophecy of Nineveh's destruction long in advance of its happening—and what delight many eighteenth- and nineteenth-century Christian writers found in such triumphantly-vindicated evidences for the truth of prophecy.[31]

Later recognition that the now-documented[32] fall of Thebes meant a date for the book after 663 still left open a range of options for its more

28. And indeed earlier by Josephus, who put Nahum's work in the reign of Jotham, making it distant prediction (*Ant.* 9.239-42).

29. So at least from Jerome, *In Naum*, p. 525 (see n. 3 above). So common was this dating that it is hardly necessary to add detailed references to its proponents (such as Calvin, Vitringa, de Wette, Bleek, Keil, A. Clarke and Pusey). Others put it later, at some time during the seventh century (e.g. some Jewish commentators, Hitzig, Ewald, S. Davidson; see the list of views in S. Davidson, *An Introduction to the Old Testament*, III [London: Williams and Norgate, 1863], p. 295), but still finding clear references back to Sennacherib and the siege in ch. 1.

30. From the Fathers on, the portrayal of the Assyrian king's death there was very often correlated with the circumstances of Sennacherib's death as reported in Isa. 37.38.

31. See, e.g., T. Newton, *Dissertations on the Prophecies which have remarkably been fulfilled and are fulfilling*, I (London: W. Tegg, 1759), diss. 9; A. Keith, *Evidence of the Truth of the Christian Religion, derived from the Literal Fulfilment of Prophecy* (Edinburgh: W. Whyte, 24th edn, 1841), pp. 264-70. To date Nahum closer to the actual fall of Nineveh was sometimes seen as casting doubt on its inspired, predictive character.

32. With the discovery (1878) and publication of the 'Rassam Cylinder' of Ashurbanipal.

precise setting—was it written only shortly after that event, or decades
later (perhaps stimulated by some crisis for Assyrian power), or very
much closer to the fall of Nineveh itself? Even then, allusion back to
the Assyrian siege of Jerusalem was often found in ch. 1. But the late
nineteenth-century and early twentieth-century scholars who postulated
the presence there of an acrostic poem commonly regarded it as a later
addition to Nahum's own words, thus opening up finally the critical gap
between prophet and text; and particularly when it was believed to be
reconstructable through the whole course of the chapter[33]—though
interwoven with other elements in its later part—such historical allusions were often no longer thought to be present. Most later scholars
would restrict the presence of the acrostic to vv. 2-8, and continue to
see its language throughout as quite general. Where historical allusions
are found in the following verses, these are often taken to refer more
generally to the continuing Assyrian oppression of Judah in the seventh
century, and to its hoped-for end.[34]

Another particularly striking result of the newer historical-critical
approach was the claim made by some scholars that Nahum, who had
now come commonly to be seen as a contemporary of Jeremiah, should
be regarded as one of the prophets condemned by the latter;[35] for did he
not promise only comfort and well-being to Judah at the very time
Jeremiah was announcing its fall? Such judgments were not always
made unambiguously—since more positive comments are sometimes
added, and it is not always clear whether the inclusion of Nahum
among the so-called 'shalom-prophets' or the like is meant descrip-
tively, or is intended to carry a theological or moral evaluation—but
they form a distinct feature of some historical-critical work. A ripe
expression of this kind of view is that of W.C. Graham in 1929:

> Nahum has grasped certain great truths. But from them he has been led
> by his emotions, prejudices, human interests, to arrive at certain unwar-
> ranted conclusions... Considerations of personal interest must have
> influenced him to ally himself with the popular party and so refrain from

33. As, influentially, in H. Gunkel, 'Nahum 1', *ZAW* 13 (1893), pp. 223-44.
34. So, e.g., S. de Vries, 'The Acrostic of Nahum in the Jerusalem Liturgy', *VT*
16 (1966), pp. 476-81 (480); J.J.M. Roberts, *Nahum, Habakkuk and Zephaniah: A
Commentary* (OTL; Louisville: Westminster John Knox Press, 1991), pp. 52-54.
35. So, e.g., K. Marti, *Das Dodekapropheton* (Kurzer Hand-Commentar zum
Alten Testament, 13; Tübingen: J.C.B. Mohr, 1904), pp. 305-306.

all moral criticism of his own nation. Consequently, Nahum provides an
outstanding example of arrested religious development...[36]

In more recent decades the specific setting of Nahum's work has been
found by many in, or closely related to, the Jerusalem cult, and this has
often been thought to cohere well with the view of him as a 'nationalist'
prophet. The impact of such historical approaches to the book is only
underlined by the counter-argument that Nahum's lack of criticism of
Judah is due to the fact that he may have been working in the shadow of
Josiah's reform.[37] All this, of course, assumes that we have a clear and
distinct profile of the 'historical Jeremiah', and that the biblical texts are
quite transparently and straightforwardly related to the history of late
seventh-century Judah, of which equally we have objective historical
reconstruction.

It assumes, furthermore, that we can extract from the book of Nahum,
seen in the setting of that historical reconstruction, the words and the
activity of the 'historical Nahum'. This, I think, is to assume too much,
too straightforwardly, both in theoretical terms about the nature of
'history' as construction of the past and the ways in which texts relate
to it, and specifically about the literary character of Nahum itself. I will
try briefly to explore this latter point a little further.

It is arguable that those older scholars were right when they saw
allusions to Sennacherib and the invasion of Judah in ch. 1. I take v. 11,
for example, to be addressing *Judah*,[38] not Nineveh as most commentators have supposed, and to be speaking of Sennacherib's withdrawal.
But my working assumption is, not that the historical Nahum spoke
independently of the same events as Isaiah his contemporary, but that
there is a form of literary link—and perhaps a rather complex one—
between the two *books*. In other words, Nahum's relationship is not
directly with some reconstructed history, but with the *portrayal(s)* of
Judah's involvement with the Assyrians in the book of Isaiah. So, to
take just one instance, the 'overflowing flood' (*šeṭep 'ōbēr*) in v. 8 I
take as literarily related to the same image and language used in Isa.
8.8; 28.15, 17-18 of the Assyrian threat to Judah, now so to speak

36. W.C. Graham, 'Nahum', in F.C. Eiselen (ed.), *The Abingdon Bible Commentary* (Nashville: Abingdon Press, 1929), p. 799.

37. See, for instance, G. von Rad, *Old Testament Theology* (2 vols.; ET; Edinburgh: Oliver and Boyd, 1965), II, p. 189.

38. Following especially W. Rudolph, *Micha-Nahum-Habakuk-Zephanja* (KAT,
13/3; Gütersloh: Gerd Mohn, 1975), *ad loc.*; so also Roberts, *Nahum*, p. 53.

reversed and made God's threat (compare Isa. 30.28) to *Nineveh* and its
'place': reading, that is, *mᵉqômâh*, rather than one of the emended forms
favoured by most modern translators and commentators,[39] and relating
the suffix back to 'Nineveh' in v. 1. The heading there, *maśśā' nînᵉwēh*,
seems to me explicitly to link Nahum with the collection of oracles
against the nations in Isaiah 13–23: these are the only places where
maśśā' is followed by a place name in this way. Now Isaiah does not
contain an oracle specifically announcing the downfall of Nineveh, but
it does announce the destruction of Assyrian power in Judah itself (see
Isa. 14.24-27). Without here going into the complex redactional questions in more detail, we might suggest that at some stage in the trans-
mission of both books Nahum was understood as supplying the 'missing' oracle which spoke of the final end of Assyrian power.

I will not argue the point more extensively here, but my impression is
that the book of Nahum has quite a densely intertextual character; and I
do not think it is easy, if it is possible at all, to discern within it the profile of a distinct individual spokesman whose words are readily and
transparently explicable in relation to one specific historical context.
Two points may be added. First, as my comment on 1.8 already suggested, the book, and especially ch. 1, has afforded scope for a good
deal of text-critical work. Sometimes this has been pursued particularly
in attempts to reconstruct the supposed acrostic,[40] but more generally in
relation to what have been perceived as textual difficulties in 1.9–2.3,
and not infrequently with claimed support from the versions, as is also
the case in 1.8, for example. It seems to me extremely difficult to get a
theoretical purchase on how the text-critical questions are appropriately
to be handled: does the concept of, and the quest for, some 'original
text' (that acutely question-begging and often inappropriately value-
laden expression!) or even a 'best text' of the book have any clear
meaning? Do we have to reckon with a fluid and protean text, with all
the difficulties and possibilities that creates for modern interpreters (and
translators)? At any rate, the idea that we have ready access to something commonly referred to as 'the final form of the text'—or to any
uniquely 'valid' form on which interpretative activity is focused—
appears to me to be problematic (as does the idea of a clear, univocal,

---

39. Mostly preferring a noun or participial form ('opposition', 'adversaries')
derived from *qûm*, in line with Septuagint *tous epegeiromenous*.

40. But see M. H. Floyd's important argument against the acrostic theory: 'The
Chimerical Acrostic of Nahum 1.2-10', *JBL* 113 (1994), pp. 421-37.

'objective' meaning of the text, determined by historical criticism). Furthermore, in any claim for the propriety of a distinctively *Christian* theological interpretation of Nahum, the question must be raised: which text-form do we take as our standard—Hebrew or Greek or other, and where *within* these traditions do we look? I have made an observation above preferring a Masoretic Hebrew to a Greek reading at 1.8; but I cannot now claim that this represents the only 'valid' reading, given both the central role played by the Septuagintal tradition in the history of Christian interpretation and, perhaps more importantly here, the fact that it cannot by any means be taken for granted that only some existing or reconstructed form of the Masoretic Text represents the authoritative 'original'—when the validity of that very concept is in question.

The second point is this: if the historical setting of the book of Nahum (which one?, we might now be asking) is less determinate than has usually been thought to be the case,[41] does that mean we leave ourselves open to the danger of allowing its ideological character to remain concealed? I shall return briefly to that question.

So far, I have reflected, albeit cursorily, on some aspects of the older Christian interpretative traditions in respect of Nahum, and raised some questions about the modern traditions of historical-critical interpretation. In the light of these reflections I want in conclusion to plead for the propriety of a distinctly theological approach to the interpretation of Nahum, and more than that, for the propriety of a distinctly *Christian* theological approach, *within the academic setting*—the university department and the learned society—as well as within the context of the church community.

Such a proposal does not imply, first, that interpretation of the Old Testament is to be controlled by one particular Christian theological system; rather, that it exists in engagement, both critical and constructive, with the central credal substance of Christian faith and theology. It

41. Most twentieth-century scholars have accepted a setting for it around the time of the fall of Nineveh (usually just before); some have preferred a considerably earlier date, during the reign of Manasseh or a little later (so, e.g., recently Roberts, *Nahum*, pp. 38-39; K. Spronk, *Nahum* [Historical Commentary on the Old Testament; Kampen: Kok, 1997]). Those who have argued for more or less complex, exilic and/or postexilic redaction in the book have often continued to work with the idea of a seventh-century core in chs. 2 and 3 (so, for instance, K. Seybold, *Profane Prophetie: Studien zum Buch Nahum* [Stuttgarter Bibelstudien, 135; Stuttgart: Verlag Katholisches Bibelwerk, 1989]).

is working within a position that regards the Old Testament as having a necessary place—theological, and not just historical—in relation to the fundamental structure of Christian faith. Such an approach will both read the text as speaking of the God of Israel who is also confessed by Christians as the God and Father of Jesus Christ, and allow its distinctive features and particularities to act in critique of, for example, neatly systematized views of the nature of God's involvement with the world and theology's ever-present temptation to speak clearly and unambiguously of that. So, for instance, I have suggested that Nahum has significant intertextual links with Isaiah, but I should also want to attend to what from a literary point of view appears as a high degree of ambiguity or polyvalence in its language (especially, perhaps, in 1.7–2.3). This is indicated heuristically by the *variety* of quite plausible understandings of what is actually being said, which exist in symbiotic relationship with the issue of what party is being addressed at a given point.[42] We should at least consider whether some of the 'oddness' of the language may be a function precisely of its capability of more than one clear reference, its polyvalence of sense.[43] The text, I have suggested, does not fit easily with a view which would see it as tied in a simple, 'objective' way with historical events—even its relationship to the historical fall of Nineveh in 612 BCE is far from clear; nor should it be turned to the service of an unambiguously clear Christian dogmatic system. The book may offer refuge and relief to the afflicted (1.7, 12), but it invites its hearers or readers to consider who is the 'you' addressed, and will not permit them too easily to assume that they are among those who find refuge in God (1.7), rather than among the 'enemies' of v. 8. Who are—may become—the inhabitants of the city of blood?[44] 'Die Mächtigen müssen mit ihm rechnen, die Machtlosen dürfen auf ihn rechnen' ('the powerful have to reckon with him; the powerless can count on him'),[45] but who is who? *Who* are the builders and maintainers

---

42. Note how REB resolves the ambiguities here by *inserting* (without comment) explicit addressees in 1.11 (Nineveh), 1.12 (Judah) and 1.14 (Nineveh). So also does the NIV, from 1.7 through to 2.1 (Eng).

43. See, famously, William Empson's comment that 'the machinations of ambiguity are among the very roots of poetry' (*Seven Types of Ambiguity* [Harmondsworth: Penguin Books, 3rd edn, 1961], p. 3).

44. See the comments of F.D. Maurice, *Prophets and Kings of the Old Testament* (London: Macmillan, 5th edn, 1892), p. 369.

45. W. Dietrich, 'Nahum/Nahumbuch', *TRE* 23 (1994), pp. 737-42 (740).

of the bloody city—or, at least, those who bring their own little bricks towards its building?[46] (Such textures of ambiguity are among the many features to which so-called 'literary approaches' to the biblical texts alert us; but they have not been well responded to in conventional Old Testament Theologies, let alone in Christian doctrinal or systematic theologies which, so far as they actually attend to the Old Testament, generally do so at a further stage of removal from the particularity of the text, in the direction of abstraction and too-easy synthesis.)

Nor, secondly, does such a claimed role for Christian theological interpretation imply or necessitate an imperialism which denies the right of existence to other interpretative stances, from other 'confessional' positions, whether of a traditionally religious kind—Judaism, obviously and especially—or of other types—conventional historical-critical, or ideological-critical, for examples. In other words, it will accept the *de facto* validity, and will wish to argue, from its own position, for the *theological* validity, too, of a *plurality* of approaches and readings. Christian theological reading need claim no more than a space among others. It need not claim some unique virgin inviolability for itself; it will do its work longing and hoping for the eschatological gift of a common language, while recognizing clearly that we do not yet have one; it cannot deny, in favour of some 'methodological atheism', its sense that it has been brought into contact with the ultimate, personal and more-than-personal Reality of things; but the authority with which it speaks cannot be that of an easy and compulsive clarity—only that of broken speech, consonant with what it confesses of that Reality and the pattern of its coming near to us.[47] It may be argued that it is most appropriate, in a pluralist (shall we call it postmodern?) context, not to bracket out specifically Christian theological engagements with the text—trying to 'do theology', so to speak, through the medium of the biblical text itself [48]—in favour of some supposed common norm for

46. A theological hermeneutic must, of course, raise and seek to answer the question: what, if anything, allows us to move from *this* Nineveh to *any* and *every* Nineveh?

47. I mean, in the darkness, desolation and brokenness of the cross of Christ.

48. I am thinking here especially of the recent work of Francis Watson, *Text, Church and World: Biblical Interpretation in Theological Perspective* (Edinburgh: T. & T. Clark, 1994) and *Text and Truth: Redefining Biblical Theology* (Edinburgh: T. & T. Clark, 1997); and of C.R. Seitz, *Word Without End: The Old Testament as Abiding Theological Witness* (Grand Rapids: Eerdmans, 1998). With these works,

interpretation; but, rather, to let them live self-consciously and in the open, and engage in debate with other approaches, not *even*, but *especially*, within the academic setting. For what is the point of a reading which brackets out or puts off indefinitely the question of *truth*? In preference to supposing that we can only work and converse at some common level of supposed neutrality, we may bring our own evaluative criteria and stances out into the open, and engage in discussion from there. If we are concerned with truth (and the nature of 'truth' and the possibility of its attainment will have to be part of the discussion, too), let that concern be expressed within the university context, and not only by those who would think of themselves as doctrinal theologians.

What my plea *does* imply, then, is that a Christian theological approach will enter into constructive engagement (even if that includes dispute) with other ways of reading the biblical text. It will be open to learning from them (which includes the acknowledgment of its failure to do so, and the reasons for that), even as it hopes they will learn from it; and it is committed by its confession to the practice of charity in every facet of its existence, including this. For if it accepts, as I think it should, a 'literal sense' of the text which includes its *practice*, and does not simply perpetuate its transmutation into a reconstuctive 'historical (-critical)' sense,[49] it really must seek to live by that practice. So, to take an instance, it will enter into debate with ideological criticism of the texts, and it will seek to learn from, say, criticism of the promiscuity of the language through which academic biblical study has commonly been pursued.[50] Rather than masking its own ideological holdings, especially under a pretended objectivity, it will seek precisely as part of its debate with other approaches to become conscious of them and make them plain.[51]

in different ways, and not uncritically, I have considerable sympathy.

49. I am alluding sketchily here to the work of Hans Frei and others influenced by him.

50. For this, see P.R. Davies on what he calls 'academic bib-speak': 'Do Old Testament Studies Need a Dictionary?', in D.J.A. Clines, S.E. Fowl and S.E. Porter (eds.), *The Bible in Three Dimensions: Essays in Celebration of Forty Years of Biblical Studies in the University of Sheffield* (JSOTSup, 87; Sheffield: JSOT Press, 1990), pp. 321-35. His point is that such language *illegitimately mixes* theological and other types of discourse. The question is whether there can be conversation without promiscuity.

51. See here the controversy between Philip Davies (*Whose Bible is it Anyway?* [JSOTSup, 204; Sheffield: Sheffield Academic Press, 1995], especially pp. 17-55)

There are, in fact, many points at which the book of Nahum might be thought to lay itself open to ideological critique: it *can* be read as the expression of religious chauvinism, say, the discourse of and for a smug élite, happy to think that the hated evil empire is tottering to destruction, and clothing its relief, and its hope of remaining in power, in conventional religious language, claiming the national god as its own, so that their enemies are his enemies. Likewise, as we have already seen, Nahum can be, and has been, subject to theological critique (which sometimes, as with Graham, verges on ideological). An obvious question which Christian theological engagement with the book must raise is whether God's only way of dealing with oppression is by destroying its perpetrators, and perpetuating the vicious and terrible cycle of violence in the world. It will, however, note also the different possibilities for Nineveh or Assyria spoken of elsewhere (Jon. and Isa. 19.23-25; but note also the oracle against Nineveh in Zeph. 2.13-15);[52] and putting those links of theme within larger settings, it will also ask how what is said in Nahum is 'shaped' by its connections with Isaiah and the book of the Twelve.[53] In addition, we should note in passing the possibility of 'eschatological' readings of the book, which make theological play of

and Francis Watson ('Bible, Theology and the University: A Response to Philip Davies', *JSOT* 71 [1996], pp. 3-16). This raises so many fundamental issues that the discussion is bound to continue—and ought to, with many participants. The web of questions takes us on ultimately (and perhaps sooner than we sometimes like to suppose) to matters about the sociology and politics of knowledge in the kind of society we have—and hope for.

52. Without supposing that such perspectives can be uncontroversially arranged in a hierarchy of value, or that 'the canon' gives clear and straightforward guidelines on this.

53. The 12 'minor prophets' have been seen as a unit in Christian theological tradition, too—though I am aware of questions possibly raised by different orderings of the books—and indeed of the issue of what might be meant by 'unit' in this context. The considerable amount of recent work on the Twelve as a group has viewed their 'unity', and hence Nahum's relation to the others, in several different ways. As examples only, see T. Collins, *The Mantle of Elijah: The Redaction Criticism of the Prophetical Books* (The Biblical Seminar, 20; Sheffield: JSOT Press, 1993), pp. 59-87; R J. Coggins, 'The Minor Prophets—One Book or Twelve?', in S.E. Porter, P. Joyce and D.E. Orton (eds.), *Crossing the Boundaries: Essays in Biblical Interpretation in Honour of Michael D. Goulder* (Biblical Interpretation Series, 8; Leiden: E.J. Brill, 1994), pp. 57-68; B.A. Jones, *The Formation of the Book of the Twelve: A Study in Text and Canon* (SBLDS, 149; Atlanta: Scholars Press, 1995).

230 In Search of True Wisdom

that note of finality expressed within it. Here we make contact again with the broad outline of the mediaeval interpretative tradition noted earlier, however differently we might wish to construe the notion of 'final judgment'; but Nahum is also—in every 'canonical' form, and in contrast to all who emphasize its supposedly sole interest in the fall of Nineveh—a book of *salvation*. Again, therefore, there may be something to learn from that 'pre-critical' interpretative tradition with which we began.

I do not think that theological readings are *easy*, since the endlessly-postponed time of final freedom from oppression might well be regarded as illusory. Like any other position, this is a matter of trust and hope, of how one chooses to read: Luther says of Nahum that 'there is nothing else here but the doctrine of faith'.[54] Luke Johnson has called for

> the appropriate apprehension of Scripture itself as a body of literature that does not primarily describe the world but rather imagines a world, and by imagining it, *reveals it*, and by revealing it, enables it to be brought into being within the physical space humans share with each other....[55]

But is this the *real* world, or a world of illusion? The biblical scholar need not vacate his or her responsibility for struggling with that question, or imagine that the book can only be handled truly if such questions are bracketed out—at least until some late stage of 'application'. I want to argue that the question of meaning and truth in Nahum can only be decided in terms of its capacity to nurture the criticism of power, on behalf of the oppressed. Now who are they, the powerful and the oppressed? There is, I suggest, no discharge—not for biblical scholars, either—from the continual asking of, and the trying to answer in life, that question.

54. *Luther's Works*, 18 (St Louis: Concordia Publishing House, 1975), p. 282.
55. L.T. Johnson, 'Imagining the World Scripture Imagines', *Modern Theology* 14 (1998), pp. 165-80 (172). I am still alert to the question of whether the *university* is a proper context in which to explore this.

WISDOM, SUFFERING AND THE FREEDOM OF GOD
IN THE BOOK OF JOB

R.N. Whybray[†]

Ronald Clements and I began serious academic publication at exactly the same time, more than 30 years ago. His particular interests have been somewhat different from mine, though I have been delighted that during the last few years he has added the wisdom literature to his repertoire. But I have gained much also from his writings on the prophets, especially Isaiah, Jeremiah and Ezekiel, and from his contributions to the history of Old Testament study and to Old Testament theology. It has been a pleasure for me since my migration to Cambridge to participate with him in the Cambridge Old Testament Seminar, and I count it a privilege to have been invited to make a contribution to this well-deserved volume of essays in his honour.

Of the views that have been put forward by scholars about the purpose and meaning of the book of Job, three will be considered in this essay. They are:

1. that the book is about the nature of wisdom;[1]
2. that it is especially concerned with suffering: suffering as a theological problem and/or how the fact of human suffering can be reconciled with faith in the goodness of God;[2]

1. So, e.g., H.H. Schmid, *Wesen und Geschichte der Weisheit* (BZAW, 101; Berlin: W. de Gruyter, 1966), pp. 171-86. For a critique of this view see K.J. Dell, *The Book of Job as Sceptical Literature* (BZAW, 197; Berlin: W. de Gruyter, 1991), pp. 73-88.

2. A classic exposition of this view is H.W. Robinson's *The Cross of Job* (1916), reprinted in *The Cross in the Old Testament* (London: SCM Press, 1955), pp. 11-54.

3.   that it is a theological discussion about the nature of God.[3]

These topics are of course not unconnected.

Wisdom

The question whether the book should be classified as 'wisdom litera-ture' has been the subject of a great deal of discussion. It cannot be set-tled by the criterion of literary form. Wisdom is not a literary genre, and what has been termed 'wisdom literature' assumes a variety of forms. The only criterion that can be applied here is that of content—what are the subjects of discourse? And even this criterion lacks specificity. However, in its reflective (and sometimes didactic) character the book most closely resembles, within the corpus of Old Testament writings, the books of Proverbs and Ecclesiastes, to which the term 'wisdom lit-erature' is applied by common consensus; and in this limited sense it may properly be so described.[4]

However, it is not my intention in this essay to maintain that wisdom is the sole or even the main subject of the book. In my opinion the author's purpose—and it is as a single whole that the book makes best sense[5]—was, in a stricter sense, to put forward in the form of a dialogue in which alternative points of view are presented, his own understand-ing of the nature of God, together with a radical reassessment of the

3.   'One cannot but affirm that Job stands face to face with a completely new experience of the reality of God' (G. von Rad, *Wisdom in Israel* [ET; London: SCM Press, 1972], p. 217). Von Rad also dismisses wisdom and suffering as the main themes of the book: 'While Job's involvement in "wisdom" questions is unmistak-able, it nevertheless recedes in view of the fact that Job introduces into the debate theological points of view of a quite different type' (*Wisdom in Israel*, p. 220). On p. 221 n. 41 he opines that the 'problem of suffering' can be said to be the subject of the book 'only in a very limited sense'.

4.   The appropriateness of the term has been consistently denied by C. Wester-mann with regard to both the book's literary genre(s) and its contents. See, e.g., his *Der Aufbau des Buches Hiob* (Stuttgart: Calwer Verlag, 1977), pp. 27-39, and more recently *Wurzeln der Weisheit* (Göttingen: Vandenhoeck & Ruprecht, 1990), pp. 119-21 (ET *Roots of Wisdom* [Louisville: Westminster John Knox Press, 1995], pp. 105-106).

5.   I do not wish to assert a single authorship for the entire book. But with the possible exception of the speeches by Elihu in chs. 32–37 it can plausibly be main-tained that after giving expression to a variety of opposing views in the debate between the friends and Job it finds its climax in the speeches of Yahweh.

conventional expectations of God current in his time.

There can be no doubt that wisdom is an important topic in the book. This is confirmed by statistical evidence alone: of the 318 occurrences of the root *ḥkm* in the Old Testament, 28 are found in Job. Only Proverbs, with 102, and Ecclesiastes, with 53, exceed that number. Moreover, these occurrences are widely spread. The noun *ḥokmâ*, 'wisdom', together with its cognates *ḥākām* and the verb *ḥākam*, occurs in the utterances of almost all the speakers, Job, Eliphaz, Zophar, Elihu and Yahweh himself. But there is no unanimity among them concerning the nature of wisdom. All agree that wisdom is an attribute of God; but when it comes to human wisdom, of which they speak frequently, they use the concept in a variety of ways. Moreover, their discussions are conducted on two quite different levels. They all claim to be wise; but they rarely discuss the relationship, if any, between divine and human wisdom.

The most obvious example of this two-level use of *ḥokmâ* is ch. 28. That chapter has frequently been regarded as exemplifying the book's multiple authorship.[6] It has, further, been widely held that its final verse, which defines human wisdom as the fear of Yahweh and the avoidance of evil, is an interpolation that directly contradicts the assertions of the preceding verses that wisdom is unattainable by human beings and that only God knows where it is to be found. But this is to misunderstand the verse. Whether or not its author was the same as the author of vv. 1-27, the wisdom to which it refers is clearly something quite different from the divine wisdom of those verses. The word *ḥokmâ* is being used in two quite different senses. Moreover, nothing in the chapter suggests that there is any link between the two: that the one may lead to the other. This is in fact specifically denied in vv. 1-11, which leave no doubt that whatever ingenuity and technical skill may be attained by human beings is not wisdom at all (contrast Isa. 3.3; Ezek. 27.8, where precisely this kind of skill *is* designated as *ḥokmâ*). These verses are perhaps intended to imply that human activity of that kind is in fact a *search* for wisdom but that it is one that is completely futile.

That God possesses a wisdom beyond human understanding and capability is acknowledged by both Job and his friends (9.4; 11.6;

---

6. J. Vermeylen, *Job et son Dieu*, II (Etudes Bibliques; Paris: J. Gabalda, 1970), p. 595 n. 3, notes that this has been the opinion of the majority of commentators.

12.13; 15.8). Yet on another level each of them claims to be 'wise' (though they do not agree about one another's wisdom!). There is little consistency in what they say about this wisdom. Job, for example, rejects the view that wisdom is peculiarly characteristic of the aged (12.12), presumably because he wants to claim that he, being younger than they, is not inferior to them. This seems to imply that wisdom is commonly available; in the next verse, however, Job is careful to distinguish human wisdom from that of God. In 13.1-2, having asserted that his own knowledge is as great as that of the friends, he contemptuously informs them that the only 'wisdom' to which they could lay claim would consist in their silence! In 26.3, in a similar vein, he ironically thanks Bildad for giving helpful advice to a fool like himself who lacks wisdom. In 15.7-10 Eliphaz directs his irony against Job's claims, asking whether, as the firstborn of the human race and auditor of the discussions held by God in his heavenly council, he has acquired God's secret knowledge and so become unique among human beings in possessing wisdom (v. 8).

In addition to these specific uses of *hokmâ* and *ḥākām*, the friends' eagerness to instruct Job about God's dealings with human beings is a further indication of their claim to be regarded as wise persons: it is on the basis of that claim that they all take it upon themselves to lecture Job. Eliphaz (4.12-17) claims that his knowledge has come to him by some kind of supernatural revelation in a night vision. Elsewhere, however, he attributes his superior knowledge to another source: traditional lore (what the sages have told, 15.17-18). This source of wisdom is claimed also by Bildad (8.8-10) and Zophar (20.4). They are claiming to possess a kind of wisdom that is either generally available or is available especially to the 'wise' in each generation and which ought to be, but apparently is not, familiar to Job.

Elihu, too, has no doubt that human beings can be wise. In 32.7-9, defending his intervention in the debate despite his youth, he asserts that the prerequisite for wisdom is not experience of life but the gift of God through his spirit. In 33.4-7 he defines this in such a way as to suggest that it is common to all human beings: he is no different from others. On the other hand, in 33.33 he seems to be confident that he is wiser than Job, and proceeds to instruct him: 'Be silent, and I will teach you wisdom!' In 34.2, 34, he addresses a group of persons (it is not clear whether he is referring to the friends or to another group) who are in some special sense 'wise' (*ḥᵃkāmîm*) and also 'knowledgeable' (*yōdᵉˤîm*) and 'men of sense' (*'anšē lēbāb*). In 35.11—though the meaning of this verse is disputed—he appears to be saying that God teaches human beings through their observation of natural phenomena—specifically the behaviour of the animals. (We may compare Yahweh's own words in ch. 39.)

From the above it has become clear that although all the human speakers claim to be wise, they use the word *hokmâ* in quite different senses. No less than six such senses may be distinguished:

1. Wisdom is a quality that certain people possess (34.2, 34) or claim to possess (26.3; 33.33) in a greater degree than others. In these verses no mention is made of a divine source of human wisdom.
2. Wisdom is the result of the experience of life, and so especially an attribute of the aged.
3. Wisdom is equated with the traditional teaching of 'the fathers' (15.8; cf. 8.8-10; 20.4). Here too there is no specific mention of a divine source or inspiration.
4. Wisdom is taught by God to human beings (35.11; cf. 4.13-17).
5. Wisdom is *inspired* by God through the gift of his spirit (32.8).
6. Wisdom is given by God to all his creatures.

There are also different views about the *range* and specific *content* of this wisdom in the speeches of the human participants in the debate:

1. Wisdom is the ability rationally to discuss problems (17.10).
2. Specifically in this book it is the ability to assess the truth of Job's claims about his innocence and God's treatment of him (32.9; 33.33; 35.11).
3. It is the deposit of traditional lore (15.18).
4. It is the result of human experience acquired in a long life (12.12; 32.7).
5. It is simple human cunning and God does not tolerate it (5.13).
6. It is identified in religious and moral terms as the fear of Yahweh and turning from evil (28.28).

The above analysis has shown that there is no agreement by the human speakers on the questions whether the uses of the term *hokmâ* can be reduced to a single, basic common feature, whether God communicates his wisdom to human beings, or, if he does so, to what extent and to whom. In the speeches by Yahweh (chs. 38–41) there is no hint that he does this. There the word *ḥokmâ* occurs only three times (38.36, 37; 39.17),[7] though it would not be inappropriate to see the whole of those chapters as a demonstration by Yahweh of his wisdom in the creation of the universe (cf. 28.25-27; Prov. 8.22), that is, of actions of his that are by definition impossible for human beings. This is also the message of ch. 28, where the word is undefined (except that vv. 25-27 also relate it to the acts of creation). The final verse of that chapter, as has been observed above, only serves to make it clear that the 'wisdom' of human beings has nothing in common with that of God.

These discussions of wisdom have something of an academic flavour. The claims to superior wisdom made by all the participants remain on a theoretical plane; they all want to demonstrate that they are wise, but unlike, for example, the speeches in Proverbs 1–9, they never succeed in defining the nature of this wisdom. Even in ch. 28, where it is claimed that wisdom is God's unique possession, its nature is not defined. It is true that the final verse of that chapter defines the nature of *human* wisdom, but that is not at all the kind of wisdom to which the other speakers are laying claim. If the author's intention had been to teach the nature of wisdom, whether divine or human, that intention cannot be said to have been successfully carried out. It is therefore necessary to look elsewhere for the book's real purpose.

Suffering

But there is scant evidence for the view that human suffering is the principal topic discussed in the book of Job. Job's suffering is, of course, a very prominent theme, and its cause is extensively debated. The views of Job and his friends about it are diametrically opposed to

---

7.   In two of these verses the reference is to the wisdom exercised by the Creator in the formation of the celestial phenomena (see, e.g., N.C. Habel, *The Book of Job* [OTL; London: SCM Press, 1985], p. 523 on the meaning of *ṭūḥôt* and *śekwî* in 38.36). In the third occurrence (39.17) *ḥokmâ* (with its parallel term *bînâ*) is used in a general sense of the intelligence conferred by God on the animals which enabled them to behave 'rationally' according to their respective natures. The observed extraordinary behaviour of the ostrich is seen as an indication that in its case God omitted that gift. It could admittedly be inferred from this that that kind of wisdom was also given generally by God to human beings; but the context shows that it was not intended that this inference should be drawn. At no point in these chapters does Yahweh speak of human wisdom, whether conferred by God or not.

one another. The latter deny categorically that the innocent have ever perished (so Eliphaz, 4.7) and maintain that suffering is always the consequence of sin. Job, who knows himself to be innocent, and whose piety has been specifically affirmed by the author of the book in the Prologue, believes that his suffering is due to the indifference or the personal malignity of God. These respective convictions are reiterated again and again. Occasionally a third cause of suffering is adumbrated: that God uses it in an attempt to persuade sinners of the error of their ways (so Eliphaz, 5.17-18; Elihu, 33.19-30; 36.8-11). It is also sometimes suggested in the book that all human suffering is the inevitable destiny of human beings from their birth (so Eliphaz, 5.7; Job, 7.1-2; 14.1). But there is no sustained discussion of these alternative explanations, and no conclusion is reached. Further, it is particularly significant that in the speeches of Yahweh, which may be regarded as representing the views of the author, the question is not even raised.

Again, if it was the author's principal purpose to discuss how human suffering can be reconciled with religious faith, his choice of plot and of Job as the central character leaves much to be desired. First, Job is not in the least an example of the typical human sufferer with whom an ordinary reader could be expected to identify and so find help or comfort in trouble. It is made clear from the outset that his troubles— though he does not know it—are not intended by God to be other than temporary. They are real enough, but they are intended to be withdrawn once the wager that occasioned them is settled. They are intended only to constitute a test of Job's purportedly genuine piety. Secondly, Job is hardly a model of how a person enduring unexpected suffering ought to behave. Although at first he accepts his afflictions in an exemplary manner which appears to be approved of by the narrator, his behaviour during the debate with the friends is far from exemplary. In his nine contributions to the debate he speaks almost blasphemously, accusing God of unjust treatment, and even of taking pleasure in his sufferings. Although later God expresses his approval of Job for having 'spoken rightly' about him, this enigmatic statement ignores a great deal of what Job has actually said. He is certainly not a model of pious resignation, and it is not certain that the readers would be entirely sympathetic towards him.

The Nature of God

Where, then, should we look for an indication of the author's purpose—
for the theological message that he wished to convey to the readers?
Throughout the dialogue the principal topic that has preoccupied the
participants has been neither the problem of suffering nor the nature of
wisdom but the very nature of the God whom they all profess to worship. About his transcendence they have been in agreement; but the
point on which they have profoundly differed has been his relationship
with his human creatures. It is surely in the speeches which the author
attributes to Yahweh in chs. 38–41 that the readers would naturally
expect to find the solution.

From the literary point of view also these chapters form the denoue-
ment of the plot. This is the moment to which everything that precedes
has pointed. Despite his feeling that God is his antagonist, Job has repeatedly wished for, hoped—or half-hoped—for, even demanded, an
answer from him. In as far as he had really expected to be granted a
direct confrontation with him he had spoken confidently of his own
ability to prove his innocence and so convict God of injustice. As the
plot proceeds the readers, too, will have been caught up in the expectation—depite its being against all reasonable probability—of God's
deigning to appear, to justify himself 'in court', and will have been
impatient to know what he will say that could convince and satisfy the
desperate Job, whom they know from the Prologue to be undeserving,
according to their notions of divine justice, of his fate. There is therefore a strong sense, when Yahweh suddenly appears, that his appearance, if not that of a *deus ex machina*, will at last bring relief from
tension and a solution to the problems that have been troubling them as
they read the debate between Job and the friends. God has been represented earlier in the book as speaking (1.7, 8, 12; 2.2, 3, 6); but these
impressive speeches have been, as it were, 'set pieces'; Yahweh is now
represented here as revealing to human beings in unprecedented fashion
the secrets of his own inimitable actions performed when and since he
formed the world. This is a theological statement comparable to the
account of the creation of the world in Genesis 1, but having the authority of the creator of the world himself. Yahweh is of course here
'merely' a character in the story; but no Old Testament writer would
have dared to attribute to him words that he did not believe to be true.

It comes as a shock to the reader to find that Yahweh's speeches appear to be entirely irrelevant to the problems raised in the preceding chapters. The longed-for reply to Job's indictment of him is entirely absent, although the speeches are stated at 38.1 to be Yahweh's 'answer' to him. In the following verse (compare also 40.2, 8) Yahweh appears to deplore Job's speeches, reproaching him with in some way 'obscuring counsel' (perhaps meaning Yahweh's universal plan) by speaking words devoid of knowledge. Otherwise throughout his speeches, apart from a brief allusion to the punishment of the proud and wicked (40.11-13) he makes virtually no allusion at all to human beings and their lives. This complete disregard for Job's troubles and for his impassioned plea for justice—and also for the arguments of the friends—will have amazed the readers, reversing all their expectations. It was, however, an astonishing but salutary signal to them that the concerns of human beings are at most peripheral to the incalculable range of God's interests.

The purport of Yahweh's speeches is to demonstrate through the massive use of irony how insignificant is Job—and by implication the whole human race—in the perspective of Yahweh's infinite power. Job is in effect repeatedly asked, in a great series of devastating questions, whether it is he and not God who created the universe and all its contents, and is taunted with the fact of his ignorance and powerlessness. Yahweh first speaks (38.4-38) of the creation of the earth and sea, and of the heaven and the cosmic phenomena. It is of interest to note the similarity of some of the details described to features of speeches made earlier in the book by participants in the debate, especially by Job and Elihu (9.5-10; 26.6-13; 28.25-26; 36.27-33; and ch. 37). Such passages were presumably derived from traditional lore which had probably already to some extent assumed a fixed literary form. There are comparable passages in the Psalms. The motif is used for a variety of purposes: simply to praise Yahweh (Ps. 29.3-9; 33.6-7), to reproach him for failing to exercise his power in a present moment of distress (Ps. 74.13-17; 77.16-19), to acknowledge his incomprehensibility (Job 26.6-13; 36.27-33), or to affirm his justice and righteousness (Job 37; Ps. 97.2-5). Job also in 9.5-12 draws the conclusion from God's cosmic power that this is so overwhelming that human beings can neither dispute with him nor prevent him from doing whatever he pleases.

All these descriptions of God's creative activity are of course necessarily based on second-hand traditions; the speakers have no *direct* knowledge of him. As Job himself finally admits in 42.5, their 'know-

ledge' is in fact only hearsay: it is not dependent on a direct vision or
divine oracle. In Job 38 the author daringly represents Yahweh as
making a direct communication to Job about these things. He confirms
some of those affirmations; however, it is significant that Yahweh does
not claim to be just or righteous, nor does he speak of exercising his
power in coming to the assistance of people in their troubles. The
emphasis of his speeches is entirely on his sovereignty and freedom, on
his incomprehensibility, and on human ignorance and insignificance as
typified by the man Job.

The final chapters of Yahweh's discourses are in the same vein.
Yahweh now proceeds to give an account of the living creatures whom
he has made, and of his care for them—but men and women are missing from the list. Although he continues to address Job and to pose
unanswerable questions to him ('Do you know...?', 'Can you...?', 'Is it
by your wisdom that...?', and the like), he almost seems to have forgotten the existence of the human beings whom also he had created, and in
particular the sufferings that he had himself inflicted on the man Job.
For him Job seems to be no more than the solitary interlocutor who has
presumptuously spoken 'words without knowledge' and attempted to
interfere with his governance of the world, but whom he has now so
unexpectedly deigned to address.

Yahweh speaks here of his personal concern and responsibility for
the creatures to whom he had given the breath of life. His failure to
include human beings in the list is strangely in contrast with other Old
Testament texts that speak of them as made in his image (Gen. 1.26-
28), as made only a little inferior to gods and as crowned with glory and
honour (Ps. 8.6), and as destined by him to rule over the animal creation
(Gen. 1.28; Ps. 8.7-9). Even Job had admitted the loving care with
which God had fashioned him as an individual in the womb and
presided over his birth (Job 10.8-12). Ironically, it is of his loving concern for the lives and nurture of the lions and ravens and their young
that Yahweh speaks here.

In a series of vignettes (38.39–39.30) Yahweh continues to over-
whelm Job, pointing out Job's ignorance of the lives and needs of a
variety of animals and birds while proclaiming his own intimate knowledge of them. It is he—and he alone—who acts as scavenger for food
for the lion cubs (38.39-41) when they might otherwise perish, and who
is familiar with such matters as the gestation period of the wild deer
(39.2-3). The list of creatures does not, of course, pretend to be exhaus-

tive. It is significant that, apart from the warhorse (39.19-25)—a passage that has been judged an interpolation by some scholars[8]—these are all wild creatures whose lives are completely untouched by human contact—except when hunted. Such creatures live in a 'world' by themselves, inhabiting remote regions far from human dwellings; and the human world is entirely ignorant of them. Significantly, particular stress is laid on the freedom of the wild ass, which 'scorns the tumult of the city'; it is contrasted with the domesticated donkey, which is at the beck and call of its brutal owner (39.5-8). Similarly the wild ox (39.9-12) is free from human domestication, and cannot be tamed to serve the demands of a human master, drawing the plough and performing various kinds of labour for him before returning meekly after its work to its designated stall.

These vignettes, in which the few allusions to human beings are wholly negative, are remarkable both for their lyrical beauty and for their perceptive description of aspects of God's providential concern of which the Old Testament is generally unaware or to which it is indifferent, though there are a few brief allusions in, for example, Ps. 104.16-18, 21, 25-27; 149.7-10. One of their most remarkable features is the unusual selection of the creatures listed to the virtual exclusion of the more familiar domestic animals except when the latter are contrasted with the former. Elsewhere in the Old Testament when animals are referred to these are mainly those with which the Israelite audience or readership would be familiar in their daily lives. The only exceptions to this are the references to dangerous animals such as bears and lions, which are mentioned only for their fierceness.

Animals are sometimes used in the Old Testament as models to be imitated. The most striking example of a completely different approach to animals from that adopted in Job 39 is Isa. 1.3. There the domesticated ox and ass, the former 'knowing' (that is, obedient to) its owner (*qōnēhû*), the latter 'knowing' the stall (*'ēbûs*) assigned to it by its owner, are models of the obedience that Yahweh expects of Israel but which they have rebelliously refused to accept. In Job 39.3-12, in contrast, Yahweh rejoices in having given freedom to their wild counterparts, the wild ass that is not forced to submit to its driver and the wild ox that refuses to serve a human master or to accept his stall (*'ēbûs*).

---

8. Even the warhorse, though 'tamed' by human beings, has a will of its own and expresses its 'freedom' by its eagerness to play its part in battle. It is not thus an entirely enslaved creature like the domesticated ox and ass.

The similarity of the two passages suggests the possibility that the Job passage has been deliberately based on that in Isaiah. In the book of Proverbs other creatures also stand as models for human behaviour, though the points made there are not dissimilar to those of Job 39. The ant, though useless to human beings, is commended as a model of independence and diligence (Prov. 6.6-9) and for its wisdom (30.24-25), and similarly the badger, locust and lizard have instructive roles (30.26-28). The lion is characterized by its courage, which is compared to that of kings (30.30).

In Job 39, then, there is a very marked emphasis on *freedom*: the freedom of the lives of the creatures described. Even the ostrich, which 'laughs at the horse and its rider' (v. 18), enjoys total freedom. There is a realism about these vignettes: the author does not idealize these creatures (in contrast to the paradisal picture in Isa. 11.6-9; 65.25). Lions and ravens obtain their food, with Yahweh's direct encouragement, by preying on other creatures; the ostrich treats its young with cruelty, and also, being devoid of wisdom, exposes its eggs to the danger of being trampled on by other passing creatures; the eagle (vv. 29-30) uses its sharp eyes to swoop down to feed on dead bodies. That is their nature, and God has created it so. But the principal point, made repeatedly, is that God has given them the freedom to roam or to fly over virtually unlimited tracts of territory at will and without hindrance. The few references to human beings in the chapter should perhaps also be taken to imply not only the bondage of the domesticated animals but also the self-imposed narrow existence of God's other creature, humankind. It is not for nothing that the wild animals scorn and keep away from the tumult of the city (v. 7).[9]

The tone of these vignettes suggests that what Yahweh values above all else in his world is freedom; that he takes a special pleasure in the uninhibited life of the creatures that he describes. We may perhaps also

---

9.　The descriptions in Yahweh's second speech of the two monstrous creatures Behemoth (40.15-24) and Leviathan (40.25–41.26 [Heb]) neither add significantly to nor detract from the theme of 38.39–39.30. It has been suggested that they have subsequently been added to an earlier version of the text. However that may be, they resemble the creatures described in the preceding vignettes in just one respect: they too are 'free'—in the sense that all attempts to capture them are unsuccessful because of their physical strength and imperviousness to assault. Their principal function in the context appears, however, to reinforce Yahweh's earlier demonstration of the wonders of his creative power.

detect here a kind of 'celebration' by Yahweh of *his own* freedom to act. Job with his problems and his endless complaints—his words devoid of wisdom (38.2)—has done his best to 'obscure counsel'; but in his speeches Yahweh pays no attention to him or to the arguments put forward by the friends. Significantly, he has chosen to display only two aspects of his creative activity: the cosmos itself, with its own unpredictability, and the world of the wild animals with their independence of human control.

Yahweh's account of himself in these chapters was one with which both Job and his friends were already familiar in some respects. But they had never before fully realized its implications: that the God who is sovereign over all that exists is unpredictable because he cannot be subjected to any restriction on his freedom. They had tried to confine him within the limits that they—or their inherited traditions—had invented. They had assumed that he *must* conform—and had in fact conformed—to their notions of justice: that he was bound to assign to human beings the rewards and punishments they had merited. Job also had made this assumption: he did not deny the principle of retribution, but he differed from the friends in his complaint that God had not observed that rule in his own, Job's, case. Moreover, he believed that he had the right to question God's conduct and had a right to an answer to his questioning. By refusing to make the slightest allusion to these claims about what he was 'bound' to do, Yahweh had by his emphatic silence implicitly rejected the very existence of human 'rights' where Job was concerned.

The omission of human beings from Yahweh's account of his creative actions, which gives the account a curiously unbalanced appearance, is clearly deliberate. That an important feature of the account was its demonstration that Yahweh's concerns are infinitely wider than Job can have imagined, and include parts of his creation that are virtually beyond human reckoning, does not sufficiently account for it. Elsewhere in the Old Testament it is taken for granted that human beings are pre-eminent in God's world.

Up to ch. 38 the book has been wholly concentrated on the affairs of a single man, Job. The impression that had been given to the readers was that these issues are supremely important. They have followed a long series of impassioned speeches by this man, and another series of discourses by the friends, all wholly concerned with Job's guilt or innocence. Now at last Yahweh speaks—and talks about something entirely different. It is difficult to avoid the conclusion—even though in the Epilogue Yahweh reverts to a consideration of Job's affairs—that the author is using chs. 38–41 to say that human affairs are only of peripheral importance in the universe and deserve at most only a tiny fraction of his attention.[10] If so, this is a revolutionary notion that stands opposed not only to the previous chapters of this book, but indeed to what was a central tenet of Israel's traditional faith. It is not just a matter of human deserts and the concept of divine justice. In the Old Testament as a whole there are two protagonists: God and humanity. These are not, of course, equal protagonists, but the relationship between them is the subject matter of the whole Bible. In these speeches of Yahweh, which, because they are placed in the mouth of God and because of their crucial position in the book, represent the author's own view, this is implicitly denied: God is all, humanity is nothing.

Admittedly the framework in which the poem of Job is set does something to mitigate this stark conclusion, though the function of the Prologue and Epilogue is somewhat obscure and has been the subject of different attempts at interpretation. In the Prologue and Epilogue God *is* concerned with the man Job, and indeed with human beings more generally: he sends the Satan out to investigate human behaviour and to make regular reports. But it cannot be denied that even there God lives up to the character of unpredictability which is the burden of chs. 38–41. Moreover, although in the Prologue he professes an interest in Job's piety and integrity, in his wager with the Satan he treats him as a mere pawn, and has no scruple about subjecting him to misery. Again in the Epilogue he is unpredictable, commending Job for speaking rightly about him and then treating him with extravagant generosity. In neither the Progue nor the Epilogue, however, does he show him the kindly concern that he shows to the lions and ravens.

The absolute freedom of God demonstrated in Yahweh's speeches, then, takes the form of unpredictability or even capriciousness when translated into the sphere of his relationship with human beings. It appears that there is *no* necessary connection between a person's behaviour and his or her good or bad fortune in life. This is the lesson that the author propounds in answer to the traditional doctrine. While it is not possible to determine precisely the circumstances in which the book was written, it clearly presupposes as its background an established

10. This has become even clearer in recent times with increased awareness of the immensity of the universe.

belief to the contrary. It is reasonable to envisage here the situation of a disillusioned people protesting, like those addressed by Ezekiel, that 'the way of Yahweh is not right' (*lō' yittāken*, Ezek. 18.25). The use of the verb *tkn*, 'to measure, adjust', in that verse implies that there is a norm to which God is expected to conform. For the author of Job there cannot be such a norm; God is bound by no rules and no conventions. It is therefore folly for human beings to complain about their lot. That is what, in the end (42.2-6), Job came to understand.

The book of Job is a polemical work. Like Ecclesiastes, it was designed to undermine a current dogma and to offer a rational defence of a revolutionary thesis. As part of the canonical Scriptures it is, of course, to be interpreted in the light of the canon as a whole. Its teaching about the nature of God and of his relationship with the world needs to be viewed in conjunction with the rest of Scripture. While the view that God is not bound by human notions of justice may seem to some readers to be destructive of faith, to others it will seem to follow from a belief in his transcendence. To those who, like Job, have suffered sudden and inexplicable blows of fortune or who have seen others suffer— for example, serious illness or bereavement—it can bring deliverance from a sense of injustice based on a view of God which sees him as bound to cater for every particular human need, and so enable them to worship him with greater understanding. This was the experience of Job, who after his agonizing struggles came to renew his initial surrender of himself to the God of whom he had been able to say: 'The Lord gave and the Lord has taken away; blessed be the name of the Lord'.

SITTING LOOSE TO HISTORY: READING THE BOOK
OF LAMENTATIONS WITHOUT PRIMARY REFERENCE
TO ITS ORIGINAL HISTORICAL SETTING

Paul M. Joyce

An emphasis on reading biblical texts in the light of their likely original
settings has, of course, been one of the defining features of the 'historical-critical' study of the Bible in modem times. But several recent
approaches have moved away from this emphasis, thereby in some
respects coming closer to some traditional handlings of the text. I
myself am committed to the pursuit of historical-critical concerns, but
not to the exclusion of other approaches. My short commentary on the
book of Lamentations[1] is in predominantly historical-critical mode,
albeit an example of (in the words of the *Oxford Bible Commentary*
editors) 'chastened historical criticism', by which is meant 'the legacy
of nineteenth- and twentieth-century critical scholarship chastened by
awareness of its limits and the legitimacy of alternative ways of reading
the texts'. I am indeed keen to explore the legitimacy of alternative
ways of reading the book of Lamentations. There follow six sections,
each considering a way in which emphasis moves away from the historical in the interpretation of this book. Occasionally comment will be
made in passing on the theological dimension of some of these reading
options. A final section will then reflect briefly on the extent to which
some of the approaches might be influenced, directly or indirectly, by
ideas associated with postmodernism, or alternatively may be shown to
share some affinities with such ideas (a discussion which will be anticipated at certain points in the body of the essay).

---

1. P.M. Joyce, 'Lamentations', in J. Barton and J. Muddiman (eds.), *Oxford
Bible Commentary* (Oxford: Oxford University Press, 2000]).

1. *Agnosticism about Dating Lamentations*

It has been commonplace to attempt to read the book of Lamentations
against a specific historical background. Some have favoured the Mac-
cabean crisis (e.g. Treves[2]) and there have been other proposals too
(e.g. Morgenstern looked to the early fifth century[3]). But overwhelm-
ingly the most common view is that these laments come from the aftermath of the fall of Jerusalem to the Babylonians in c. 587 BCE. This has
survived as a consensus position,[4] long after the traditional ascription to
the prophet Jeremiah has been abandoned by almost everyone.

Recently, however, there have been moves away from the attempt to
locate the work in a known, particular historical period. For example,
Iain Provan has argued that we have no clear idea of the period of
ancient Israel's story to which this text might primarily relate.[5] He
regards the evidence to be such as not to allow certainty concerning
either the period spoken about or the time of writing. The most he is
willing to chance is that: 'The second poem, and therefore the book as a
whole, may, with a degree of certainty, be dated between the 6th and
the 2nd centuries B.C.'.[6] S.J.D. Cohen has argued along comparable
lines, that the author was not narrowly interested in specific historical
events, but rather in 'all falls from divine grace, all disasters inflicted
upon a sinful humanity'.[7] It must indeed be admitted that specific clues
to dating are difficult to discern in Lamentations. This is one of several
features which Lamentations shares with the Psalms, which are of
course notoriously hard to pin down to particular periods of Israel's history. Indeed Psalms 74 and 79 raise very similar dating debates to those
prompted by Lamentations, concerning which particular crisis may be

2. M. Treves, 'Conjectures sur les dates et les sujets des Lamentations', *Bul-
letin Renan* 95 (1963), pp. 1-4.

3. J. Morgenstern, 'Jerusalem—485 B.C.', *HUCA* 27 (1956), pp. 101-79; 28
(1957), pp. 15-47; 31 (1960), pp. 1-29.

4. E.g., D.R. Hillers, *Lamentations* (Anchor Bible, 7a; Garden City, NY:
Doubleday, 2nd edn, 1992).

5. I.W. Provan, 'Reading Texts against a Historical Background: The Case of
Lamentations 1', *SJOT* 1 (1990), pp. 130-43; Provan, *Lamentations* (NCB; London:
Marshall Pickering; Grand Rapids: Eerdmans, 1991), pp. 7-19.

6. Provan, *Lamentations*, p. 19.

7. S.J.D. Cohen, 'The Destruction: From Scripture to Midrash', *Prooftexts* 2
(1982), pp. 18-39.

in view. Both the Psalter and Lamentations feature traditional and for-
mulaic language; but as with the Psalms, so with Lamentations: the
very feature of unspecificity means that the poems lend themselves to
use and reuse in ever new contexts, and to multiple reference. This is
indeed part of their abiding power. In the case of Lamentations, we
know for sure that they were applied, for example, to the fall of the
Temple in 70 CE; this is clear from the rabbinic Midrash *Lamentations
Rabbah*, which relates that disaster to the long story of the suffering of
the Jews down the ages.[8]

   This first example poses sharply the important question: does it really
matter if we cannot know much at all about the historical setting of a
biblical text? Provan, speaking with particular reference to Lamentations 1, argues that dating may indeed be significant in so far as our
concern is with historical reconstruction of one kind or another. 'But',
he continues, 'does it matter...from the point of view of *meaning*? The
answer seems to be no.'[9] Provan's move away from reading in the light
of a specific historical situation in some ways reminds one of the ahistorical aspect of some approaches influenced by postmodernism. In
other respects though, most notably the affirmative theological stance
adopted in his work, Provan clearly stands far from postmodernism.

2. *Liturgical Use*

Though developed within a historical-critical context, Provan's agnosticism about dating Lamentations in some ways brings us back closer to
styles of reading which characterized the period before the rise of the
historical-critical method in modern times. The book of Lamentations
has had an important role in liturgical usage in both Judaism and Christianity for many centuries. Indeed this could have been a feature of this
work from its inception, for the book may have had its very origin in
liturgical commemoration of the fall of Jerusalem in 587 BCE.[10] Within
Jewish liturgy it certainly came to be associated with the ninth day of
Ab, the anniversary of that event, and the liturgical function of the book

   8.   Cf. J. Neusner, *Israel after Calamity: The Book of Lamentations* (The Bible
of Judaism Library; Valley Forge, PA: Trinity Press International, 1995). (This
work deals with *Lamentations Rabbah* rather than with the biblical book directly.)
   9.   Provan, 'Reading Texts', p. 141.
   10. Though there is Talmudic evidence which seems to suggest that, at least in
one period, the book was read only in private (*b. Ta'anit* 30a).

may have been a key feature in its achieving canonical status.[11] The role of this text in articulating corporate Jewish identity and memory in a whole sequence of tragic situations in the story of the Jews down the centuries is well documented, as for example in the work of Mintz.[12] Within Christianity too the book has had a liturgical function. Quotations from Lamentations have had an important place in the service of Tenebrae ('shadows'), a sequence of lessons accompanied by the gradual extinguishing of lights, historically associated with the evenings of Wednesday, Thursday and Friday of Holy Week. In some newer liturgies, too, the book has retained a place; for example, the Anglican *Alternative Service Book 1980* made provision for the reading of Lam. 3.22-26, 31-33 at certain funerals.

Such liturgical use is very different from historical-critical reading. The text is a vehicle for communal and personal devotion. There is of course an awareness of the past, but no focus on a reconstructed situation in which the text was created and no preoccupation with the probable original meaning of the text, or indeed awareness of that as a distinct issue. It is interesting to note in this context the work of Brevard Childs; with particular reference to Lamentations 3, Childs wrote in 1979:

> A shift has been effected from the communal focus to an individual, and from the events of 587 to an individual's personal history. This is not to suggest that the writer has moved from historical concerns into a timeless era—the historical quality of the lament is dominant—but rather that he has incorporated history within liturgical language. The suffering of one representative man is described in the language of worship which transcends any one fixed moment in history.[13]

---

11. The same may well be true of all five short texts which comprise the Megilloth, the others being the Song of Songs, Ruth, Ecclesiastes (Qoheleth) and Esther.

12. A. Mintz, *Hurban: Responses to Catastrophe in Jewish Literature* (New York: Columbia University Press, 1984). Chapter 1 (pp. 17-48) is entitled 'The Rhetoric of Lamentations'.

13. B.S. Childs, *Introduction to the Old Testament as Scripture* (Philadelphia: Fortress Press; London: SCM Press, 1979), pp. 594-95. We may suggest that the general trend of Childs's work in more recent years has been to distance him ever further from the emphases of historical criticism, and in this regard—if no other— to increase an affinity with postmodern approaches. Incidentally, quotation of the above words does not necessarily imply agreement with Childs in all the details of his interpretation of the reference to 'the man' in Lam. 3.

Such factors, which may in this way already feature in the shaping of the text, gain a heightened place during its subsequent life, once the book is used as Scripture within worship.

In liturgical reading we have at the very least a loosening of the moorings of the text within ancient history, when compared, say, with historical-critical study; in this respect liturgical usage might be said to have an affinity with some approaches influenced by postmodernism. On the other hand, worship has of course a transcendent referent, namely God, and the text is seen to bear upon ultimate truths as perceived by the believer; and these features place liturgical reading very far from postmodernism.

3. *Psychological Interpretation*

Among the many new methods that have arisen within biblical studies over recent decades has been the application of the insights of psychology to the task of reading the Bible.[14] Though evidently in many respects a new development, it is important to acknowledge some features shared with commentators earlier in the history of interpretation, including Augustine and Ignatius Loyola, for whom psychological insights, albeit differently expressed, certainly had an important place.

It is the potentially ahistorical nature of the psychological approach which makes it relevant to the present context. I have elsewhere attempted to bring the insights of pastoral psychology to bear on the book of Lamentations, arguing that the book's contradictions and inconsistencies may be understood more readily in the light of what has been learned of how human beings react to experiences of radical loss.[15] That contribution was presented primarily in terms of historical-critical issues, that is to say the emphasis was on how new understandings of the way human beings respond might help us better understand how the book of Lamentations emerged in ancient Israel. However, it would also be possible (either as an alternative or as a complement) to develop a psychological approach to reading the book of Lamentations which was not tied to historical questions in that way. Some of the lines

14. Cf. D.K. Miell, 'Psychological Interpretation', in R.J. Coggins and J.L. Houlden (eds.), *A Dictionary of Biblical Interpretation* (London: SCM Press; Philadelphia: Trinity Press International, 1990), pp. 571-72.

15. P.M. Joyce, 'Lamentations and the Grief Process: A Psychological Reading', *BibInt* 1/3 (1993), pp. 304-20.

along which such reading might be developed are indicated by Clines and Exum:

> Just as psychoanalytic theory has shown the power of the unconscious in human beings, so literary critics search for the unconscious drives embedded within texts. We can view texts as symptoms of narrative neuroses, treat them as overdetermined, and speak of their repressions, displacements, conflicts and desires. Alternatively, we can uncover the psychology of characters and their relationships within the texts, and ask what it is about the human condition in general that these texts reflect, psychologically speaking. Or we can turn our focus upon empirical readers, and examine the noncognitive effects that reading our texts have upon them, and construct theoretical models of the nature of the reading process.[16]

One could go on from here to consider roleplay, Gestalt therapy, drama and dance as ways of engaging in imaginative exploration of the text and of the psychological 'inscapes' of participants. The book of Lamentations offers much scope for such work, which might draw further inspiration from Walter Hollenweger's dramatic use of other biblical materials.[17]

In the present context, of course, the extent to which such psychological handlings of texts 'sit loose' to history is of particular interest, and one becomes aware here of affinities with certain features of postmodernism. Some may be surprised to find psychology discussed in connection with postmodernism, for psychology is commonly perceived as a typically 'modernist' enterprise. Psychologists since Freud have, it is said, worked with a grand 'metanarrative', whereas postmodernism is often characterized by the abandonment of all 'metanarratives'. It is important to recognize, though, that psychology has not stood still over recent decades, and it has not been immune from the influences of postmodernism.[18]

As for theology, psychological reading of the Bible may or may not have a theological dimension. This is excluded, for example, by Hal-

16. D.J.A. Clines and J.C. Exum, 'The New Literary Criticism', in Exum and Clines (eds.), *The New Literary Criticism and the Hebrew Bible* (JSOTSup, 143; Sheffield: Sheffield Academic Press, 1993), p. 18, and the related Select Bibliography (pp. 23-24).

17. E.g., W.J. Hollenweger, *Conflict in Corinth, and Memoirs of an Old Man* (ET; New York: Paulist Press, 1982).

18. See 'Psychoanalytic Criticism', in The Bible and Culture Collective, *The Postmodern Bible* (New Haven: Yale University Press, 1995), pp. 187-224.

perin's reductionistic psychological reading of Ezekiel,[19] but it would be perfectly possible to have a creative engagement with Scripture, profoundly informed by the insights of psychology, which, though sitting loose to history, very much retained theological reference.[20]

4. *Literary Approaches*

One of the most distinctive developments in biblical studies over the last quarter-century has been the strong influence of literary studies in English, French and other modern languages upon the assessment of meaning in biblical interpretation.[21] One important feature has been a move away from the notion of fixed and precise meaning, defined as the original meaning or even the author's intention, to a recognition of openness of meaning in biblical material. Robert Alter, among others, has helped us appreciate the 'multivalency' of Hebrew poetry, that is, its capacity to carry many possibilities of meaning at one and the same time.[22] Whereas many biblical scholars of an earlier generation would wrestle to the death with semantic ambiguity in a Hebrew word or phrase, determined to pin down its one precise meaning in the particular

19. D.J. Halperin, *Seeking Ezekiel: Text and Psychology* (University Park, PA: Pennsylvania State University Press, 1993).

20. Cf. my critique of Halperin's reductionism in P.M. Joyce, 'Reading the Bible within the Public Domain', in F.M. Young (ed.), *Dare We Speak of God in Public? The Cadbury Lectures for 1994* (London: Mowbray, 1995), pp. 67-79. Halperin's psychological approach to Ezekiel is historical in its reference (it attempts nothing less than psychoanalysis of the historical Ezekiel), but it excludes theology; I, on the other hand, am hinting at a psychological reading of Lamentations which might be theological but not necessarily historical in its reference.

21. A best-selling if relatively conservative representative of this trend is R. Alter and F. Kermode (eds.), *The Literary Guide to the Bible* (London: Collins, 1987). Francis Landy provided the section on Lamentations (pp. 329-34). Within the context of the present discussion, it is noteworthy that it remains very historical in its application of literary insights. It begins: 'Lamentations is as historical as the Song of Songs is ahistorical; it marks, with untempered immediacy, the focal calamity of the Bible, the destruction of Jerusalem in 586 B.C.E.' (p. 329). In his discussion of ch. 4, he writes: 'These insistent comparisons set the catastrophe in a context that is partly literary, partly historical' (p. 332). For an indication of the more thoroughgoing, and generally more ahistorical, nature of much of the broader range of literary approaches, see Clines and Exum, 'The New Literary Criticism', pp. 11-25.

22. R. Alter, *The Art of Biblical Poetry* (New York: Basic Books, 1985).

text, we are now more inclined to enjoy the rich possibilities and multiple echoes of a passage, aware that—especially in poetry—it would be a thin piece indeed which was entirely univocal. We have come to understand more, too, about the way in which interpretative choices are shaped by the situation and perspective of the interpreter. In practice, interpretation has of course always been influenced by such factors to a much greater degree than has been consciously acknowledged, but recent years have seen a more overt recognition of this.

Jannie Hunter has given particular attention to the possible implications of radical literary theory, especially postmodernism and deconstruction, for reading the Bible.[23] His work demands special attention here, both because it is particularly well informed and also because he focuses on the book of Lamentations. Hunter begins by reviewing examples of methods of interpretation in 'the modern era'. In historical-critical mode, Kraus's work on Lamentations certainly sought to elucidate the precise meaning of the book and its parts.[24] Even the 'structural' method employed in Renkema's large commentary seeks to establish the definitive meaning of the text.[25] In contrast to these, Hunter argues that in 'the postmodern era' biblical scholarship must face fresh challenges. The central idea he emphasizes is intertextuality, both in the creation of a text and in the reading process. 'Texts', he writes, 'are...always part of a sequence and group of texts which all have influence on the meaning in a specific text'.[26] He argues that this phenomenon of intertextuality tends to 'disseminate' or 'destabilize' meaning, 'as no single text uses words in exactly the same sense and meaning'.[27] The biblical scholar can trace a good deal of the literary dependence of a text (though even this quest inevitably has its limits), but when one takes account of other 'disseminating' factors, such as the interpreter's own projections onto the text, one realizes that any search

23. J.H. Hunter, *Faces of a Lamenting City: The Development and Coherence of the Book of Lamentations* (BEATAJ, 39; Frankfurt-am-Main: P. Lang, 1996).

24. H.-J. Kraus, *Klagelieder (Threni)* (BKAT, 20; Neukirchen–Vluyn: Neukirchener Verlag, 3rd edn, 1968).

25. J. Renkema, *Klaagliedern* (Commentaar op het Oude Testament; Kampen: Kok, 1993; ET: Leuven: Peeters, 1998); cf. Renkema, 'The Literary Structure of Lamentations (I-IV)', in W. van der Meer and J.C. de Moor (eds.), *The Structural Analysis of Biblical and Canaanite Poetry* (JSOTSup, 74; Sheffield: JSOT Press, 1988), pp. 294-396.

26. Hunter, *Faces*, p. 27.

27. Hunter, *Faces*, p. 32; cf. p. 38.

for precise and final meaning is doomed to failure. In such ways, Hunter concedes much to the insights of postmodernism and deconstruction.

How then can the interpreter operate? Two features of Hunter's strategy may be highlighted. One is that he adopts what we may call a 'realist' stance, arguing that (in spite of all the above) we still as readers seek meaning, and, he comments, 'these interpretations are normally communicated to other people, who are thought to understand the interpretations'.[28] Hunter's second emphasis is that every text has what he calls its 'individuality'; that is, an element of originality and particularity is always present. Meaning is still elusive, but '...a text features individuality as much as it features intertextual references'.[29] 'Practically therefore,' he writes, 'the search for meaning...means looking for the distinctiveness or peculiarity of the text within both the signifying process and the intertextual references of the text'.[30] 'Instead of calling for the final and exact meaning of the text...as that of the text or that of the author, an intertextual meaning is proposed...one that says that meaning does exist, even if it is for an interpretive moment through the...interpretation of intertextual associations'.[31]

The particular approach and vocabulary adopted by Hunter may not commend themselves to all, but it is to be hoped that his work will receive the attention it deserves. In a less sophisticated way and yet one also influenced by literary approaches, I too wish to find a place both for the rigorous quest for meaning in interpretation and also for a recognition that the final and exact meaning of material, especially poetic material such as Lamentations, may always elude us. Let me briefly illustrate this with two cases. In Lam. 4.6a, a pair of Hebrew words is used, each of which is ambiguous. The English of the Revised Standard Version runs: 'For the chastisement of the daughter of my people has been greater than the punishment of Sodom'. The Hebrew word '^{a}wôn, translated 'chastisement' here, can also be translated 'iniquity' (as RSV margin); whilst the Hebrew word ḥaṭṭā't, translated 'punishment' here, can also be translated 'sin' (as RSV margin). The context clearly demands a pair of synonyms, but are they two words meaning

28. Hunter, *Faces*, p. 37.

29. Hunter, *Faces*, p. 38; cf. also p. 34.

30. Hunter, *Faces*, p. 38. For a fuller articulation of Hunter's position and its theoretical undergirding, see J.H. Hunter, 'Escaping the Abyss: Beyond Deconstruction in Old Testament Studies', *Acta Academica* 24 (1992), pp. 62-76.

31. Hunter, *Faces*, p. 37.

'sin' or two words meaning 'punishment'? Interpretation of this verse depends in part upon one's theological assessment of the message of the book as a whole. On such a basis, Gottwald asserted that two words for 'sin' are found here;[32] on the other hand, it can be argued that the context (with its additional detail on the fate of Sodom in the latter part of the verse, and with the general picture of Zion's tragic state in the surrounding verses) favours the RSV's option of taking the pair of synonyms to refer to 'punishment'. We may strive for certainty, but we have to recognize that semantic ambiguity remains; indeed perhaps both senses of the words (sin *and* its punishment) should be heard. Another case is provided by 5.7, where the RSV runs: 'Our fathers sinned, and are no more; and we bear their iniquities'. Does the Hebrew word '*ᵃbōtênû*, translated 'fathers' here, refer to ancestors, now dead, or to leaders, now in exile? To take the word to mean leaders rather than ancestors would cohere with the blaming of leaders in 4.13-16, but, on the other hand, texts such as 2 Kgs 23.26 and Jer. 31.29 may suggest that the blaming of ancestors is equally likely. Again we have to recognize more than one possible meaning. Of course, reading within a broader context and humility about exegetical certainty have long been features of historical criticism, but this has been as part of the quest for final meaning. I am here suggesting something rather different, highlighting the ultimately inconclusive and unstable nature of all broader frames of reference. Perhaps we can never reach a definitive and final interpretation. One strives to elucidate the meaning of the words, while acknowledging the provisionality of such findings, but not merely in the negative sense of falling short of the real aim, but in a more positive way, that allows one to play heuristically and imaginatively with possibilities, and to hear multiple echoes in a richly-laden poetic text.

5. *Reading in the Light of a Particular Ideological Agenda*

Alice Miller's remarkable essay on 'the mistreated child in the Lamentations of Jeremiah' shares some of the features of both literary and psychological approaches. But more especially it provides a good example of a reading conditioned by a particular ideological agenda, for it is profoundly influenced by her personal commitment to the fate of

32. N.K. Gottwald, *Studies in the Book of Lamentations* (SBT; London: SCM Press, 1954), p. 69.

abused children in our own modern societies.[33] So far removed is Miller's essay from the concerns of historical criticism that, although this is in some respects the most radical item discussed here, it assumes Lamentations to be written (as tradition had it) by Jeremiah. Equally significant and even more surprising, the essay does not focus at all on the fate of actual children within the book; the two dreadful references to the cannibalistic eating of babies in Lam. 2.20 and 4.10 go unmentioned. Rather Miller finds in the protests of the book of Lamentations a powerful expression of rebellion against cruelty, this being the voice of the 'vital, feeling and seeing child' within each of us. This is a concept which she projects onto the text, in terms of which she reads it within our modern setting. She perceives the book of Lamentations as a whole to be emphasizing the acceptance of suffering; this she resists, and instead gives a privileged status to the voice of protest which she hears within the text. She argues that, in our situation as readers, acceptance of the unacceptable must be rejected. Miller contends that mistreated children typically cling to the hope that the torture they suffer is no more than a just and necessary response to their own guilt, that they are being chastised out of love. In so far as the book of Lamentations encourages this sad delusion, she says, it must be resisted. It is important to stress that Miller's discussion here is in no way related to the historical judgments of redaction criticism. She does not claim that the voice of protest has been overlaid by later editors, but rather makes a readerly decision to 'foreground' one feature of a holistic text. This raises the fascinating question of 'who has the last word?', both within the text and in the business of interpretation, and, furthermore, 'on what grounds are such questions to be decided?' For Miller, ideology (one might substitute the word morality) is quite evidently a more important criterion than history. In her apparent indifference to the original context of Lamentations, Miller shares something with postmodernism; on the other hand, her passionate commitment to a moral stance might seem to place her some way from postmodernism.[34]

33. A. Miller, 'The Mistreated Child in the *Lamentations of Jeremiah*', in *idem*, *Breaking Down the Wall of Silence to Join the Waiting Child* (London: Virago, 1991), pp. 114-26.

34. See, though, Z. Bauman, *Postmodern Ethics* (Oxford: Basil Blackwell, 1993). Bauman presents a postmodern perspective on ethics which challenges the assumption that postmodernism need imply an abandonment of moral responsibility.

6. *A New Approach to Textual Criticism*

One can tend to think of textual criticism as the archetypal 'modernist' scholarly discipline, attracting those people who like matters cut and dried and to know where they are with things. However, one perhaps has to view textual criticism somewhat differently in the light of some recent developments, exemplified by the work of the New Testament scholar David Parker.[35] He argues that the quest for the original text is illusory. He writes: 'Generally, debate has centred on the meaning of a single authoritative text...such a text does not exist today, and never has existed'.[36] Again, he speaks of how 'the differences in emphasis, not between [the Gospels] but between different versions of those Gospels, show the oral period and the first centuries of the written period to have been a continuum of re-interpretation'. He highlights 'the difficulty of establishing a fixed point in the tradition that has any unique "authority"'. 'What we have', he says, 'is a collection of interpretative rewritings of a tradition'.[37] Within Old Testament studies, some comparable moves have been made by, for example, Johan Lust, who argues that the striving for an original 'pure' and uncorrupted form of the text must ultimately be regarded as an abstract ideal.[38] We may never have the original text, then. But excitingly what we do have, in all the multiple textual possibilities, is a window on developing tradition; we are permitted to eavesdrop, as it were, on the conversations of interpretative communities in the early church or, in the case of Lamentations, ancient Israel. Both Parker and Lust arrive at such conclusions by a practical route, wrestling with particular textual cruces, and moreover the uncertainties they introduce remain, of course, uncertainties within an ancient—albeit now dynamic—historical context; but it is interesting

35. D.C. Parker, 'The Early Traditions of Jesus' Sayings on Divorce', *Theology* 96 (1993), pp. 372-83; Parker, *The Living Text of the Gospels* (Cambridge: Cambridge University Press, 1997). See also Parker, 'Scripture is Tradition', *Theology* 94 (1991), pp. 11-17. A particularly stimulating feature of Parker's work is his suggestion that as texts become electronic resources we can rediscover a sense of their dynamic nature.
36. Parker, 'Early Traditions', p. 372.
37. Parker, 'Early Traditions', pp. 378-79.
38. Cf. J. Lust (ed.), *Ezekiel and his Book: Textual and Literary Criticism and their Interrelation* (BETL, 74; Leuven: Leuven University Press/Peeters, 1986), pp. 8, 16-17, 19, 53-54.

to note an intriguing analogy with the more theoretical and of course more thoroughgoing emphasis on the elusiveness and intangibility of text which characterizes much work influenced by postmodernism.[39]

The possible implications of contributions such as Parker's may be illustrated briefly by reference to a specific line from Lamentations, namely 1.14a, which in the RSV reads: 'My transgressions were bound into a yoke; by his hand they were fastened together'. The problematic phrase is that translated 'My transgressions were bound into a yoke'. Several factors here contribute to uncertainty of meaning. The most important is that the Hebrew word found in the Masoretic text, *niśqad*, translated 'were bound' here, seems to be the niphal of a root found nowhere else in the Hebrew Bible. The plural word *pᵉšā'ay*, translated here 'my transgressions', is obviously difficult to construe as the subject of the singular verb *niśqad*, even though many, including the RSV, attempt to do so. And, further, the absence of a preposition (itself, of course, common in poetry) increases the ambiguity; the RSV supplies 'into', but this is simply to sustain the translation it has chosen. Other manuscripts, translations and commentaries, ancient and modern, offer alternatives for the difficult word *niśqad*. Some Hebrew manuscripts read the root *šqd*, 'watch', and this is reflected in some of the versions: the Septuagint has the equivalent of 'watch was kept over my sins' (implying the preposition *'al*, 'over', instead of the Masoretic text's noun *'ōl*, 'yoke'). The Targum, on the other hand, has the equivalent of 'the yoke of my rebellion is heavy', apparently implying the Hebrew root *qšh*. It is clearly very hard then to know what to make of this phrase in Lam. 1.14; this case is one where the original text may well be genuinely beyond our reach. Indeed the evidence of the versions (and even the variation in the Hebrew manuscript tradition) is probably best seen as giving a glimpse of early uncertainty and puzzlement in line with our own, rather than as offering genuinely helpful clues to the original text.[40] This section provides yet a further example, then, of

---

39. Cf. S. Fish, *Is there a Text in this Class? The Authority of Interpretive Communities* (Cambridge, MA: Harvard University Press, 1980).

40. It is interesting that Provan, after a careful discussion of possibilities (in which he stresses that the plural *pᵉšā'ay* cannot be taken as the subject of the clause in question, and that the context favours reference to the yoke's construction), feels able to be no more definite than this: 'I would suggest the following: "a yoke was fashioned out of my transgressions". This is, however, only a guess' (Provan, *Lamentations*, p. 51).

'sitting loose' to history, distancing from absolute original. Of course, we must acknowledge that traditional textual criticism has, at its best, always remained modest about its aspirations and achievements. But, in the light of Parker's contribution, the difference is twofold: we may need to admit that 'the original text' is simply not to be had, and then, moreover, positively enjoy the possibilities which this opens up for overhearing and indeed engaging in interpretative conversations, ancient and modern.

Concluding Reflections

Apart from liturgical reading, all the cases we have briefly reviewed have been essentially developments of recent decades. It is worth asking about the general intellectual climate within which they have arisen. We have already in passing noted possible affinities between some modes of reading the book of Lamentations and what we might call 'postmodern approaches'. I am no specialist in postmodernism, but I affirm the importance of striving to do our biblical studies, so far as possible, in the light of the cultural and intellectual context within which we live and work.[41] In speaking of 'postmodern approaches', I have in mind especially but not exclusively one particular feature, namely the tendency to read texts without reference to historical context. The emphasis on reading biblical texts in the light of their historical contexts has, as we have observed, been one of the defining features of the 'historical critical' study of the Bible, a phase often styled as that of 'modernism'. That 'postmodernism' is to be defined in contradistinction to 'modernism' is not uncontroversial, but it is commonplace. And for biblical scholars this has some attractions, since we are often particularly aware that 'sitting loose' to historical concerns constitutes a prominent feature of postmodernism as it impinges upon biblical studies. Strictly speaking, 'sitting loose' to the historical context of a text is associated with an earlier phase of criticism, namely that of structuralism, itself a feature of modernist rather than postmodernist thinking (postmodernism itself could, indeed, be said to 'sit loose' to meaning as a whole, or at least to fixed and final meaning). But, although the place

---

41. For an introduction to postmodernism, see M. Sarup, *An Introductory Guide to Post-Structuralism and Postmodernism* (New York: Harvester Wheatsheaf, 2nd edn, 1993). Valuable materials are assembled in R. Young (ed.), *Untying the Text: A Post-structural Reader* (Boston: Routledge and Kegan Paul, 1981).

of the historical in postmodernism is complex, it is generally true that 'sitting loose' to historical matters is a feature of postmodern approaches and, moreover, that it is through encounter with such approaches that biblical scholars have most commonly become familiar with this emphasis over recent years.

As biblical scholars, we have much to learn from encounter with recent critical theory, and not least with postmodernism, even though many will wish to be discriminating about what they take on.[42] There is a growing literature on the interface between biblical studies and post-modernism.[43] With regard to theology more generally, a thoroughgoing postmodernist stance is generally regarded as incompatible with most if not all forms of religious commitment, but there is certainly a lively theological debate under way on this broader front too.[44]

In particular, it has been 'sitting loose' to history, the reading of texts (specifically, of course, the book of Lamentations) without primary reference to original historical context, which has been our concern. Each in its way, agnosticism about dating, liturgical use, psychological interpretation, literary approaches, reading in the light of an ideological agenda, and the newer textual criticism, have illustrated this phenomenon.

It is no bad thing that the dominance of historical matters in biblical studies has been much questioned of late. Over recent decades many have become more aware of the potentially negative side of the histori-cal-critical approach. In some ways, as this enterprise developed, espe-

42. Self-critical discrimination is certainly necessary. Within a more general context, Terry Eagleton has recently warned of the dangers of casual and facile borrowing from postmodernism: T. Eagleton, *The Illusions of Postmodernism* (Oxford: Basil Blackwell, 1996).

43. For a range of attempts to relate postmodern issues to biblical studies, very varied in both emphasis and style, see: W. Brueggemann, *The Bible and Postmodern Imagination: Texts under Negotiation* (Minneapolis: Fortress Press; London: SCM Press, 1993); The Bible and Culture Collective, *Postmodern Bible*; J. Barton, *Reading the Old Testament: Method in Biblical Study* (London: Darton, Longman and Todd, 2nd edn, 1996), pp. 220-36; R.P. Carroll, 'Poststructuralist Approaches: New Historicism and postmodernism', in J. Barton (ed.), *The Cambridge Companion to Biblical Interpretation* (Cambridge: Cambridge University Press, 1998), pp. 50-66.

44. The work of Graham Ward in particular might be mentioned here, especially G. Ward, *Barth, Derrida and the Language of Theology* (Cambridge: Cambridge University Press, 1995).

cially in the nineteenth century, the Bible became just another historical text, as though a relic of a bygone age. Through being placed within its original setting, it lost for many much of its immediate religious impact. Moreover, there developed a widespread sense that only the experts could interpret this collection of ancient texts, while others came to feel de-skilled. The Bible, which had emerged within the context of the life of God's people, their struggles and their hopes, now often seemed far removed from that life of faith. The functioning of Scripture was undermined and stultified. Traditional meanings were disallowed; material was now 'properly' understood in terms of the immediate situation in ancient times, and its later traditional use widely regarded as misguided. Appeal was commonly made to likely original meaning to exclude particular interpretations, and the cry 'That is not what it meant originally!' came to be regarded as a 'knock-down' argument in some quarters, even though original meaning can only be given this power (at least in an unqualified way) at the cost of the very functioning of Scripture, with its capacity to address readers afresh in ever new situations.

And yet historical criticism has contributed much and continues to do so. The rise of the historical-critical method was itself in many ways an exciting process of liberation. The process of historical distancing had—and can still have—a very positive side to it. By being set within their original historical situations, the biblical materials can be brought to life in new and exciting ways. Far from these texts being robbed of meaning in this process, they can be the better understood for being seen in their historical contexts, in the light of the theological questions their authors were facing. As historical criticism has subjected the Bible to the same kind of scrutiny as any other ancient literature, ecclesiastical and other distortions have often been swept away, and the dust of the centuries blown off, revealing a strangely unfamiliar text. We can sit humbly before the text in its 'otherness', in a way that can sometimes be profound, even spiritual.

There are thus good things as well as bad about a historical emphasis in reading the Bible. And so it is important to reflect on the different tasks which are served or hindered by a historical emphasis, and to adjust accordingly. Such a clearly articulated pluralism of method can equip one, indeed free one, to enjoy the many varied ways in which a fertile text such as Lamentations has been and is being read.[45]

45. A pluralism of distinct, legitimate 'interpretative interests' is championed by M. Brett, in, e.g., 'Four or Five Things to do with Texts: A Taxonomy of Interpreta-

What, then, of the place of the historical in biblical interpretation? I myself am committed to according a continued 'place of honour' to historical-critical concerns, albeit a carefully circumscribed place.[46] I have no serious doubt that the book of Lamentations was shaped by the crisis of 587 BCE and its immediate aftermath; and, while acknowledging that such a setting can never be more than a plausible hypothesis, I believe that the text is illuminated by being read in the context of the exilic crisis and moreover that, carefully handled, it can contribute to an understanding of the theology of that age. But that is just the start of the story of this text, a story which comes to include uses from the liturgical to the psychological. An exclusive or excessive preoccupation with original setting and original meaning can do little to equip us for appreciating many of these. But, kept in its honoured if limited place, as part of a self-critical pluralism of method, a historical concern for the text in its likely original setting will continue to shed invaluable light on the book of Lamentations, without stultifying its life as religious Scripture or literary classic.

It is a great pleasure to contribute this short study to a volume honouring Ronald Clements. His written work was among the first to attract me to the field of Old Testament study—I think perhaps especially of *Abraham and David*[47]—and over subsequent years his encouragement and example, as scholar and teacher, editor and friend, have been an inspiration.

---

tive Interests', in D.J.A. Clines, S.E. Fowl and S.E. Porter (eds.), *The Bible in Three Dimensions: Essays in Celebration of Forty Years of Biblical Studies in the University of Sheffield* (JSOTSup, 87; Sheffield: JSOT Press, 1990), pp. 357-77. Cf. S.E. Gillingham, *One Bible, Many Voices: Different Approaches to Biblical Studies* (London: SPCK, 1998).

46. P.M. Joyce, 'First Among Equals? The Historical-Critical Approach in the Marketplace of Methods', in S.E. Porter, P.M. Joyce and D.E. Orton (eds.), *Crossing the Boundaries: Essays in Biblical Interpretation in Honour of Michael D. Goulder* (Biblical Interpretation Series, 8; Leiden: E.J. Brill, 1994), pp. 17-27.

47. R.E. Clements, *Abraham and David: Genesis XV and its Meaning for Israelite Tradition* (SBT; London: SCM Press, 1967).

THEOLOGY AND HERMENEUTICS IN THE BOOKS OF CHRONICLES

R.J. Coggins

Changing interests in the study of the Hebrew Bible have affected the work of the Chronicler to a remarkable extent. A generation or so ago at least three propositions relating to 1 and 2 Chronicles would have been generally agreed. First, they were to be seen as part of a larger whole, embracing also the books of Ezra and Nehemiah. Secondly, the Chronicler's purpose was to be a recorder of his people's history. And thirdly, partly because the Chronicler was not a reliable historian and partly because much of his work seemed to be exceedingly tedious, these books could safely be marginalized in any study of the theology of the Hebrew Bible.

All these views have now been called into question. I am not here greatly concerned with the relation between Chronicles and Ezra-Nehemiah, but the second point—the Chronicler's 'historical' frame-work—does invite further consideration. As for the theological marginalization of Chronicles, one can only comment that among the many privileges of working for more than 30 years in the Biblical Studies Department at King's College, London was that of working alongside two professors whose work has played an important part in bringing about a new appraisal. Peter Ackroyd's extensive work on the Chronicler has been fundamental in challenging existing assumptions and inviting fresh scrutiny of the material; Ronald Clements has been one of the most influential figures in bringing about a new theological appraisal of much of the Hebrew Bible, and it is a great pleasure to offer these reflections to him.

I

In some sense it seems apparent that the Chronicler's purpose is histori-cal. His[1] work starts with Adam, and goes forward to the advent of

---

1. The masculine pronoun is used deliberately; whatever may be the case in

Cyrus of Persia. The historical structure is obvious, and has long been recognized, though much criticized ever since Wellhausen's famous dismissal more than a century ago of the books of Chronicles as no more than midrash.[2] Less instantly clear is evidence of any theological concern which could play a significant part in building up a 'Theology of the Old Testament'. (The Christian title for the collection of books is appropriate here, for, as is well known, Jewish scholars have for the most part not used the biblical material as the basis for a unified theological presentation.) Thus, when the influence of scholars such as von Rad was at its greatest in persuading us that the key to a theological understanding of the Old Testament was to be found in *Heilsgeschichte* no significant contribution to that understanding was allowed to the Chronicler. The greatest complex of saving events in the people's history was the deliverance from Egypt, the Exodus, the journey through the wilderness and the conquest of the Promised Land. But this found little conscious reference in Chronicles. In that collection the role of Moses appears to be marginalized; Joshua seems to feature not at all. One of the most widely used handbooks for this kind of understanding of the Bible as 'the Book of the Acts of God' does indeed devote a brief chapter to 'The Chronicler's history of Judah', but makes it clear from the outset that 'Theologically, the Chronicler adds little that is new or fresh'.[3] In the older fashion of historical theology, therefore, the Chronicler was regarded as having little to offer.

Two kinds of response to that judgment seem relevant. The first is a warning against too limited a reading of what were perceived to be God's saving acts. It is undoubtedly the case that in most of the surveys

some other parts of the Hebrew Bible, it is difficult to envisage a significant feminine input in 1 and 2 Chron. To what extent that weakens or even invalidates a theological message will be for readers to determine. The masculine pronoun is also used when referring to God; literary sensitivity rather than any particular theological standpoint has dictated this usage.

2. J. Wellhausen, *Prolegomena to the History of Israel* (ET; Edinburgh: A. & C. Black, 1885), p. 227. I was helped in tracing this reference by the article of I. Kalimi, 'Was the Chronicler a Historian?', in M.P. Graham, K.G. Hoglund and S.L. McKenzie (eds.), *The Chronicler as Historian* (JSOTSup, 238; Sheffield: Sheffield Academic Press, 1997). The book contains several other interesting references to Wellhausen and his attitude to the Chronicler. I am also grateful to Dr Kalimi for sending me a copy of his article prior to publication.

3. G.E. Wright and R.H. Fuller, *The Book of the Acts of God* (London: Gerald Duckworth, 1960).

of the people's history in, for example, the 'historical' Psalms such as 78, 105 and 106, greatest emphasis is placed upon the events described in the Hexateuch, but already in the closing verses of Psalm 78 the importance of David comes to the fore. The Chronicler, with his great emphasis on David, can legitimately be seen as developing an existing tradition.

For our present purposes, however, a second type of response is more immediately relevant. The Chronicler's theological strengths lie less in his direct presentation of the great events of the people's history than in his creative use of existing traditions, of making them appropriate and relevant to the situation of the community for which he wrote. Much of this essay will be concerned with some of the ways in which the work of the Chronicler offers a measure of theological understanding for a community; there are other theological insights to be gained from Chronicles to which only the briefest reference can be made here.

The nature of the group with which the Chronicler was involved is worthy of attention. Much attention has been paid in recent years to the sociology of the Second Temple community; one may think, for example, of the work of Weinberg, whose 'Citizen-Temple Community' terminology has given rise to much debate.[4] Perhaps somewhat less attention has yet been paid to the sociology of the relevant literature: from what sort of background did the work of the Chronicler emerge? Is it possible to discern in that work anything of the circumstances which impelled him to write?

The greatly varying dates proposed for the compilation of 1 and 2 Chronicles offer a strong hint that little is known for certain in this area. The valuable survey by Kleinig[5] shows that dates ranging over more than two centuries have been proposed by recent scholars. Thus, if we were to follow Braun,[6] who very tentatively ('it is at least

---

4. J.P. Weinberg, *The Citizen-Temple Community* (JSOTSup, 151; Sheffield: JSOT Press, 1992). I assume that this is an accurate representation of the Russian in which Weinberg's original studies were written. Such works as the two volumes of *Second Temple Studies*, I (ed. P.R. Davies; JSOTSup, 117; Sheffield: JSOT Press, 1991), II (ed. T.C. Eskenazi and K.H. Richards; JSOTSup, 175; Sheffield: Sheffield Academic Press, 1994), reflect something of the debate which Weinberg's work has generated.

5. J. W. Kleinig, 'Recent Research in Chronicles', *Currents in Research: Biblical Studies* 2 (1994), pp. 43-76. His discussion of dating is at pp. 46-47.

6. R.L. Braun, *1 Chronicles* (WBC; Waco: Word Books, 1986), p. xxix.

interesting to consider') proposes a date c. 515 BCE for the body of the work, we should have to think of Chronicles as a kind of prospectus for the newly reconstructed temple, addressed to its potential worshippers. But such a view needs to posit extensive later additions to the Chronicler's work, and—though the interest in the temple is undeniable—there is little that would most naturally be associated with the period of building or rebuilding the Second Temple.

A later date has therefore been generally agreed, set by Kleinig as 'between 350–300 BCE'.[7] At first it seems reasonable enough that a spread of half a century should be allowed where greater precision is unattainable, but a moment's reflection shows what a curious choice this is. For this was exactly the period during which the long-established Persian control of Palestine came to an end and Alexander's conquests became effective. If it really is the case that any time during that period, 350–300, is the likely date of the Chronicler's work, then we can only assume that as far as the religious community in Judah was concerned, it was not a matter of major concern who was exercizing political authority; their concerns lay elsewhere.

It may of course be that the Chronicler's work was actually completed before the downfall of the Persian empire. The lack of even incidental references to a new situation of Hellenistic rule makes that quite likely. Nevertheless, the absence of reference to the current political situation makes an important theological point, even if it may strike us as being negative: the effective political power of the day is not a matter of concern to the Chronicler. It is one view of the religious community/ state relation which has had much resonance later in the Judeo-Christian tradition.

Not least is this of importance in our perception of the biblical period itself. There is a widespread popular assumption that ancient Israel was preoccupied with matters which we should call 'religious'. If they were not so preoccupied there were prophets and others whose task it was to recall the people to that concern. Such a perception owes much to the way in which both the Deuteronomistic Historian and the Chronicler appear to be addressing the whole people. In fact, as far as the Chronicler is concerned, it seems clear that he wished to address a particular group, whether or not we identify them as a 'Citizen-Temple Community'. When it comes to the all-pervading nature of religious interests, an

---

7.	Kleinig, 'Recent Research', p. 46.

obvious contrast can be drawn with the community at Elephantine, in Egypt, from a period probably only slightly earlier than the time of Chronicles. There too, we have a community from the Second Temple period, but the texts which have been discovered betray no particular interest in the historical reconstruction and the religious concerns which provide the main structure of Chronicles.

Chronicles is, of course, much closer to 1 and 2 Kings, but when we look at the two works more closely the contrast with the viewpoint of the editor of the earlier work is a striking one. Kings too was surely primarily addressed to a religious community. I need not here enter into the debate concerning the time and place of origin of that work, but it is clear that its complete form cannot have emerged before 562 BCE, in view of the reference to Jehoiachin in the closing verses (2 Kgs 25.27-30). By that time Judah was no longer even nominally an independent nation-state. The addressees of 1 and 2 Kings must have been those whom the final editors wished to claim as adherents of the god Yahweh. But the message of Kings was emphatically set out in terms of the political concerns of that time. They were seen directly as the means of God's judgment on what should have been a loyal community of worshippers.

Put another way, the story in Kings does not have a happy ending. Certainly the last four verses, referring to Jehoiachin in exile, have been seen as a consciously 'up-beat' conclusion, but this seems improbable. (How these concluding verses should appropriately be interpreted was a topic of dispute between Noth and von Rad some 40 years ago.) Jehoiachin was given enough to eat (25.29-30); good! But how slightingly it is expressed. No reference is made to any possible successor, though we know from 1 Chron. 3.17-18 that he had children. Instead we are simply told that 'he dined regularly in the king's presence'. 'The king' is not the Davidic monarch, the recipient of the great promises first spelled out in 2 Samuel 7 and alluded to frequently in Kings. Now 'the king' is the Babylonian ruler known to the Hebrew Bible as 'Evil-merodach'. We know the Akkadian form of his name, 'Amel Marduk', and that he ruled for a mere two years. And that is all. In short he is a figure of so little consequence that he is otherwise scarcely known. As happy endings go this has a lot to learn.

The Chronicler's work also has a brief epilogue. But what a contrast this offers! Now we are concerned not with who gets what to eat under conditions of house-arrest in Babylon. Now we have God's word through his prophet being fulfilled. The prophets, pictured in their own time as bringers of woe, at least according to their editors (Jer. 23.16-17), are now seen as looking forward to restoration. A great ruler is being raised by God's spirit. The climax of that ruler's edict is the building of a house for God in Jerusalem and the promise that all his scattered worshippers are to 'go up', that is, to Jerusalem (2 Chron. 36.22-23). This is a real happy ending.

Plenty of scholars have seen major problems in taking this as a reliable account of the events that actually took place in Cyrus's reign, but at the narrative level it is powerfully effective. Thus, to take just one of the historical problems, there is no way in which these events took place 'in the *first* year of King Cyrus', for he became king in or around 550 BCE, and a decade passed before Babylon was overthrown. But such a presentation conveys a powerful sense of immediacy. It gives a real justification for that quietism in relation to politics that we have seen to be characteristic of the Chronicler. God has seen to all of that; the ordering of statehood and political control can safely be left to him. Though attempts have been made to find a 'messianic' expectation in the Chronicles, they seem to be misplaced. In 1 Chronicles 3 it is noted of Jeconiah (=Jehoiachin) that he was *'assīr* ('captive', v. 17), but otherwise the list of David's descendants is offered in the concluding verses of that chapter without any highlighting of their role, or suggestion that they might be the forerunners of greater things to come.

Against the proposal that the interest of the Chronicler cannot be set out in political terms, it might be objected that there are in Chronicles many stories which appear to be political, in the sense of referring to the achievements and failings of state rulers. This is certainly the case, but there is a real sense in which these stories are totally 'unworldly'. The overall structure of the Chronicler's work was provided for its author by existing literary conventions. Originality was no virtue; what was needed was the clarification and making applicable to his own community of the traditions of the past.

I may mention just two ways in which that need was met. Sometimes stories from the past could be amplified to make clear just how God was at work in the proper structuring of his community. An obvious example here would be the account of King Uzziah's affliction. In 2 Kings 15 we are told how Azariah[8] 'did what was right in the sight of

___

8.   The king is regularly called 'Azariah' in Kings and 'Uzziah' in Chronicles, as in Isa. 6.1. Many proposals have been made to account for this variation in

the Lord' (v. 3), but was stricken with leprosy[9] (v. 5), and replaced as ruler by his son Jotham. The Chronicler saw in this a good opportunity to show that this was not an arbitrary event. God had punished Uzziah for usurping the priestly role (2 Chron. 26.16-21). Does such a story as this imply a political dimension to the Chronicler's work after all? Not necessarily, for it will have had little direct relevance to the circumstances of his own day. There was no king who might aspire to take over the duties properly assigned to the priesthood. Thus, the story should be seen, not only as providing an example of the Chronicler offering an explanation of a development unexplained in Kings, but also as stressing the need for proper boundaries to be observed, for appropriate roles to be performed. We are in the world of the clean and the unclean, made familiar by Leviticus, rather than in any more directly political scenario. The Chronicler's God was a great maintainer of proper boundaries, as is already made clear by the genealogies in the opening chapters of 1 Chronicles. (To them I will return in a moment.)

The second type of apparently political story is to be found in those episodes where no direct link with Kings can be traced. The classic example here would be the fate of King Zerah the Ethiopian (2 Chron. 14.9-13). Here, surely, we are in a story world pure and simple. Neither in other parts of the Hebrew Bible nor in any other ancient source is there material which would offer us a clue to a possible historical nucleus here. No doubt there will have been some source lying behind the story, for few of us are capable of indulging in wholly free composition, but this seems to be a tale with a religious moral told in terms of kings and armies. We need look no further for that being the kind of language used for the story than to remember that this was the structure imposed upon the whole corpus.

This first theological concern may seem to have been largely negative. That is not wholly true, for an independence of political involvement can also be construed in positive terms. But when we turn to consider the Jerusalem temple the picture is certainly a positive one. This is the centre of the author's concerns. It was at one time widely maintained that it is possible to detect an underlying ideological rivalry here, perhaps directed against the Samaritans with their temple on Mt

naming, but as far as I am able to judge they are all guesses. We do not know the reason for the change.

9.   We need not here concern ourselves with the identity of the disease, now widely acknowledged not to have been true leprosy.

Gerizim. Thus Rudolph maintained that the speech of Abijah in 2 Chronicles 13 should be seen as an apologetic on behalf of the ministers of the Jerusalem temple as the true 'keepers' (*šōmᵉrîm*) of God's charge to his people. Certainly at a later date the Samaritans' self-description was as *šāmᵉrîm* (of the Law); was Abijah's speech therefore aimed against them?[10]

Many more recent studies have shown that the emergence of the Samaritans as a distinct and identifiable group only took place later than any plausible date for the Chronicler. Even if the Chronicler were to be dated in the Hellenistic period (a view already seen to be unlikely) this would still be the case; only with Sirach in the second century BCE do we have clear evidence of animosity against the Samaritans (Sir. 50.26). Similarly their self-designation as *šāmᵉrîm* is only attested in much later sources. So it is improbable that Abijah's speech should be seen as specifically aimed against the Gerizim community. Nevertheless the general point may be acknowledged, that it is likely that the Chronicler will have been mounting a defence of the Jerusalem temple against any possible rival readings of the divine will. We have been reminded by various recent studies of the diversity of what is customarily lumped together as Second Temple Judaism, and it is important to see the Chronicler's claim as one among a number of rival claims to true insight.[11]

Indeed, there is a sense in which the expression 'Second Temple Judaism', widely used as it is, can be misleading. It gives the impression that whatever other divisions there may have been within the overall community of Judaism, on this, at least, they were in accord: that the Jerusalem temple was central to their standing before God and to their self-identity. But this is clearly not the case. We have already noted that at a later date a community identifiable as the Samaritans

10. W. Rudolph, 'Problems of the Books of Chronicles', *VT* 4 (1954), pp. 401-409 (404). The same position was maintained in his 1955 commentary (*Handbuch zum Alten Testament*), ad loc.

11. The implications of this diversity are discussed by D.M. Carr, 'Canonization in the Context of Community: An Outline of the Formation of the Tanakh and the Christian Bible', in R.D. Weis and D.M. Carr (eds.), *A Gift of God in Due Season: Essays on Scripture and Community in Honor of James A. Sanders* (JSOTSup, 225; Sheffield: Sheffield Academic Press, 1996), pp. 22-64. The considerations that he applies specifically to the matter of canon-formation are relevant to other aspects of the religious life of the community.

would emerge, maintaining that Mt Gerizim was the true place for the worship of God, and even if it is unlikely that the later Samaritans were in existence as such by the fourth century, we may surely assume that claims on behalf of Gerizim were already being made. This is the point being made by J. van Seters, when he says that 'the demonstration of continuity for Jerusalem's temple underscores a discontinuity for rival sanctuaries and communities and their respective claims to represent the true Israel'.[12]

In a comparable way, it is now widely held that the Enoch literature came into existence during the period from the fourth to the first centuries BCE, and that it, too, was hostile to the claims of the Jerusalem temple, though in this case it is not possible to identify any other holy place with which the Enoch material should be linked.[13]

That other claims were made on behalf of other sanctuaries during this period seems probable; in addition to the Egyptian evidence from Elephantine (and later from Leontopolis) there may well have been a sanctuary at 'Araq el-emir in Transjordan, associated in some way with the Tobiads.[14] In short, there seems no reason to modify the conclusion which I expressed more than 20 years ago: 'Perhaps the viewpoint of the Chronicler, with its great emphasis on Zion, has too readily been taken as the accepted standard of orthodoxy'.[15]

Though it may be unlikely that Chronicles should be seen as anti-Samaritan polemic, there is another sense in which a parallel with the Samaritans may be relevant. It is greatly disputed whether the Samaritans in the last centuries BCE are better understood as an 'ethnos', a political group maintaining and developing some of the traditions of the old northern kingdom, or more specifically as a religious community centred on their venerable sanctuary on Mt Gerizim.[16] Similar uncer-

---

12. J. van Seters, 'The Chronicler's Account of Solomon's Temple-Building: A Continuity Theme', in Graham *et al.* (eds.), *Chronicler as Historian*, p. 283-300 (283).

13. A helpful outline of study of the Enoch literature is provided in the section 'Provenance and Social Setting' of G.W.E. Nickelsburg's article 'First Book of Enoch', *ABD*, II, pp. 508-16 (515).

14. The evidence relating to the Tobiads is summarized and evaluated by J.A. Dearman, 'The Son of Tabeel (Isaiah 7.6)', in S.B. Reid (ed.), *Prophets and Paradigms: Essays in Honor of Gene M. Tucker* (JSOTSup, 229; Sheffield: Sheffield Academic Press, 1996), pp. 33-47, especially pp. 37-40.

15. R.J. Coggins, *Samaritans and Jews* (Oxford: Basil Blackwell, 1975), p. 112.

16. I have discussed some of these issues in 'Jewish Local Patriotism: the Sam-

tainties affect our understanding of the Chronicler, but it does seem as if it is appropriate to put greater stress on his role as the spokesman of a religious community than has often been customary.

However that may be, it is presented as a matter beyond argument that the Jerusalem temple provided the context in which God's requirements were to be honoured and the place in which the community was to find its true identity. This ties in with another important element in the work of the Chronicler: the genealogies.

Here is another area in which the previously dominant historical understanding of a genre has been replaced by a different approach. First of all, it is important to bear in mind that, though the extended genealogies in 1 Chronicles 1–9 are much longer than any other such lists, it is by no means unique to begin a text in this way. Exodus 1.1-5 provides a much briefer parallel, and of course in the New Testament Mt. 1.1-17 has often been compared with the method of the Chronicler in setting out the parameters of his subject. But then, secondly, a close reading of 1 Chronicles 1–9 reveals that the usual dismissal of these chapters as 'no more than a list of names' is seriously misleading. They do, in fact, contain a number of other elements. These have been scrutinized by Kartveit, the very title of whose book is relevant here.[17] After a brief introduction, he devotes his longest chapter to a detailed source-critical analysis of the material, which is not relevant to the present discussion. It must in any case remain a matter of doubt whether such precise analysis as that which he undertakes can yield such exact results as is claimed. More important for my purposes is his second main chapter, in which he speaks of the 'land theology' of Chronicles. He draws attention in particular to the place-names and city-lists which are scattered through these chapters. There are, of course, similarities with the information supplied in Joshua 13–21, but also important divergences. The significant point is that the collection as a whole offers a developing theology of the land. The area of that land is conceived differently here from what is found elsewhere, and this is in itself an important theological point. The Hebrew Bible as a whole sets out the conviction that God had promised to his people a particular land, but finds no

aritan Problem', forthcoming in S. Jones and S. Pearce (eds.), *Jewish Local Patriotism and Self-Identification in the Graeco-Roman Period* (JSPSup, 31; Sheffield: Sheffield Academic Press, 1999), pp. 66-78.

17. M. Kartveit, *Motive und Schichten der Landtheologie in 1 Chronik 1–9* (ConBOT, 28; Stockholm: Almqvist and Wiksell, 1989).

difficulty in offering a variety of pictures of the extent of that land. One hesitates to put too much weight on a mere inversion of order in the use of a common phrase, but it is interesting that for the more usual 'from Dan to Beersheba' when describing the extent of the land, the Chronicler has 'from Beersheba to Dan' (1 Chron. 21.2), as if Beersheba was the important point of reference.

Another important theological point emerges from these genealogies. H.G.M. Williamson has rightly drawn attention to the much more open attitude to be found in Chronicles, as compared with Ezra-Nehemiah, to those who might be regarded as excluded from its membership.[18] The main thrust of his argument related to the concept of Israel, and the fact that those who lived in the territory of the former Northern kingdom were regarded much more positively in Chronicles than in Ezra–Nehemiah. In the build-up of his argument, moreover, he notes on several occasions that in the genealogies he records various of those listed were involved in mixed marriages with those who were quite outside the community, and that 'the Chronicler nowhere condemns mixed marriages, but if anything rather condones them'.[19]

Williamson's point can be taken further in the light of studies by E.A. Knauf and others who have looked at those named in the genealogies who are otherwise unknown. Knauf has drawn attention to 'the high frequency of Arabian names in 1 Chronicles 2 and 4'.[20] Similarly, the list of David's 'warriors' in 1 Chronicles 11 includes an Ammonite (Zelek, v. 39) and a Moabite (Ithmah, v. 46). All of this adds detail to the point already made by S. Japhet in her discussion of 'Foreigners and Aliens' within the Chronicler's ideology.[21] Here again there is an interesting development away from the Deuteronomistic History. In the earlier work great emphasis was placed upon the list of Canaanites and other peoples who were to be dispossessed by the incoming Israelites. This theme is much less prominent in Chronicles; instead, in Japhet's words, 'No distinct, separate foreign population exists in the land.

18. H.G.M. Williamson, *Israel in the Books of Chronicles* (Cambridge: Cambridge University Press, 1977). He has elaborated and refined the point in various later writings on Chronicles.

19. Williamson, *Israel*, p. 61.

20. E.A. Knauf, 'Ephah' [person], *ABD*, II, p. 534.

21. S. Japhet, *The Ideology of the Book of Chronicles and its Place in Biblical Thought* (Frankfurt: P. Lang, 1989). Her extended discussion is summarized on pp. 346-51.

Everyone who lives there, whatever his origins, is part of the people of Israel'.[22]

In all this we can see important theological implications: people and land are intimately bound together in a particular understanding of the service of God. There is, however, a tension which is perhaps not wholly resolved. On the one hand, we have the presentation of Hezekiah as restoring the unity of the whole nation which had been broken after the death of Solomon. 2 Chronicles 30 describes the dispatch of couriers to the furthest corners of the land. Though the great majority of the northerners 'laughed them to scorn and mocked them' (v. 10), there were those who 'humbled themselves and came to Jerusalem' (v. 11), and by v. 18 their numbers seem to have increased, for that speaks of 'many' from these northern tribes. They are made welcome; the festal calendar is modified (v. 23) in order to accommodate them. Williamson describes the situation thus: 'In principle the whole population was reunited in worship at that time at the Jerusalem temple'.[23]

But of course the exile was to follow. In Ezra we find another description of those who joined in worship in the—by now restored—Jerusalem temple. Ezra 6.19-21 refers to the worshippers as the $b^e n\bar{e}$ $hagg\hat{o}l\hat{a}$, 'the exiles'. (NRSV has 'returned exiles'; one can point out that there is nothing in the Hebrew equivalent to 'returned', but equally it might be argued that since they were in Jerusalem, they must have returned.) It is clear that for Ezra the experience of exile was a necessary condition: 'true membership of the Jerusalem community...can only be granted to those who have the experience of having passed through exile'.[24]

Now it may legitimately be pointed out that this picture comes from Ezra, and not from Chronicles, and that, as we saw at the beginning of this essay, the close linkage between Chronicles and Ezra–Nehemiah is no longer accepted in the way that was once usual. Nevertheless, it remains likely that there are close connections between the two presentations, and in any case the fact of the exile is, as we have already seen,

22. Japhet, *Ideology*, p. 351.

23. Williamson, 'The Concept of Israel in Transition', in R.E. Clements (ed.), *The World of Ancient Israel: Sociological, Anthropological and Political Perspectives* (Cambridge: Cambridge University Press, 1989), pp. 141-61 (157).

24. Coggins, 'The Origins of the Jewish Diaspora', in Clements (ed.), *World of Ancient Israel*, p. 163-81 (167).

an important datum for the Chronicler. It seems scarcely likely that he envisaged the devastation and exile of all the former land of Israel, and so the tension already alluded to is not wholly resolved.

II

My main concern in the greater part of this essay has been to draw out some of the ways in which the historical structure of Chronicles has conveyed significant theological messages. It has, however, been characteristic of a number of recent studies to discern other ways in which Chronicles makes a contribution to our theological understanding. A starting-point here may be found in the widespread recognition that a central concern in these books relates to the identity and welfare of the community. That community was blessed by God, yet it had also been severely punished. Why should this have been so, and what steps should be taken to avoid a recurrence of such events?

A significant pointer in this regard is provided by the very title of an essay by W. Johnstone: 'Guilt and Atonement: the Theme of 1 and 2 Chronicles'.[25] In it he notes the use by the Chronicler at significant points in his story of the term *ma'al*, found in Chronicles as both verb and noun, and customarily translated by NRSV as 'be unfaithful/unfaithfulness'. In Johnstone's judgment it should be understood as 'failure to accord God what is his due'. It is pictured as being the cause of the exile (1 Chron. 9.1: 'Judah was taken into exile in Babylon because of their unfaithfulness'[26]); it is the way in which the unacceptable behaviour of various individual kings is described (e.g. Ahaz: 2 Chron. 28.19; Manasseh: 2 Chron. 33.19). The pattern of usage of *ma'al* forms in Chronicles is also striking: 11 out of a total of 17 references are found in the closing section of the books, from 2 Chronicles 26 onwards, as attention is more and more focussed on the exile and its causes. (Indeed, even those references which come earlier do not

25. In J.D. Martin and P.R. Davies (eds.), *A Word in Season: Essays in Honour of William McKane* (JSOTSup, 42; Sheffield: JSOT Press, 1986), pp. 113-38. The quotation is from p. 118. Johnstone has developed his point much more fully in his two-volume commentary, *1 and 2 Chronicles* (JSOTSup, 253/54; Sheffield: Sheffield Academic Press, 1997), the second volume of which has the sub-title *Guilt and Atonement*.

26. The plural translation here reads awkwardly, but follows the Hebrew text. The difficulty may have arisen because at some point the phrase 'and Judah' was construed with the preceding phrase, referring to 'the kings of Israel'.

detract from this conclusion, since, as we have just seen, 1 Chron. 9.1 refers to the exile, and is surely intentionally placed as an indicator of the way in which the story is to develop.)

There is another aspect of Johnstone's article to which it is appropriate to draw attention in view of what has been said above. We have already noted the importance of the genealogies in 1 Chronicles 1–9 as markers concerned with the land and the community that was to occupy it. Johnstone notes that already in the setting out of these concerns the theme of *ma'al* is already present. Those chapters set out the ideal constitution of the community, but stress also that from its very inception that community has fallen away, so that 'there are a number of details in 1 Chron. 2–8 which stress Israel's *ma'al* and its deadly effects'.[27] Johnstone provides several illustrations of his point, for example, the treatment of the trans-Jordanian tribes in 1 Chron. 5.18-26.

But the recurring pattern of guilt and the subsequent need for atonement is not confined to those groups which might be regarded as marginal. In a more recent paper,[28] Johnstone has explored various reasons for the condemnation of David in 1 Chronicles 21 and reaches the conclusion that the basic concern is to show that even the Chronicler's model king, David, is not free of guilt in matters holy. The overarching pattern of guilt and atonement, which he sees as fundamental to the Chronicler's presentation, is to be found even in the most propitious circumstances.

The theological significance of such an understanding scarcely needs to be underlined. Its applicability may be another matter. It could certainly be argued that religious communities have been only too ready to associate their story with a self-incriminating tale of hopes disappointed and failures of different kinds. To discover yet another one may confirm our worst suspicions concerning the self-imposed burdens which litter so much of religious history. But the purpose of this essay is not to justify, but to describe, the purpose and aims of the Chronicler.

In any case, there seems to be a danger that Johnstone may overstate his case. Guilt and atonement are certainly major themes in Chronicles, but it is important to place them in the context which I have tried to establish. Things had gone horribly wrong in the past, and an explanation of why that should have been so was an important element in the

27. Johnstone, 'Guilt and Atonement', p. 130.

28. W. Johnstone, '1 Chronicles 21: What Did David Do Wrong?', a paper read to the Society for Old Testament Study in January 1997.

Chronicler's work. But, as we have already seen, his work has a happy ending. Punishment for wrong-doing had been inevitable and it had taken place; now, as a faithful religious community fulfilling its obligations, it might look forward to a future of blessing.

This conclusion may be supported by brief reference to another way in which the study of Chronicles has been significantly modified in recent years. As long ago as 1972 T. Willi published a work largely devoted to an exploration of the exegetical technique of the Chronicler.[29] The explorations which he then undertook have been carried much further more recently by several authors writing on the theme of inner-biblical exegesis. Explicit reference to 'the law of Moses' is made on several occasions (e.g. 2 Chron. 23.18). It is striking that, just as the theme of *ma'al* is prominent in the closing chapters of the work, so also reference to 'the law of Moses' is particularly frequent in those final chapters: nine times in 2 Chronicles 23–36. It is as if the Chronicler brings his work to an end with a warning and an encouragement. Just as the *ma'al* of the people had led to its punishment through exile, so now the assurance is repeated that the community has the Torah as its guide.

In addition to the specific encouragement offered by these references to the Torah we can note more generally that allusions without specific reference throughout the book show how dependent the Chronicler was on sources which we should describe as 'biblical'—what Fishbane has described as 'the infusion of 'Torahistic' values into the book of Chronicles'.[30] Not everyone would agree with Fishbane's terminology when he speaks of 'Aggadic exegesis', but the phenomenon he describes has come to be a well-recognized one. The Chronicler's community was one whose roots were secure in its possession of what it claimed as the sacred traditions of the whole people. As we have seen already, it may well have been that other groups within the spectrum of Second Temple Judaism would have challenged such claims, but this was the pattern that was to become normative.

The acceptance in Judaism and Christianity of the Chronicler's own work as 'Scripture' may in a sense be seen as completing the chain. The Chronicler, and those for whom he wrote, were trying to shape their

29. T. Willi, *Die Chronik als Auslegung: Untersuchungen zur literarischen Gestaltung der historischen Überlieferung Israels* (FRLANT, 106; Göttingen: Vandenhoeck & Ruprecht, 1972).

30. M. Fishbane, *Biblical Interpretation in Ancient Israel* (Oxford: Clarendon Press, 1985), p. 424.

understanding of their place in God's purpose. The traditions of the people were incorporated, with a clear recognition that they pointed to an ongoing story. How far the continuation of that story should be seen in the work of Ezra and Nehemiah need not here concern us: Japhet, Williamson and others have rightly warned against over-simplified readings of 'Chronicles–Ezra–Nehemiah' as a single whole, but that does not exclude some close links between the constituent elements. In any case, for our present purposes, we have seen that the end of 2 Chronicles is certainly to be envisaged as a hopeful ending. The later religious communities, by taking the Chronicler's work on board, have made their own claim to be part of that tradition whose distinctive concerns he had spelt out.

A concluding reflection may perhaps be permitted. When I was invited to contribute to this volume the provisional title was 'Studies in Old Testament Theology and Hermeneutics'. It may not be too fanciful to claim that the Chronicler incorporates both of those concerns in a unique way. We have seen that his work has often been neglected in the past, but many recent studies have done something to put that right, and any theology of the Old Testament now written must give due place to such issues as the Chronicler's concern for the Jerusalem temple; his understanding of and explanation for the disasters that had befallen the community; and his claim that the group which he represented were the true heirs of the ancient traditions of the people. But it is also proper to see in the Chronicler the beginnings of the long and complicated process which we may describe as Old Testament hermeneutics. As we have already noted, the phenomenon known as 'inner biblical exegesis' has attracted increasing attention in recent years, and it is surely proper to see in the creative way in which Chronicles and other later parts of the Hebrew Bible used the traditions they inherited as the beginnings of such hermeneutics.[31]

31. In addition to works cited earlier, the volume of essays in honour of Barnabas Lindars is devoted to this theme: D.A. Carson and H.G.M. Williamson (eds.), *It is Written: Scripture citing Scripture* (Cambridge: Cambridge University Press, 1988). Williamson's own essay, 'History' (pp. 25-38), offers a valuable discussion of Chronicles in this context.

INDEXES

INDEX OF REFERENCES

OLD TESTAMENT

INDEX OF AUTHORS

JOURNAL FOR THE STUDY OF THE OLD TESTAMENT
SUPPLEMENT SERIES